Published By Longstreet Press

ISBN-1-56353-057-5

CAPTIONS:

Page   1. *Dominique goes against Larry Bird in the 1988 playoffs.*
Page   2. *The Hawks' lockerroom of yesterday.*
Page   4. *Pete Maravich drives on Dick Barnett.*
Page   6. *Moses Malone inside.*
Page   7. *Mike Fratello directs the troops.*
Page   8. *Eddie Johnson shoots over Henry Bibby and Dr. J.*
Page   9. *Dazzling Spud Webb.*
Page 10. *Tree Rollins over Hakeem Olajuwon.*
Page 11. *Doc Rivers rebounds.*

FROM SWEET LOU TO 'NIQUE

Text by Jeffrey Denberg, Roland Lazenby
and Tom Stinson

Edited by Arthur Triche

Longstreet Press 1992

The Hawks' new uniform design.

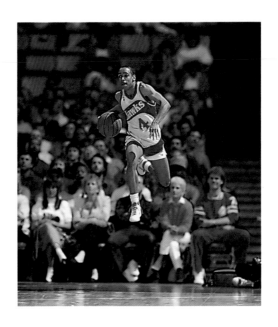

Contents

1. A Tale of Seven Cities 17
   by Roland Lazenby

2. Oh Atlanta! 31
   by Roland Lazenby

3. Ted Takes Charge 45
   by Tom Stinson

4. Fratello and the Air Force 63
   by Jeffrey Denberg

5 The U-Nique Factor 73
   by Jeffrey Denberg

6. Records 88

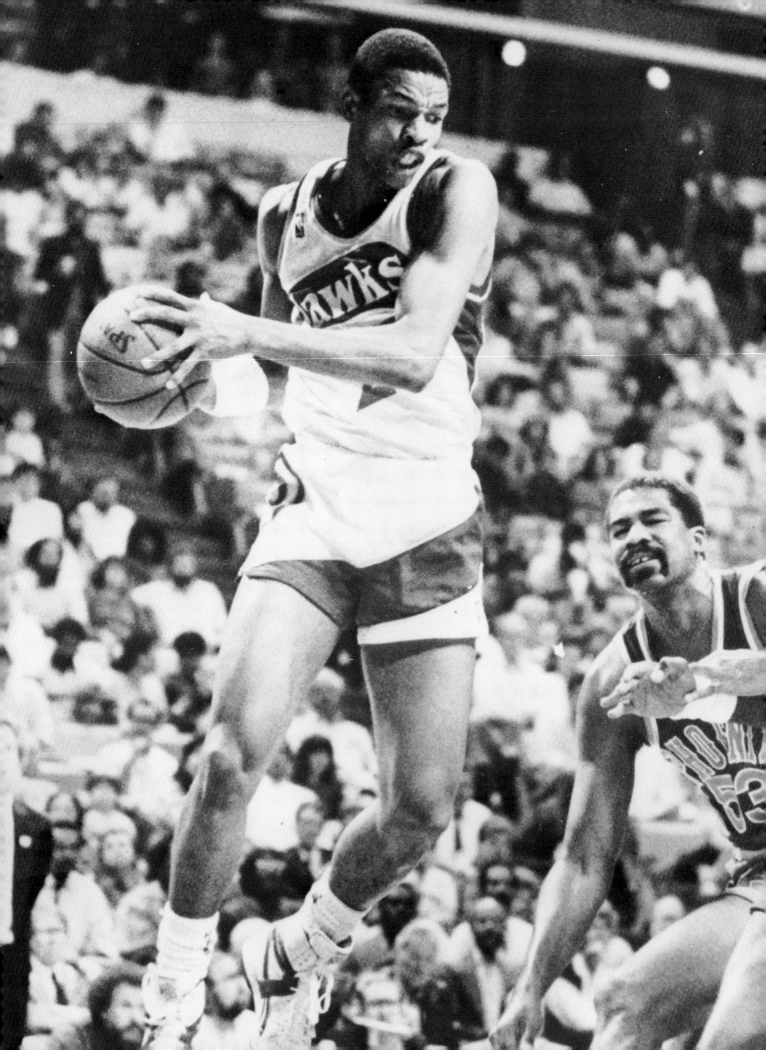

Foreword

When the Hawks were transported from St. Louis to Atlanta in 1958, it was all a part of the Big Picture. Tom Cousins, one of the men who helped to build modern Atlanta, had another one of his visions, and the Hawks were like a piece of a puzzle, the first piece, as a matter of fact. Cousins had to plan to bring new life to downtown, a sports coliseum was the centerpeice, and to have a coliseum, he had to have teams. In the company of Carl Sanders, the former governor, he went for it.

First, the Hawks of basketball. Later, the Flames of hockey.

The news first reached this correspondent at a peculiarly unforgettable Kentucky Derby, the only time a winner has been set down for drug abuse. (Dancer's Image was replaced by Forward Pass.) The following week in New York, the NBA team completed its transformation from the original Tri-Cities Blackhawks to the Atlanta Hawks, from a firetrap called Wharton Fieldhouse to the spacious Omni, and eventually, from Red Auerbach to Bob Weiss. It isn't easy now to comprehend that this team has its roots in the river cities of Davenport, Iowa, and Moline and Rock Island, Ill., in days of bus travel and 24-cent gasoline.

The Hawks had no home at the time, but became tenants at Alexander Coliseum through the good nature of Georgia Tech. At dinner one evening during the NBA meeting in New York, Tom Cousins asked, "How do you think the Hawks will draw in Atlanta?"

Gushing with enthusiasm, I said, "Oh, gosh, they'll fill the house every night. This is something Atlanta has never seen before."

My prediction was somewhat off the mark. In the first place, playing on a college campus made pro basketball seem somewhat less than professional and more like an exhibition. The Hawks arrived with no established identity, though they had won their conference championship the previous season, and Richie Guerin had been elected Coach of the Year. He might as well have been the prime minister of Italy, far as Atlanta was concerned. Frankly, the NBA had not made a resounding impact on Atlanta journalism.

The city was slow warming up to these towering professionals. Winter had customarily been the quiet season between football and baseball, though Georgia Tech had managed to arouse an occasional whoop with some of Whack Hyder's challenging teams. It was five years before Tom Cousins managed to bring off Step Two, the opening of The Omni, which the Hawks then shared with the Iceman of NHL. The Big Picture was in focus, for the nonce.

As for memories, there was the time Richie Guerin had to insert himself into the lineup during the playoffs against Los Angeles and then a creaking 36 years old, matched his age in points; the celebrated arrival of Pistol Pete Maravich, which sadly created a team divided rather than a team united; the brief ownership of Slick Selig, who followed Cousins, but for only three days or so; the passing through of Mike Storen; the blue-ing of the atmosphere by Hubie Brown along the sideline, and finally, the arrival of Ted Turner, his pals Mike Gearon and Bud Seretean, and the extensive world of cable.

There was little more saddening than the sorrowful turn of some of the star-crossed Hawks who passed this way, the late Terry Furlow, the pitiable John Drew, and the unpredictable Eddie Johnson, from gold and glitter to the pits. But there has been the redeeming presence and citizenship of Lou Hudson, of Mike Glenn, of Jim Washington, of Dominique Wilkins, of the now departed Doc Rivers. It was the Hawks who introduced the midget Spud Webb to the league of behemoths, against the odds. And I have only agitated the surface.

What you have here is a compendium of all this, the sometimes grand and the sometimes not-so-grand 25 years of the Hawks in Atlanta. If there is one major regret, it is that Bob Pettit was born not to fit into this time frame. As we reach this era, it may be that he is not the greatest of all the Hawks, but I would like to have seen for myself.

Furman Bisher, Atlanta Journal

In 1958, the Hawks beat the Celtics in six games to win the NBA title. Here the Hawks' Ed Macauley (20) loses a rebound to Boston's Bill Russell (6).

A Tale of Seven Cities

1946-68

With the opening of the 1992-93 NBA season, the Hawks will have made Atlanta their home for 25 years. That, in itself, should surprise some observers, considering the hasty manner in which the city and the team arranged their relationship in 1968.

If anything, though, the years have revealed that the two were made for each other. The city wanted to adorn itself with another professional sports team, and the Hawks—one of pro basketball's original vagabond clubs—were road weary and looking for a clean, well-lighted place to settle down.

Atlanta didn't exactly provide the clean place right away. Neither did it offer stability and security. The club would have to earn those things. Yet the city wasn't stingy either. What Atlanta offered foremost was the interest of its talented young entreprenuers. First, there was Tom Cousins. Then, when no one else would have it, Ted Turner took the team and gave it the dignity it deserves.

The Hawks, after all, are one of pro basketball's grand old franchises. Of the 27 modern NBA teams, eight began life in the 1940s during the pro game's vagabond days. The other 19 teams are merely expansion franchises in one form or another.

The oldest team is the Detroit Pistons, founded in 1941 as the Fort Wayne Pistons. The second oldest is the Sacramento Kings, which got their start in 1945 as the Rochester Royals.

Then in 1946 came the Boston Celtics, New York Knicks, and Philadelphia Warriors (Golden State, today). Also that fall, three obscure teams were given franchises in the old National Basketball League—the Detroit Gems, the Syracuse Nationals and the Buffalo Bisons. The Gems became the Lakers; the Nationals transformed into the Philadelphia 76ers; and the Buffalo Bisons exist today as none other than your Hawks.

In all, the Hawks' story is a tale of seven cities. From its beginnings in Buffalo, New York, the team's wanderings stretched to Moline and Rock Island, Illinois, and Davenport, Iowa, then on to Milwaukee and St. Louis and finally Hot-lanta.

Along the way, the cast of characters came to include all the usual suspects—wiley owners, tough-talking coaches and an assortment of stiffs and stars. It's a story of thrown punches and hasty deals, of ancient arenas and cold showers, of made shots and missed opportunities.

"We struggled and we fought," said Ben Kerner, the man who started the team 46 years ago, "but we had a mind to succeed."

The team's travels seem fitting, considering that the original owners were two nomadic ad men, Ben Kerner and Leo Ferris. Both had worked for Jacobs Brothers Sports Service, one of the companies that dominated sports concessions during the 1940s. Kerner was a "hustler and Ferris was an idea man," recalled Sid Goldberg, who worked for them briefly. "Ferris always had a lot of pencils. One in his ear and several in his pocket. I always called him Leo 'Pencils' Ferris."

They traveled across the Northeast and Midwest selling program ads for sporting events, all the while learning the cities with the good crowds. Eventually they formed a small company to produce programs for auto races and wrestling bouts. After they sold programs for a couple of semiprofessional basketball clubs, Kerner and Ferris hatched a notion of starting their own team.

"We thought it might be a good idea," Kerner explained.

World War II had ended just a few months earlier, and already there was a demand for new entertainment. The

Red Auerbach once coached the Blackhawks.

Hawks owner Ben Kerner (right) with Bob Pettit.

basketball business seemed to hold promise, mainly because it was cheap. Salaries were tight (the average player earned about $5,000), and the equipment amounted to little more than a few hastily stitched satin uniforms and a half dozen balls.

The old National Basketball League had struggled through the war, at one point dropping to a mere three teams. But peacetime had brought a flourish of expansion to a dozen franchises. And a new league—the Basketball Association of America—quickly formed with 11 brand new teams.

Joining this surge of hoops mania, the ad men pooled their resources and spent about $1,500 to purchase a franchise in the National Basketball League. Then they kicked another $5,000 into the league coffers for a performance bond, and the team that would become the Hawks was off and running. Ferris and Kerner decided the Bisons would be a good name for a Buffalo team.

There was little to distinguish the Bisons from the dozens of other quickly hatched pro teams of the era, except for the fact that they were one of pro basketball's first integrated clubs. Their roster included Pop Gates, who had played for the famed Harlem Renaissance barnstorming team.

"He was available, so I signed him," the 78-year-old Kerner said in a 1992 interview from his St. Louis home.

The two ad men soon realized that this new business of pro basketball was a strange and frustrating venture. Teams literally opened one week and closed the next. "There were

a lot of vagabond teams," Goldberg explained. "They operated out of one city and played their games in another. They had to, to find a crowd."

The Bisons suffered most of the usual setbacks. By January, they had five wins, eight losses and almost no fan following. "We were doing very bad. We weren't drawing at all," Kerner recalled.

From his travels in the Midwest, Kerner had learned that three small cities—Moline and Rock Island, Illinois, and Davenport, Iowa—were sportsminded and might support a pro team. They sat clumped together along the banks of the upper Mississippi River, and combined they just might be big enough, Kerner reasoned. Plus, Rock Island had the 6,500-seat Wharton Fieldhouse.

So in midseason, Kerner moved the team and renamed it the Tri-Cities Blackhawks.

Unfortunately, the integration experiment ended in Moline because the local hotels didn't want to house Gates. For a time, some of his teammates joined him in a hotel in Rock Island, but Gates wasn't invited back to the team for the 1947-48 season.

The Blackhawks won 66 and lost 58 over the next two seasons, and Kerner, working as a full-time owner, somehow managed to pay the bills. "Pencils" Ferris, however, wrote off his interest in the team and returned to Buffalo.

Kerner, on the other hand, "had a mind to succeed." In his 30s, with only his mother to support, he was willing to work the long hours to keep the Blackhawks going. The early pro teams couldn't afford any of the front office staff, or scouts, or assistant coaches that populate modern franchises. So Kerner did most of the chores himself. Somehow, tickets got sold.

Within months, Kerner's persistence began to pay off. When the National Basketball League and the Basketball Association of America merged in 1949 to form the NBA, the Blackhawks were healthy enough to join the new league.

But their introduction to the competition was a bit rough. When they opened the 1949-50 season at 1-6, Kerner, already known as a man with little patience for coaches, promptly relieved Roger Potter and hired a fiery young fellow named Arnold "Red" Auerbach, who had coached the Washington Capitals to the 1949 league finals. When the Washington team folded that fall, he had become available.

His reputation already established, Auerbach was considered quite a coup for Kerner. He coached the Blackhawks to a 28-29 record down the stretch and even helped them to a brief appearance in the playoffs.

That spring, however, league commissioner Maurice Podoloff called a meeting. The Boston Celtics were struggling terribly. Podoloff had decided that the league needed Boston to survive. To do that, they had to win. To win, the Celtics needed Auerbach as coach, Podoloff told Kerner.

Then he asked the owner to give up his coach, who had another year on his contract. Some owners might have taken umbrage at such a brazen attempt to raid his business. But not Kerner.

"I said, 'Sure,'" he recalled. "Auerbach went to Boston, and the rest is history."

Auerbach said Kerner agreed to let him go because the owner knew he was mad. It seems Kerner had traded center John Mahnken after promising Auerbach he wouldn't.

Within a decade, the Hawks and Celtics would emerge as the two best teams in the league. But pro basketball teams were living through troubled times, and both feared for their existence in 1950.

Without Auerbach, the Blackhawks lived another losing season in Tri-Cities, and Kerner went through another three coaches. Despite the losses, the team continued to draw well. But the NBA wanted to think of itself as a big-town league. Kerner was encouraged to move the franchise to a major city, where it would have a better chance for survival.

He chose Milwaukee and shortened the name to the Hawks. Unfortunately, Wisconsin proved to be a wrong turn. The Hawks averaged 48 losses for each of their first three seasons in Milwaukee, and Kerner went through three more coaches.

But the third coach was veteran player William "Red" Holzman. Preoccupied with defense, he directed the Hawks to a 26-26 record for 1954-55.

After nine seasons, a dozen coaches and five home cities, Kerner decided to move again. The times were dangerous for pro basketball. In 1950, the NBA had consisted of 17 teams. By 1955, only eight survived.

Kerner decided to abandon Milwaukee when he heard the Boston Braves had plans to move there. Teetering on the verge of bankruptcy, the owner was sure his team could never survive in Milwaukee's small market with competition from baseball.

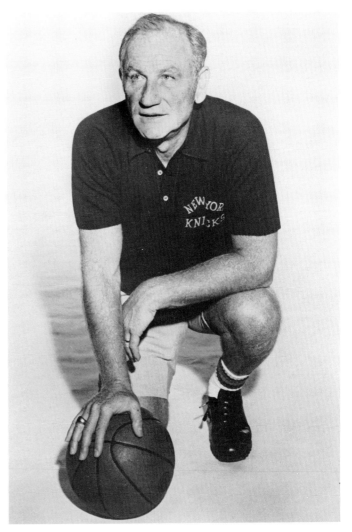

Red Holzman, another early Hawks coach.

So he packed up again, this time for St. Louis.

Before leaving Milwaukee, Kerner made two decisions that would boost the franchise's fortunes. In 1954, he drafted forward Bob Pettit out of Louisiana State. Later that year, Kerner hired a short, chubby, eccentric youngster named Marty Blake to help run the team. Despite his youth, he had been a promoter and scout and had even managed fighter Joe Louis' career briefly. Blake's official title with the Hawks was public relations man. But he was much more. As Richie Guerin, who served the Hawks as player, coach and general manager during his career, explained, "Marty Blake was a very, very astute judge of basketball talent."

Blake was immaculately organized and kept note cards seemingly on anyone who had ever played the game. The stiffs he called "Humpties," and he was given to phrases like, "He couldn't play dead."

He was gregarious and known to turn his mouthy wit on opposing teams. "He could start a riot in a convent, that Marty," Paul Seymour recalled. Kerner was rough on Blake sometimes, but he laughed it off and became chief scout, general manager and overall wheeler-dealer. With Blake helping to make the basketball decisions, the Hawks would become very good in St. Louis, and in the process they would make Ben Kerner a very rich man.

Hall of Fame center Easy Ed Macauley came to St. Louis in the Bill Russell deal.

THE RUSSELL DEAL

Perhaps the defining moment in Hawks history came when they traded away their rookie draft pick, Bill Russell, in 1956. Somewhat weary of how that trade has been portrayed over the years, Marty Blake, then the team's general manager, says the Hawks never figured to have Russell.

The Rochester Royals had the first pick in the 1956 draft and were set to take Russell. So the Hawks felt safe in agreeing to give the second pick in the draft to the Celtics in return for veteran center Easy Ed Macauley.

At the last minute, Rochester owner Les Harrison decided not to draft Russell, because the University of San Francisco center was playing in the Olympics in Australia and would not be able to sign a pro contract until December. Instead, the Royals drafted Sihugo Green out of Duquesne.

Suddenly, the Hawks had to draft Russell, the best young player to come along in years, then turn him over to the Celtics. It hurt Kerner, knowing that the Hawks had already given Auerbach to Boston in 1950. Now, they had to give up Russell, too.

Instead, the Hawks owner balked. The Celtics would have to give up another player if they wanted to close the deal, he said. Rather than tarry, Auerbach coughed up the rights to another talented young player, forward Cliff Hagan, who was just coming out of the service.

Together, Russell and Auerbach led Boston to 11 NBA titles over the next 13 seasons.

"Fortunately, it was great for basketball," Blake said in a 1992 interview. "If the Hawks had taken Russell, the Celtics might have folded."

As it turned out, the trade worked quite well for the Hawks, too. Macauley and Hagan both became Hall of Famers, as did Pettit. Even better, the revamped Hawks would battle Boston four times for the league championship.

THE GREATEST EVER

Marty Blake has little trouble identifying the greatest NBA Finals ever. It was the classic seven-game series between the Hawks and Celtics in 1957.

Blake recalled that just minutes before Game 3 of the series, CBS radio approached him and asked him to be the color commentator for its broadcast. The pay would be $25, he was told. The glib Blake readily agreed. "That's what basketball was like back then," he said of the informality. "And I never saw the twenty-five bucks."

Despite the lack of hype and publicity, the pro game staged a great series in 1957.

With their newly rebuilt team, the Hawks battled to the Western Division championship after tying for first place during the regular season with only a 34-38 record. But the Hawks had needed time to adjust after Blake acquired guard Slater Martin (a future Hall of Famer) before the season. The team jelled in the playoffs with wins over the Lakers and Pistons.

On paper, the Finals matchup didn't seem like much. The Celtics had finished the schedule 10 games better than the Hawks. But there was so much more to the 1957 NBA Finals than face value. The fortunes of the players and management of the Hawks and Celtics had become entwined over the years. Auerbach had worked for Kerner. Macauley had played six seasons in Boston. Hagan had been brought into the league by the Celtics, then dealt to the Hawks. St. Louis had drafted Russell, then handed him over to Boston. Chuck Share, who played in the St. Louis frontcourt, had been drafted by Boston and then released. Even Bob Cousy had once been the property of Kerner's Blackhawks, who had traded him to Chicago. Just about every player, it seemed, had a history with the other team.

The Hawks matched up well with Boston, too, despite their record. They had Pettit at forward, as well as Macauley, Hagan, Jack Coleman and Share in the frontcourt. Their guards were excellent, as well. Slater Martin ran the team. At guard with him was Jack McMahon, a solid pro the Hawks had gotten from Rochester.

About the only question mark was at coach, where Kerner set a record for changes that only George Steinbrenner of the Yankees could admire. Red Holzman began the season with the job, but lasted only until early January with the team's record at 14-19. Kerner replaced him with Martin as interim player/coach. Martin, however, loved to play and had little interest in the other headaches. Finally, the job fell to Alex Hannum, a Hawks' sub who had been claimed on waivers earlier in the season. He was a veteran journeyman with a good idea of the game, and that was enough for Kerner.

In the championship series, the Hawks wasted no time in establishing their toughness. Bill Sharman scored 36 for the Celtics in the first game at the Garden, but Pettit scored 37, and Macauley and Martin added 23 apiece. With that kind of firepower, the Hawks pushed the home team to double overtime. Miraculously then, St. Louis won it, 125-123, on a long shot by Jack Coleman as the 24-second clock expired. The Celtics got the ball back but couldn't score.

Immediately, it was clear the matchup would be intriguing. St. Louis would do most of its scoring in the frontcourt with the offensive touch of Macauley and Pettit, who had been effective against Russell in Game 1. Most of Boston's offense came from the guards. St. Louis had excellent defenders and floor people in Martin and McMahon. Boston answered with defense in Game 2, held Pettit to 11 points and won 119-99 to tie the series at one.

Game 3 was another zinger, however. The St. Louis crowd in Kiel Auditorium had its rough edges, which included a reputation for racial and anti-Semitic epithets. "Those fans in St. Louis screamed some strange things at you," recalled Earl Lloyd, one of the league's first black players. (The Hawks would become the last all-white team to win a title.)

Auerbach stirred this cauldron during pre-game warmups when he complained that one of the goals was too low. "I knew it was too low when Sharman and Cousy told me they could touch the rim," he explained. Auerbach took his complaint to the officials, who agreed to check the height. They found no problem. Kerner, though, was angered by the delay and stalked out onto the floor to scream that Auerbach was embarrassing him in front of the home fans.

Then Auerbach abruptly punched Kerner.

"Benny went up to argue with him, and Red hit him in the mouth," Blake recalled with a chuckle.

"He bloodied my lip," Kerner said. "You have to know Red

Bob Pettit

In his era, Bob Pettit epitomized basketball success. His statistics alone bear that out, although the numbers are only one indication of his greatness.

"In his day, he was the best power forward that was," Red Auerbach said of Pettit. "Elgin Baylor was a close second. Pettit could do more things than Baylor, because he could play some center. And he was a better rebounder than Baylor. Pettit was Mr. Clean. Mr. All America. He was a clean liver, just a super guy. But very, very competitive. He would play all out, whether he was 50 points ahead, or 50 behind. It didn't matter. That's the only way he knew how to play—all out."

At 6'7", he had entered Louisiana State as an unsung prospect. But Pettit grew to 6'9" and retained his mobility. He averaged 27.4 points per game over his college career, outstanding numbers in the era of slower basketball and good enough to make Pettit a three-time All-American center.

He averaged 20.4 points his first pro season (fourth best in the league) and finished third in rebounding. That performance earned him rookie of the year honors and presaged his stardom. He made the All-NBA first team for 10 of the 11 years he played. In 1956, he became one of only three players in NBA history to lead the league in both rebounding and scoring. (He retired in 1965 as the leading scorer in NBA history, although he knew the record wouldn't last long with Wilt Chamberlain in the league.)

"He kept coming at you," Syracuse Nationals Hall of Famer Dolph Schayes said of Pettit. "There was no way you could stop him over the course of a game. He was just too strong."

He used that strength to average better than 15 rebounds over his 10-season pro career. The Hawks ran a double pick offense that helped him get his shots (he was a streak shooter). "But if you asked him to dribble the ball twice, he wouldn't know where it was on the second bounce," joked former Hawks coach Paul Seymour.

When the Hawks moved to St. Louis after Pettit's rookie season, he became the favorite of crowds there. He came to be known as "Big Blue" because of his insistence on wearing a ratty old blue overcoat. That affection increased during the height of Pettit's career, from 1957-61, when he led the Hawks to four NBA Finals.

Auerbach. It was his style."

"I was talking to the refs," Auerbach explained. The officials chose not to throw him out, he said, because the incident occurred before the game. The blow brought blood but no permanent damage to Kerner, who was a friend to Auerbach both before and after the incident. "When I retired he gave me wonderful gifts," Auerbach said.

With this exchange as a backdrop, Game 3 quickly developed into a tense defensive struggle. There were numerous fouls and both teams did well at the line. But at the end, Pettit hit a long shot to give the Hawks a 100-98 win and a 2-1 lead. Boston came right back to win the fourth game, in St. Louis, 123-118, to tie the series again. Cousy scored 31 to counter 33 by Pettit. Then the Celts zipped St. Louis 124-109 in Game 5 for a 3-2 Boston lead. The series returned to St. Louis, where the Hawks waged another defensive battle and held Cousy to 15. Still, he could have won it with 12 seconds left and the score tied at 94, but he missed at the free-throw line. As expected, the Hawks gave Pettit the desperation shot, which missed, but Hagan tipped it in for a 96-94 win.

Tied at 3-3, the series returned to the Garden. Game 7 was a classic, except for the performance of the Boston backcourt. Cousy shot 2 for 20 and Sharman 3 for 20. Combined they made only 12.5 percent of their field goals. The championship load fell on Boston's rookies, Russell (19 points and 32 rebounds) and Tommy Heinsohn (37 points and 23 rebounds).

The Celtics had jumped out early, but the Hawks led 28-26 at the end of the first. Boston went on a tear from there, moving up 41-32. Hagan put the Hawks back in it with a six-point outburst in the closing minutes of the half. They led, in fact, 53-51 at intermission. The Celtics found another edge late in the third, 73-68, and pushed that lead to eight points early in the fourth. The Hawks answered again with a 9-0 run to take the lead and held a four-point edge with less than two minutes left. Boston hit three free throws to trail 101-100.

At less than a minute, the Hawks had the ball and Coleman took the shot to win it. But Russell blocked it and scored at the other end to give Boston a 102-101 lead. The Hawks couldn't score, and Boston again got possession. Desperate, the Hawks fouled Cousy, who had a chance to clinch the title at the line. He made one of two.

With the Celtics leading 103-101, Pettit sank two free throws in the closing seconds to send the game into overtime. Foul troubles caught up with the Hawks from there. McMahon went first, then Hagan fouled out. Still, they stayed close. As the first extra period wound down, Boston again held a lead, 113-111, but Coleman, who had won Game 1 for the Hawks, hit another clutch jumper for another overtime. With just seconds to go in the second extra period, Macauley went to the bench after fouling Boston's Jim Loscutoff. The muscular forward hit two free throws for a 125-123 Boston lead. For their only hope to tie, the Hawks had to inbound the ball with a full-court pass to Pettit. Player/coach Alex Hannum, the last eligible player on the Hawks' bench, entered the competition for the first time in the series. He planned to bank the pass off the backboard and hope that Pettit could tip it in. Incredibly,

Alex Hannum was a deep sub on the Hawks' bench when he was promoted to head coach in 1957.

Hannum banked the pass off the board to Pettit, but the final shot rolled off the rim.

Russell, Auerbach and the Celtics had won their first title, but the Hawks had come incredibly close to derailing Boston's championship tradition before it ever got rolling.

CHAMPIONSHIP

The 1957-58 season was one in a chain of Pettit's outstanding campaigns. He averaged 24.6 points and 17.4 rebounds per game while boosting the Hawks to the Western Division crown with a 41-31 record.

By no means, though, were the Hawks a one-man team. Both Slater Martin and Jack McMahon returned at guard. To go with this backcourt, the Hawks still had Ed Macauley, Chuck Share and Jack Coleman in the frontcourt. Also there was 6'4" forward Cliff Hagan, the team's other major threat, averaging 19.9 points per game. Despite his height, Hagan found a way to dominate inside. "He was the Adrian Dantley of his day," Auerbach said, comparing Hagan to one of his favorite modern players. "He played the game the same way. He was a very powerful man. And a proud man. He was always a hard worker, and another Mr. Clean in Pettit's mold."

Hagan had begun perfecting his inside moves as a high school center in Owensboro, Kentucky. He joined Frank Ramsey at the University of Kentucky, where they starred on three of coach Adolph Rupp's best teams. Hagan had a deadly hook shot and a rebounding fierceness that earned him consensus All-America honors in 1951-52.

Drawing their strength from Pettit and Hagan, the Hawks blasted the Pistons, 4-1, in the 1958 Western Division finals and advanced to the championship series for the second consecutive year.

The Celtics, meanwhile, dominated the Eastern Division with a 49-23 record. Many observers figured the Celtics probably would have won the 1958 title if Russell hadn't suffered an ankle injury in the third game of the series. Auerbach, however, found no comfort in that opinion.

"You can always look for excuses," he said. "We just got beat."

The results support that opinion. The Hawks upset the Celtics, with a healthy Russell, in Game 1 in Boston Garden, 104-102. Boston cracked back with a wipeout in Game 2, 136-112. Back in St. Louis, the Hawks held serve in Game 3 when Russell injured his ankle, 111-108.

Then, without Russell, the Celtics evened the series with a 109-98 surprise in Game 4. Still, Boston was drastically undermanned in the frontcourt. Even so, it was no cakewalk. The Hawks forced a 102-100 win in Boston Garden to take a 3-2 lead.

Back home in Kiel Auditorium on April 12, the Hawks weren't about to miss their opportunity. Pettit guaranteed that, turning in a solidly spectacular performance. He scored 31 points in the first three quarters, then zoomed off in the final period, nailing 19 of his team's last 21 points. His last two, a tip-in with 15 seconds remaining, put the Hawks ahead, 110-107. The Celtics scored a meaningless bucket and could do no more. Ben Kerner's team finally had a title, 110-109.

Pettit's 50-point performance tied the single-game playoff scoring record set by Cousy against Syracuse in 1953. But Cousy's record had been set in a four-overtime game, an event so foul-plagued that he hit 30 of his points from the free-throw line. In pure basketball prowess, Pettit's 50-point performance was stunning. Better yet, it had delivered his team a championship.

The celebration was the crowning moment for Kerner. "We beat 'em in six," he said 35 years later. "That I'll never forget."

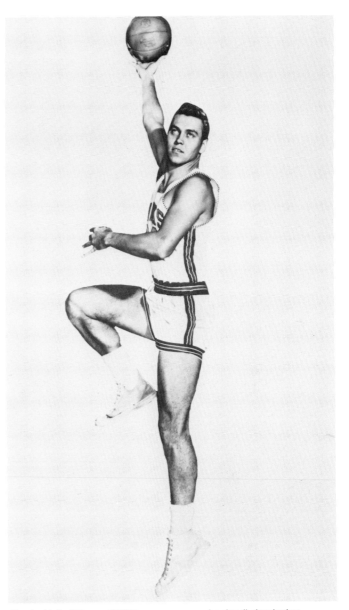

Hawks Hall of Famer Cliff Hagan possessed a deadly hook shot.

THE BATTLE RESUMES

For 1958-59, the Hawks underwent several major changes, the biggest of which was the retirement of Macauley. Also Hannum had left as coach because he wanted more control over the team, and Kerner wouldn't give it to him. Kerner first hired Andy Phillip to coach, but he lasted only a few games into November. The mercurial owner then selected Macauley.

"Every day was an experience," Paul Seymour said of Kerner. "He was an emotional guy. You never knew what mood he was gonna be in. I think he fired a coach a year. Sometimes two."

The team had changed its look in the frontcourt with the addition of Clyde Lovellette, a future Hall of Famer who had been picked up in a trade with Minneapolis. During the regular season, the Hawks were nearly as powerful in the West as the Celtics were in the East. Pettit had perhaps his best season ever, breaking the league scoring record by averaging 29.2 points. But the Hawks lost in the semifinals to the Minneapolis Lakers with rookie sensation Elgin Baylor, who had averaged 24.9 points in his first season.

Kerner's team came back strong in 1960, and again the Hawks and Celtics met for their third league Finals in four years. "At the time, the Hawks were the most intense rivalry we had," Cousy said.

Nothing better epitomized this rivalry than the matchup of Cousy against the Hawks' Slater Martin.

"Slater was the guy I most disliked to play against, in terms of his skills matched against mine," Cousy said.

Cousy often looked forward to matching up with the bigger guards around the league, because his speed and quickness would usually win over their size and strength. Martin, though, was smaller than Cousy and matched his quickness. "Slater was the only one I used to call for help on," Cousy said. "I used to tell my big people to set picks as often as they felt like it."

Although Martin was an older veteran, Cousy said he

never noticed a diminishing of his quickness. Nor a slackening of his fierce competitiveness.

But for the first time in his 11-year career, injuries began to nag Martin in 1960. "I'd never wrapped an ankle as long as I played basketball," he told writer Charles Salzberg. "Never had a sprained ankle, never put a piece of tape on it. I could get dressed for a game in 30 seconds. I'd put on my jockstrap, slip on the jersey, and I was ready to go."

He pulled a hamstring during the 1960 All-Star game in St. Louis, and that took a few weeks to heal. Then he pulled another leg muscle during the playoffs. But the team was in a tight series with the Lakers and needed a road win. Martin said Kerner asked him to play the next game with a shot of novacain to kill his pain. He agreed. The Hawks won. But Martin was left on crutches the next day and was through for the season, his last in the league.

Even without Martin, the Hawks squeezed past the Lakers and returned to the Finals once more to face the Celtics. Ed Macauley was now in his second season as the Hawks' coach. In a bold television interview after his team had eliminated the Lakers, Macauley predicted that St. Louis would whip Boston. But privately, he knew his team would be outmanned in the backcourt.

"We'll be lucky if we win one game," he later told his wife.

The St. Louis lineup had changed considerably since their '58 championship. Pettit and Hagan were still in the frontcourt. But Coleman, Share and Macauley were gone. McMahon's playing time had diminished (he appeared in

Hall of Famer Slater Martin.

only 25 games). And with Martin injured, Si Green and Johnny McCarthy ran the backcourt.

True to expectations, Boston dominated the first game of the series, 140-122. But the Celtics got notice they were in for a scrap in Game 2, when the Hawks broke back and upset them, 113-103, in Boston Garden. To reaffirm their dominance, Boston thumped the Hawks again, 102-86, in Kiel Auditorium in Game 3. St. Louis won their second home game, 106-96, to send the series back to the Garden tied at 2-2. Boston again won big there, 125-102, which left things secure enough. Even if the Celtics lost Game 6 in St. Louis—which they did, 105-102—they returned to the Garden for number seven.

There on April 9, the Celtics claimed their second consecutive championship and third overall with a comfortable win, 122-103. With Martin out of the lineup, Cousy had been able to maneuver unhampered. He finished with 19 points and 14 assists. All the same, the Hawks had nothing to be ashamed of. They had won three more games than Macauley figured they could.

ENTER WILKENS

The Hawks again dominated the Western Division in 1960-61, but Kerner changed coaches once more. During the '60 playoffs, he had hired Paul Seymour, only he didn't inform Macauley until after the season ended.

Macauley later said he would have preferred to remain coach, but he agreed to move up to general manager (a position he held only briefly). Seymour wanted the team to run a little more, and they finally had the guy to do that in rookie guard Lenny Wilkens out of Providence College.

Seymour had spotted Wilkens at a college All-Star game and told Blake that he was the guard the team needed. "He could steal your sneaks if you put 'em on the floor," Seymour said. "He was really quick."

But Wilkens was quiet and couldn't shoot, and Kerner became angry early in the season when Seymour began playing him. The owner told the coach to bench the rookie. But Seymour started Wilkens against the Knicks in a game in Detroit, and the rookie responded with bunches of steals that propelled the Hawks to a win.

"Kerner was sort of an arrogant guy," Seymour recalled. "He stood at midcourt after the game, smoking a big cigar and bellowing out, 'I wouldn't trade Lenny Wilkens for the whole Knick team and $50,000.'"

At first the Hawks veterans had been cool to Wilkens, until they realized how well he could run the team. With Wilkens' superb basketball mind directing the action, Pettit averaged a whopping 27.9 points, while Hagan and Lovellette each scored about 22 a game. The veterans liked the rookie guard even more when they realized he didn't shoot much, Seymour said.

The Hawks might have made a better showing in the championship series if they hadn't gotten caught in such a fight with Los Angeles in the Western finals. Rookie Jerry West and Baylor pushed the Hawks through a seven game series before falling 4-3.

The Hawks arrived at Boston Garden April 2 after just completing their series with the Lakers the night before in St. Louis. They were blown out by the Celtics, 129-95. For

Game Two, they improved a bit but still lost, 116-108. Their single victory was a tight win in Game 3 in St. Louis. But the Hawks lost Game 4 at home by 15 (119-104), then succumbed in Boston Garden to fall 4-1.

It had been a remarkable run. Four times in five years they had battled for the world championship. Arguably, Russell's Celtics were the greatest team in the history of the game, and the Hawks had given them all the challenge they wanted.

FALL AND RISE

From the height of their championship bouts, the Hawks' fortunes plummeted precipitously the next season, 1961-62. Lenny Wilkens was called to military duty and appeared in only 20 games, and Clyde Lovellette spent much of the season nursing an injured back. They finished with 51 losses. Kerner responded with his usual frantic coaching shuffle. Paul Seymour was fired after 15 games (when he refused Kerner's demands to bench rookie guard Cleo Hill), then Fuzzy Levane guided the team to a 20-40 record. He, too, was let go with six games left, and Bob Pettit took over as player/coach.

Kerner (seated) with Pettit, Hagan and Wilkens.

All of which left Marty Blake searching far and wide for the right answer to the team's personnel problems that spring of 1962. From little Prairie View College in Texas, he drafted 6'9" center Zelmo Beaty, and from the University of Kansas, he took 6'5" strong man Bill Bridges. He also got guard John Barnhill from Tennessee State. To go with the new cast, Kerner hired Harry "the Horse" Gallatin to coach. The results were immediate. With Wilkens back from military duty, the offense again ran smoothly. Pettit enjoyed one of his best seasons, averaging 28.4 points and 15.1 rebounds. The Hawks finished 48-32 and played their way to the 1963 Western Division finals, where they lost to the Lakers in a seven-game series.

They slipped slightly early in the 1963-64 season, but Blake acquired Richie Guerin, a tough veteran guard, from New York during the campaign. By playoff time, they were strong enough to defeat the injury-riddled Lakers in the first round. But the balance of power had shifted in the Western Division with the movement of Wilt Chamberlain and the Philadelphia Warriors to San Francisco. Still, the outsized Hawks fought the giant Warriors (rookie Nate Thurmond also inhabited the San Francisco frontcourt) through a seven-game Western final before losing.

Later that spring of 1964, Blake drafted Paul Silas, a bulky power forward out of Creighton. His presence would help to make the Hawks of the future one of basketball's best rebounding teams.

The 1964-65 season was Pettit's last. Injuries limited the great forward to appearances in only 50 games. Regardless, Kerner had high expectations. When the team opened with

a 17-16 record, he discarded Gallatin (who had directed the team to 96 wins over the two previous seasons) and promoted the 32-year-old Guerin as player/coach. Under Guerin, they went 28-19 to finish 45-35. But Pettit's career ended when the Hawks lost to Baltimore in the first round of the Western playoffs. "He worked at both ends of the floor," Kerner said wistfully of Pettit. "You don't get players to do that very often."

Certainly, superstars of Pettit's caliber didn't come along very often. But there were a number of good players available, if you looked close enough. And Marty Blake knew where to look. His trades and drafts funneled a steady stream of talent onto the roster.

During the 1965-66 season, Blake acquired marvelously versatile guard/forward Joe Caldwell from Detroit. Caldwell's leaping style (his nickname was "Pogo Joe"), his defense and his hustle made him a quick fan favorite. At the same time, the general manager added Rod Thorn, a veteran guard.

Still, the Hawks were a team in transition. Pettit had retired, and Hagan was playing his last season. They finished a disappointing 36-44 and were swept by the Bullets in the first round of the playoffs.

It was then that Blake made perhaps his best move as general manager, with the drafting of Lou Hudson out of the University of Minnesota. He was a pure shooter and could play both forward and guard, although he was most dangerous in the frontcourt.

Hawks fans witnessed the emergence of a rookie superstar over the course of the 1966-67 season. With a sugary shot, "Sweet Lou" Hudson led the team in scoring with 18.4 points per game. Although they finished only 39-42, the Hawks came together at the close of the season,

Standing, left to right, Bill Bridges (32), Pettit (9), Zelmo Beaty (31) and Hagan. Kneeling are Wilkens and player/coach Richie Guerin.

Lou Hudson starred at the University of Minnesota.

Center Zelmo Beaty came out of Prairie View in Texas.

battling their way to the Western finals before losing 4-2 to San Francisco.

All of which served as a set-up for the next season, 1967-68, when the Hawks got off to a 16-1 start and finished 56-26 (a club record) to claim the Western crown. The stellar Wilkens enjoyed his best season, averaging 20 points and 8.3 assists. He was perfect in setting up shots for Zelmo Beaty, Bill Bridges, Joe Caldwell and Paul Silas.

In recognition, the writers voted Wilkens second behind Chamberlain in the league's MVP balloting.

If anything, that 1967-68 team reflected balance and Guerin's love of tough, smart players. The Hawks were a solid rebounding team, with Bridges (1102), Silas (958) and Beaty (959) all ripping big numbers off the boards. Even Wilkens averaged better than five rebounds per game.

As a result, their image was all workmanship. Which should have been enough in a blue-collar town like St. Louis. But during a 56-win season, they had averaged just a little better than 5,000 fans per night in old Kiel Auditorium, which seated about 9,000. Even that modest draw was enough to turn a nice profit for Kerner. But the owner wanted

out. Now in his 50s and married, he had put better than 20 years into the game and that was enough. The American Basketball Association had just gotten started, plus hockey and baseball were eating up the entertainment dollars in St. Louis.

Despite all of that, Kerner could have stayed on and kept making money. He had tried unsuccessfully to get the city of St. Louis to build a new arena. But it wasn't just the small building. Kerner had lost the fire in his belly and wanted to sell.

The only problem was, with ABA franchises going cheaply, there weren't many people willing to pay top dollar for an established NBA team.

Then late one week, a young man from New Orleans contacted the Hawks. He said he was a son of a Louisiana state senator and he wanted to buy Kerner's team. He mentioned his net worth of $40 million, or so. Almost the weekend, there wasn't time to check him out completely. But he talked a good game, so management invited him to town to discuss specific numbers.

Somehow, word even got out to the newspapers.

Guerin—The Player/Coach

To say the least, the record was daunting when Richie Guerin took over as the player/coach of the St. Louis Hawks in 1964-65. Over the Hawks' previous 15 seasons in the NBA, owner Ben Kerner had hired and fired 16 coaches.

The casualty list included Red Holzman, Red Auerbach and Alex Hannum, who between them would coach 13 NBA championship teams.

But Guerin was different.

He was a tough New York city ballplayer who averaged 18 points over 11 NBA seasons and had once scored 56 points in a game. Where the others failed, he survived eight straight seasons coaching the Hawks. They earned a playoff spot for every season he was in charge. In addition, they won two divisional titles. His 327 career victories means he has won more games than any other Hawks coach.

He was only able to accomplish that because he established a rapport with Kerner right away.

"I became player/coach in December 1964 after Harry Gallatin was fired," Guerin recalled. "I told Mr. Kerner I would do the coaching for the balance of the season and see how it worked out. One of our first games was an embarrassing loss in Baltimore. Afterward, I had to go in and explain to Mr. Kerner what happened. I told him, 'We're gonna lose sometimes by 30 points. If I have to explain it every time we have a tough loss, forget it. I'll go back to being a player and you can find someone else to be coach.'"

Kerner quickly agreed not to interfere, and Guerin had the freedom he needed to succeed.

"I was always trying to find the right coach, trying to win," Kerner said of his penchant for changing coaches. "It was a combination of things.

"But there was no bull about Richie. He told it the way it was. He was all business, a great coach."

Guerin remained a player/coach long after his quickness had gone. Whenever injury left the Hawks roster a little thin, or whenever lackluster play got up his dander, Guerin would break his uniform out of moth balls and show his team how to do it.

It was this special fire that cast the Hawks as a force. They hustled and punished their opponents with defense. Best of all, they played together.

Outside of a championship, that was all Guerin ever wanted.

"He was one hell of a coach," said former Hawks general manager Marty Blake.

After stepping aside as coach, Guerin became the team's general manager, a position he held for two seasons. Upon leaving the NBA, he became a successful stockbroker in his native New York.

Kerner met with him briefly, seemed pleased and asked Marty Blake to talk to him. Blake recalls it was a Sunday afternoon.

"The first thing he says to me," Blake recalled, "is that he wanted me to stay on as G.M. Then he said I would have my own plane to scout talent all over the country, and he offered me $225,000 over three years. At the time, I was making about $14,000 a year.

"I said to myself, 'This guy's crazy.' I called Bennie [Kerner] and told him what he had offered me. 'He is crazy,' Bennie said.

"As it turned out, the guy had about six cents in his pocket. He lived in a shack, a complete nut."

After that embarrassing fiasco, Kerner resumed his search for a buyer, only the next time around he was determined to move swiftly and silently.

As a result, the Hawks' move to Atlanta would catch nearly everybody by surprise.

Hall of Famer Bob Lovellette.

Hudson introduced Atlanta to sensational hoops.

Oh Atlanta!

1968-76

Historian William Manchester once described 1968 as "the year everything went wrong."

He wasn't overstating the situation.

The year opened with a string of tragedies and horrors. Then things got worse. The U.S.S. Pueblo was captured by North Korea on January 23rd. A week later, the Viet Cong launched the Tet Offensive in South Vietnam. Later, the U.S. submarine Scorpion would be lost at sea with her crew of 99. And a coal mining disaster in West Virginia would leave 78 miners entombed.

On April 4, America's great non-violent Christian leader (and Atlanta's own son), Dr. Martin Luther King, Jr., was slain in Memphis by assassin James Earl Ray. His murder set off riots in 168 cities and towns across the nation. An estimated 120 million television viewers watched a throng of between 50,000 and 100,000 march in his funeral procession in Atlanta.

Just two months after King was felled, Robert F. Kennedy was murdered in Los Angeles as he celebrated an impressive string of Democratic presidential primary victories. That summer, the Vietnam war became the longest war in United States history. The ensuing months were marked by anti-war protests and demonstrations at college campuses, by municipal worker strikes in major cities, and by a tumultuous Democratic national convention in Chicago.

All of this, of course, occurred during a presidential election year, with Kennedy, President Lyndon Johnson, Richard Nixon, Eugene McCarthy and Hubert Humphrey all playing major roles in the drama.

Amid this chaos, the St. Louis Hawks became the Atlanta Hawks in a simple announcement on Friday May 3.

In light of the events in society at large, it seems almost ludicrous that the local papers would describe the announcement as a "bombshell."

Yet, in terms of pro sports, it was a bombshell. Thomas G. Cousins, a 36-year-old real estate developer, and former Governor Carl E. Sanders, a one-time University of Georgia quarterback, had agreed to purchase the Hawks for a reported $3.5 million.

The highly secretive negotiations had taken just one week to complete, and the Atlanta press was left dumbstruck and disappointed at being kept in the dark about a major story.

It was a bombshell because Atlanta and the South seemed an unlikely market for pro basketball. At its best, the region was thought to be Southeastern Conference football country.

At its worst?

Sid Goldberg, a basketball promoter, recalled that he staged a series of pro games in the South in 1947. Houston and New Orleans produced good crowds that warmed to the athletes in short pants. But everywhere else the sport was a bomb. Nowhere was it worse than Atlanta.

Goldberg didn't recall exactly where he staged the game in Atlanta. But he did recall the gate—84 paying customers. During the game, one of the players threw a full-court pass that knocked out several lights. "We didn't take in enough at the gate to pay the light repair bill," Goldberg recalled with a laugh.

Needless to say, there were no plans for a return engagement to the city. "We thought Atlanta was a Ku Klux Klan city," Goldberg explained. "And our teams had mostly Jewish players."

Whatever of that image was accurate, a goodly portion of it had been shed 21 years later. Atlanta had become a city of the future by 1968, with developers scrambling to reclaim downtown neighborhoods or to transform outlying farms into suburbs.

At 36, Tom Cousins was one of the youngest and brightest of these developers. And he made no bones about why he wanted the Hawks.

"I was concerned with developing 60 acres of downtown Atlanta," he told Furman Bisher. "A coliseum was the key to the whole thing, some focal point to build around."

Cousins planned to build a coliseum, then find a pro basketball team or hockey team to play in it. He took that idea to then-mayor Ivan Allen, who had played a role in bringing the Falcons to town.

"Oh no!" Allen said when he heard the plan. "I almost had

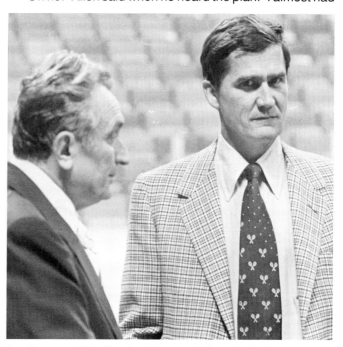

Ben Kerner and Tom Cousins, the men who brought the Hawks to Atlanta.

Paul Silas (above) and Bill Bridges (right) gave the Hawks an excellent set of power forwards.

a stadium without a team. Get your franchise first. Then we'll build a coliseum."

"That's what I did," Cousins told Bisher. "That's the reason I bought the Hawks. I needed them to get the development going."

Still, it didn't happen right away. Cousins approached St. Louis Hawks owner Ben Kerner but was turned down. Kerner figured that the NBA would never approve a sale of the team if there was no suitable building immediately available. Promises to build an arena would never work.

Undaunted, Cousins backtracked and secured an agreement with Georgia Tech to allow the Hawks to use ancient Alexander Memorial Coliseum. Then he returned to St. Louis and struck a deal with Kerner. Even then, Hawks General Manager Marty Blake didn't think it would work. "There was no way the NBA should have approved the Hawks playing at Georgia Tech," Blake said recently. "The Tech people were great to us and very gracious. But it was a bad building. It had terrible locker rooms and only seated about 7,200. The league wouldn't have approved it, but Benny Kerner was one of the pioneers of pro basketball, and the league people wanted to see him get out of the business with some money."

The NBA approved the transaction based on promises that Cousins would have a new building ready in two years. The papers reported that Cousins was planning a "modern, Madison Square Garden type arena."

To many Atlantans, the most startling thing about the deal was that the city suddenly possessed a divisional championship team. Two other cities, Phoenix and

Milwuakee, were entering the NBA with expansion franchises, but it would take time and luck to build competitive teams there.

"It's really amazing to me that they could acquire a strong established team like that," William C. Fox, an insurance representative, told the Atlanta papers.

"We're an exciting club, the kind, I feel sure, all the fans in Atlanta are really going to like," coach Richie Guerin said.

They were a very good team, with potential to get better. Lou Hudson had become one of the premier shooters of that era. Joe Caldwell was on the verge of blossoming into an all-star. Zelmo Beaty had proven to be just the quick, smooth-shooting center to give Wilt Chamberlain fits. And Bill Bridges and Paul Silas gave the Hawks a pair of smart, robust power forwards.

"We were a close-knit team, which made us a tough team," said Guerin, who had been named the league's coach of the year for 1968. "We were smart and physical but not dirty."

Yet, even as the team moved, Guerin's lineup was beginning to show the stress that would break it apart. Team captain Lenny Wilkens had evolved into one of the best players in the game after eight pro seasons, as evidenced by the fact that he finished second only to Chamberlain in the 1968 MVP balloting. A poor shooter as a rookie, he had developed his shooting skills and made himself a 20-points-per-game scorer. But his real contribution was as a playmaker and leader. He knew how to exploit mismatches on the floor so that Beaty and Caldwell could score.

"He's the one who makes this team unselfish," Beaty said of Wilkens.

Hudson was a hit in Atlanta.

But for his skills and experience, Wilkens was vastly underpaid at $30,000 per year. He asked for a raise in his new contract, and the team mentioned $40,000. Wilkens wanted $60,000 (Chamberlain was making $250,000).

With negotiations at an obvious impasse, Wilkens became the first holdout in Hawks history. And that sealed the team's fate.

When the Hawks brought their players to Atlanta to introduce them to the media, Kerner told them to leave Wilkens in St. Louis because he was unsigned.

"Pay me or trade me, " Wilkens told reporters by phone from his St. Louis home. "We have a championship caliber team, and I would like to play on it."

Behind the scenes, the real problem was between player and coach.

"For some reason, he didn't get along with Richie Guerin," Marty Blake said. "Wilkens deserved a hell of a raise. They wouldn't give it to him. We should have signed Wilkens. It was a stupid move."

Instead, the Hawks traded the 33-year-old Wilkens to Seattle for 26-year-old Walt Hazzard. On paper, it looked like a decent deal. But Hazzard couldn't compare with Wilkens as a playmaker.

"Lenny was our leader and a great basketball player," Guerin said in a 1992 interview. "But he held out, and we had to make a trade. That was the start of our demise."

Guerin confirmed that he and Wilkens were in the midst of a spat, but it was a problem the two men later worked out.

As if the Wilkens trade wasn't enough, other things conspired against the Hawks. That summer of 1968 Wilt Chamberlain was traded from the Philadelphia 76ers to the Lakers, creating a super team in Los Angeles. With Wilkens, the Hawks just might have been successful in the Western Division. Without him, they were still a good team.

But not good enough.

With the expansion of Milwaukee and Phoenix, the NBA became a 14-team league in 1968, with the San Diego Rockets, Lakers, Warriors, Phoenix Suns, Chicago Bulls and Seattle SuperSonics joining Atlanta in the Western Division.

The Hawks first draftees, including Skip Harlicka, Bob Warren and Rusty Parker, failed to distinguish themselves. But there was still plenty of bravado from Guerin during the exhibition season. The team would survive without Wilkens, he said.

Publicly, other coaches and executives around the league agreed. "The Hawks run, run, run and have a strong defense," Boston's Red Auerbach said. But privately they were elated to see the Hawks grow weaker.

Their first exhibition game was played in Salem, Va., a victory over the defending world champion Celtics. But a few days later, again facing Boston in Knoxville, Tenn., the Hawks had 32 turnovers, revealing the void Wilkens had left.

The season opened October 16 at Memorial with a 125-110 loss to Oscar Robertson and the Cincinnati Royals. Among the 5,606 in attendance were Ben Kerner and Bob Pettit. The Hawks' first victory came three nights later against the Milwuakee Bucks expansion franchise.

An early rash of injuries further thinned the lineup, taking center Zelmo Beaty with a badly sprained ankle and guards George Lehmann and Don Ohl. The situation forced the 36-

year-old Guerin, who had averaged 18 points over 11 pro seasons, back into uniform.

It was then that the Hawks showed Atlanta their toughness. Silas, Bridges, Caldwell and Hudson stepped up their intensity. By mid-January, they had a 12-game winning streak and were drawing capacity crowds. Through December and January, they won 20 of 23 games. The display earned Caldwell and Hudson spots on the Western All-Star roster.

"We did it with togetherness," Guerin said proudly. "But eventually talent overcomes a lot of that."

Whenever the emotional pace slowed, Guerin found a way to pick it up. In January, he roughed up a Philadelphia sportswriter, causing a minor ruckus. Regardless, the Hawks played on, finishing 48-34, good enough for second place in the Western Division behind the Lakers.

In the first round of the playoffs, they shook off the San Diego Rockets, 4-2, and tried to come up with a way of neutralizing Chamberlain in the Division finals against the Lakers. Silas, Bridges and Beaty took turns boxing him out.

The officials called the series tightly, which left Guerin fuming. Atlanta led by 20 points in Game 1 in the Forum, before losing 95-93. "That was a crucial loss that was tough to overcome," Guerin recalled. "They shot 30 more free throws than we did. That officiating set the tone for our players."

The Hawks dropped another two-point game in the Forum, then won at home by 19, 99-80. But the Lakers

Herm Gilliam, Hawks point guard of the early 1970s.

controlled the series from there and advanced, 4-1.

The offseason brought an even bigger setback when Zelmo Beaty jumped ship to the Utah Stars of the ABA. Then Guerin compounded the problem by insisting that Silas be traded to Phoenix for Gary Gregor. "That was the worst deal I made as a coach," Guerin said "Gregor had played well in his first two years, and I wanted him as another big scoring forward. But the trading of Paul Silas was another part of the team's demise."

Bridges averaged 14.4 rebounds to pick up the slack, but the team needed more. With 23 games left on the 1969-70 schedule, Marty Blake acquired 6-foot-11 veteran Walt Bellamy from Detroit to patch the hole in the middle.

"Big Bells" was an immediate hit with Atlanta fans, as the Hawks finished 15-8 down the stretch to claim the Western title over the injury-riddled Lakers. Atlanta easily handled the Chicago Bulls in the first round, 4-1. But the Lakers were healthy by the Western finals and overwhelmed the Hawks, 4-0.

Guerin had actually believed they could beat West and Chamberlain and Baylor. "I was devastated," the coach said two decades later, the pain still obvious. (In frustration, with his team far behind, he had entered Game 4 of the series and scored 39 points to close out his playing career.)

Complications and controversy continued apace for the Hawks that spring. They possessed the third pick in the draft and hoped to use it to stake out their future. Blake recalled that he wanted to pick Florida State center Dave Cowens. Guerin recalled that the team's thinking ran toward Dan Issel of Kentucky.

But Tom Cousins figured that LSU All-American Pete Maravich would sell tickets. "It was not my decision," Guerin said. "I found out the night before the draft that we were taking Pete Maravich."

Neither was it Blake's. The general manager resigned that summer, after 16 years with the club. The Hawks gave Maravich a $2 million contract over four years, just two years after declining to give Lenny Wilkens a $60,000 contract.

Atlanta also had another first-round pick in 1970 and used it to draft UCLA guard John Vallely, another move opposed by Blake. "He couldn't play dead," Blake said. The team gave Vallely $300,000 over two years and ended up eating the second year of the contract.

But the big blow came later, when it was discovered that a loophole in Joe Caldwell's contract allowed him to become a free agent. "Joe wanted to stay in Atlanta," Guerin recalled. "But he also wanted a lot of money."

The Hawks' first game in Atlanta, a loss to Oscar Robertson (14) and the Cincinnati Royals on Oct. 16, 1968.

Having seen the money the team was giving its rookies, the popular Caldwell, who was again selected to the All-Star team in 1970, was offended by the offers to him and jumped to a fat contract with the Carolina Cougars of the ABA.

"Lou Hudson and Joe Caldwell gave us great flexibility," Guerin said. "They both could play guard and forward. Losing Joe was a great loss."

It could be argued that no NBA team was hit worse by the rival league. Over six seasons, the Hawks would lose starters and top draft picks to the ABA, yet when Atlanta attempted to retaliate by signing young ABA star Julius Erving, the NBA stepped in and stopped the move.

In 1971, the Hawks traded Bridges to Philadelphia for Jim Washington, signaling the end of an era. Wilkens, Silas, Caldwell and Bridges had been the heart of a great team. "We had a lot of good players," Guerin said. "But we may have been one or two players away from a league championship. We could never get over the hump with the Lakers and the Warriors."

The sting of breaking up their close group stayed with the players for some time. Caldwell later had an opportunity to return to the team but declined.

A year after his trade, Bridges was still out of sorts. "You know," he told reporters one night in New York, "I turned around with a rebound tonight and started to toss that long pass downcourt, and I swear I thought I heard Joe Caldwell's familiar yelp to let me know it was there. You know what happened to that pass? It fell into an empty court."

THE PISTOL ARRIVES

From the start, the chemistry was bad.

The Atlanta Hawks were a team of underpaid veterans, with a coach who demanded defense and hustle. And Pete Maravich had been schooled in the run-and-gun game at LSU by his father, coach Press Maravich. "The Pistol" was used to dominating the ball and showboating for the crowd. He took shots when he wanted (which was often) and

Although only 6-foot-6, Bill Bridges used his great strength to become a powerful rebounder.

Guerin and assistant Gene Tormohlen.

entertained himself by entertaining the fans with no-look passes and fancy ballhandling.

"He knew how to play one way," recalled Richie Guerin. "His dad turned him loose at LSU, and that's the only way he knew."

From the moment he entered the Hawks' training camp in 1970, Maravich drew the resentment of veterans who made far less than he. Already aloof, he became more so.

"It was a long season," Guerin said.

The Hawks had moved to the Eastern Conference's Central Division for 1970-71, where they had a legitimate shot at contending. But their chemistry was rotten. It seemed that Maravich was constantly catching his teammates unawares with a no-look pass, bouncing the ball off their hands and faces. They made no attempt to hide their dislike.

"Pete's style of play offended me as a coach and our players," Guerin said.

By February, their record stood at 19-39, and for the first time since he had become coach six seasons earlier, Guerin was faced with not making the playoffs.

Regardless, the fans loved to watch Maravich work. Even with their record, the Hawks were transformed overnight into the second-best drawing road team in the league. Fans came out in droves to see the Pistol.

And even Guerin had to admit that as time passed, they began to play better together. Typical of his teams, these Hawks closed the regular season with a flourish, going 17-7 through the final third of the schedule to finish 36-46, good enough for a second place finish in the weak Central.

Somehow they had salvaged yet another playoff appearance. But the New York Knicks dismissed them 4-1 in the first round.

Still, Guerin had reason for optimism. At the close of the season, the team had pulled together, and Maravich had shown some willingness to change.

"It was a battle," Guerin said. "He would try to change and then revert to the old ways."

The hope, however, quickly vanished in training camp that fall of 1971, when Maravich was diagnosed with mononucleosis. He returned to the lineup after Thanksgiving, but was obviously weak.

By late winter, the Hawks were in another deep hole with a 21-38 record. The frustration was punctuated that season after a loss to the Lakers, when Atlanta Journal sports editor George Cunningham punched out Hawks business manager Irv Gack.

Fortunately, Maravich began to come around in January, scoring 50 in a win over Philly with only 3,665 fans watching in the Coliseum. A few nights later, he did it again, this time against Cleveland.

Hudson works on John Havlicek. (Herm Gilliam in background).

Hudson, the Super Sweet Star

The only great debate over Lou Hudson was his nickname. Was he "Super Lou"? Or "Sweet Lou"?

Actually, to Atlanta fans he was both. His game was Super, and his shot was Sweet.

That combination made the 6'5", 215-pound Hudson one of the premier players of the era.

"Lou Hudson is a superstar in the NBA, ranking up there with Jerry West, John Havlicek and Elgin Baylor," veteran coach Alex Hannum once remarked.

"Lou Hudson was one of the greatest shooters in pro basketball history," agreed his coach of eight years, Richie Guerin.

A native of Greensboro, N.C., Hudson and Archie Clark integrated University of Minnesota basketball in the erly 1960s. As a Golden Gopher, Hudson quickly built a reputation for greatness.

Former Hawks general manager Marty Blake recalled scouting Hudson as a college senior. Although Lou had a cast on his broken left hand, he still scored 30 points that night. Blake and Hawks coach Richie Guerin were so excited by the performance, Blake wrecked their rental car returning to Atlanta.

That spring of 1966, they selected Hudson with the fourth pick of the first round. He never disappointed. Over a 13-season pro career, he averaged 20.2 points, with 4.4 rebounds and 2.7 assists. Beginning with his first season in Atlanta, Hudson earned six straight NBA All-Star appearances.

"I scored the first basket for the Atlanta Hawks," he told writer Bill Kreifeldt in 1992, "the first two points at Alexander Memorial Coliseum on a 20-foot jumper from the left side of the key. Zelmo [Beaty] was open under the basket, but I couldn't get the ball to him."

He remembers his early years in Atlanta as among his favorite. "We were a close-knit team," he said. "There was great camaraderie. We didn't draw much in those early seasons in Atlanta. But we weren't as close later on. Those five years at Georgia Tech before the Omni was built were special."

Hudson spent the final two seasons of his career with the Los Angeles Lakers. He retired in 1979, and the Hawks called him back to retire his number (Pettit and Hudson are the only two Hawks to enjoy the honor).

"They'll do Dominique one day," Hudson said. "That's good. He's one of my all-time favorites. It's a big-time honor. It means you made a mark that will last forever. They can't take that away from you. It's like it's written in stone."

Hudson today lives in Park City, Utah, where he is actively involved in high school coaching, youth work and numerous other charitable activities. In recognition of his efforts, Park City named Hudson its "Citizen of the Year" for 1992.

Coach Cotton Fitzsimmons works from the bench, with trainer Joe O'Toole.

Significantly, the Hawks won both games.

As a point guard, Maravich was learning to penetrate and dish off or draw the foul. He earned his millions at the line. Even better, he played with fire that spring. As did Bellamy and Hudson.

And once again, Guerin's Hawks came alive down the stretch, winning 15 of their last 23 games to finish 36-46 in the Central, good enough for another playoff appearance.

In eight years of coaching, Guerin's teams had made the playoffs eight times. But even the latest resurgence couldn't save him. Already the rumors had started about a coaching change. Al McGuire, Oscar Robertson, Dave DeBusschere and Jerry West were said to be among the leading candidates.

The Hawks battled the Celtics in the first round of the playoffs, but Boston center Dave Cowens was too quick for Bellamy. The Hawks fell, 4-2, and Guerin's coaching career went with them.

OMNI TIME

When Tom Cousins first purchased the Hawks from Ben Kerner in 1978, he said that he planned to keep the team a short time, then find a wealthy Atlantan to buy it.

Kerner replied that Cousins would find that the ownership of a pro basketball team was intoxicating, that it would get in his blood because it was too exciting.

"It is exciting," Cousins later admitted. "It has been a great adventure. But I don't choose it for me."

He had worked feverishly to develop Atlanta and had even brought pro hockey to town in the form of the National Hockey League's Atlanta Flames (later to move to Calgary).

But by 1972, Cousins had reduced his share of the Hawks to 20 percent and had sold a sizeable chunk to a group headed by local businessman Bill Putnam, who took Cousins' place in management.

Cousins' plan for a "Madison Square Garden-type arena" had taken longer to build than the two years first promised. But construction crews were working feverishly on the Omni that summer and fall of 1972 in hopes of getting it open for the Hawks' fifth season in Atlanta. The space-age building would accommodate better than 16,000 in plush lavender and orange seats.

A new building wasn't the only change, however. That July, the team announced new colors and a logo for the third time in five years. When the Hawks arrived in 1968, they wore red and blue uniforms. In 1970, they adopted a "mod" look in blue and green. Now, in style with the Flames, the Hawks switched to red and white and a "touch of gold."

To all this newness was added a new coach. Guerin, 41, was promoted to general manager, and hired in his place was 39-year-old Cotton Fitzsimmons, who had just coached the Phoenix Suns to a 49-win season.

Like the Hawks, Fitzsimmons had lived his formative years along the Mississippi River. Raised in Hannibal, Mo., he had grown up a local gym rat, then gone on to coach nine years at nearby Moberly Junior College. His excellent record there had led him to Kansas State, where his team

For Whom The "Bells" Toils

When Walt Bellamy played for the Baltimore Bullets, he owned a funeral home. To promote its services, he came up with a catchy advertising slogan: "I'm the last to let you down."

Yet over the course of his lengthy professional basketball career, a number of critics claimed that letting them down was precisely what the 6'11" center had done.

Bellamy played 14 full seasons in the NBA, with a total of six different teams. He scored 20,941 points and pulled down 14,241 rebounds. Despite these impressive numbers, most of this time was spent dealing with the incredibly high expectations of coaches, teammates and fans. Only with the Hawks did Bellamy outdistance his critics. Only in Atlanta was he loved.

His appearance in a Hawks uniform in the spring of 1970 marked his fifth NBA team in nine pro seasons. At each of his previous stops—in Chicago, Baltimore, New York and Detroit—Bellamy had been labeled by the press as both "brilliant" and "lazy," just the kind of guy to drive his coaches and fans to bitter disappointment.

"He has been burned, second degree perhaps, but the scars linger within his complicated body," wrote Hawks beat writer Jim Huber (now a CNN sportscaster). "And he does not forget them easily."

An Indiana University graduate and a gold-medal Olympian, Bellamy broke into the NBA with a bang in 1962. He played for the expansion Chicago Packers and earned rookie-of-the-year honors by averaging 31 points and 19 rebounds.

"He was a great shooter and a good defensive rebounder," recalled Hall of Famer Jim Pollard, his coach in Chicago.

But Bellamy was reluctant to pass out of the numerous double teams that came his way, which led to complaints that he was a selfish player. Al Bianchi, another critic, charged that Bellamy didn't play if he didn't feel like it. The New York Knicks often remarked that the secret to their championship teams in the 1970s was the trading of Bellamy to Detroit for Dave DeBusschere.

But the Hawks never saw the difficult Bellamy. His arrival in 1970 marked a miraculous turnaround for the team that propelled Atlanta to the regular-season divisional title. He rebounded, played defense, scored when necessary and passed. "Walt Bellamy did everything in the world that I asked him to do to help the team," recalled Richie Guerin, his coach. "He was one of the big reasons we won the title that spring. Bellamy could be an awesome offensive player at times, but he did the other things for us, too."

Marty Blake, then the team's general manager, recalls the thrill of watching Bellamy's big debut in Atlanta: "I got a railroad bell and painted it gold. Every time he got a rebound, I rang it."

Almost immediately, "Dr. Bells" became a fan favorite.

But it wasn't just his inspired play. His off-court activities also offered plenty of reason for admiration. In addition to holding an Indiana business degree, he could speak four languages. He had been a friend of the late Dr. Martin Luther King, Jr., and aided the efforts of the Rev. Jesse Jackson. Bellamy worked behind the scenes with organizations such as the NAACP, the Southern Christian Leadership Conference and the Urban League. His main efforts went toward the vital voter registration drives of the era. He found that he couldn't march and picket, but his athletic celebrity enabled him to open doors to contribute other things to the effort.

"I devoted myself to promoting peace and good hope around the world," he once explained.

Atlanta, with its broad range of universities and foundations, offered the perfect base for doing that. "This city certainly has one of the more knowledgeable black communities in the world," he once explained to a reporter.

In return, the city had no ambiguous feelings about Bellamy. Forget "lazy" or selfish. In Atlanta, he was just brilliant.

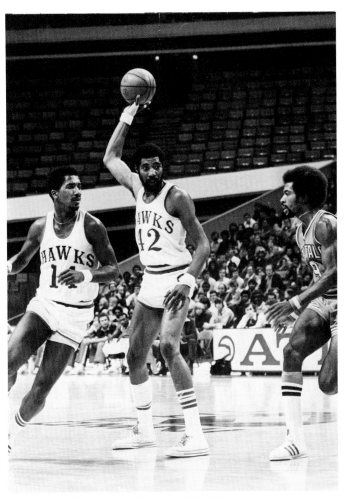

Hall of Famer Connie "The Hawk" Hawkins as a Hawk.

Tom Van Arsdale in 1974.

won a Big Eight championship in 1970. From there, he had established his reputation in Phoenix as a solid pro coach (And a fiery one to boot. He had once gotten a technical foul just 12 seconds after tipoff.) But two big seasons in Phoenix had convinced him that no matter how much he won, life in the Western Conference would be miserable so long as the Lakers dominated. So he agreed to take the job in Atlanta.

After all, it seemed to hold immediate promise.

That June of 1972, the Hawks had come to $2 million terms with Julius Erving, the brightest young player in the ABA. Erving, it seemed, could do everything. Glide through the air for stupendous dunks. Rebound like a demon. Even play a little guard when necessary. Then he could discuss his performance with the eloquence of an Ivy Leaguer (which he was, having played at the University of Massachusetts).

But his signing set up an immediate and gnarly legal battle. Erving's ABA team lay claim to his rights, as did the Milwaukee Bucks, who had drafted him after Atlanta signed him.

The NBA came down immediately against the Hawks and levied a $25,000 fine for every day they kept him in training camp that fall.

But Erving was the kind of player worth paying through the nose for. In his first two exhibiton games with the Hawks that September, he recorded 51 points and 32 rebounds.

In the first game, the Hawks said goodbye to Alexander Memorial Coliseum with a victory over the Kentucky Colonels of the ABA. In the second, the Hawks opened the Omni to basketball with a crowd of 13,867.

Alas, the Erving case went to court, and the Hawks lost. Erving went back to the Nets and on to the greatness for which he was destined.

The Hawks somehow gathered their broken hearts and charged off to a 46-36 season, still only good enough for second place behind Baltimore in the Central.

Again, their demise in the playoffs was Boston. Again, Dave Cowens' quickness helped do them in, 4-2.

It seemed like a wonderful beginning for Fitzsimmons. Little did anyone guess that it would be his best season in Atlanta, that it would be all downhill from there.

In Cotton's mind, the fall guy for the troubles would be the Pistol. The coach once remarked that watching Maravich's style of play made him want to throw up.

In 1973-74, the Hawks finished 35-47 and were out of the playoffs for the first time in a dozen years. Guerin was fired as general manager, and was replaced by John Wilcox, a lawyer and a member of Putnam's ownership group. After the season, they traded Maravich to the expansion New Orleans Jazz for a host of players and picks, a move that dismayed the fans who had become mesmerized by his dazzling floor game.

Atlanta's Young Gun

There were two distinct views of Pete Maravich: that of his coach and teammates, and that of the fans.

His coaches and teammates found it difficult to relate to Maravich. "Pete's style of play offended me as a coach and our players," recalled Hawks coach Richie Guerin.

Maravich had averaged an NCAA record 44.2 points per game in college while playing for his father, Press Maravich, at Louisiana State in the late 1960s. The Hawks selected him third overall in the 1970 NBA draft and signed him to a multi-million dollar contract that his pro teammates openly resented.

"It created a lot of animosity, it did for sure," Guerin recalled.

Maravich was the quintessential showboat. "He felt like he had to score 30 or 40 points every night to please the fans," Guerin said. "Every where he went they expected a lot of him."

But it was the fans who understood and appreciated "Pistol Pete."

"Personally, I would trade any number of wins for the thrill of having seen Pete Maravich a few times at his very best," wrote fan Keith Coulbourn after the Hawks traded Maravich to New Orleans in 1974. "That incredible pass between his legs while in midair is simply unforgettable—though I couldn't care less whether they won or lost the game. Those beyond-the-backboard reverse shots I'll never forget either."

Coach Cotton Fitzsimmons said the Hawks traded Maravich because they concluded they couldn't build a winner around him. But Coulbourn ended his essay by saying that Maravich cared deeply about winning.

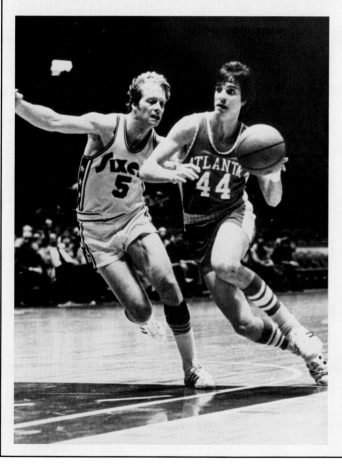

The record seems to bear that out. He fought off injury and illness to play a major role in the Hawks making the playoffs during his four seasons in Atlanta. And after the team traded him, Atlanta missed postseason play for four straight seasons.

Maravich, meanwhile, went on to win the league scoring title while transforming the expansion New Orleans Jazz into a competitive club.

Coulbourn pointed out Maravich's contributions went beyond mere winning and losing. In short, he showed Atlantans how much fun the game could be.

"And that's what we'll miss," Coulbourn said.

Maravich retired from pro basketball after a brief tenure with the Boston Celtics in 1979. He died in 1988 at age 40 while playing pickup basketball. It was later determined that a heart defect contributed to his untimely death. He was elected to the Naismith Memorial Basketball Hall of Fame in 1986.

Time has worn away the irritation that his Atlanta teammates felt over his big contract in 1970. "Those were really exciting times," Lou Hudson said recently of playing with Maravich. "Pistol was showtime then. Once we were on a fast break and he rolled the ball down the floor. Another time he took a hook shot in Buffalo as he was running off the floor—and it went in!"

Assistant coach Gene Tormohlen took control of a sinking ship in March 1976.

"I like Pete," Fitzsimmons said afterward. "But he was here four years. This is not meant to be derogatory, but in those four years the Hawks could not build a team around him to win."

Those who disagreed with Fitzsimmons' assessment point out that the Hawks' fortunes took a steep dip in the seasons after the Pistol's departure. They had drafted John Drew in the spring of 1974, and he was hot from the start, averaging 18.7 points over the 1974-75 campaign and earning rookie of the year honors.

The team's record, though, headed south. They finished 31-51, just a few games better than the brand new Jazz. Their solace was two number one picks (first and third) in the 1975 draft, which they used to take superstar David Thompson of North Carolina State and Marvin "The Human Eraser" Webster of Morgan State. It was just the kind of talent harvest to secure the team's future. Instead, it soon became a disaster. The agent for both players claimed they had been insulted by the Hawks and abruptly cut off the negotiations. Both players signed with Denver of the ABA,

and the Hawks got nothing.

"In my opinion, that was the demise of the franchise," Guerin said.

The 1975-76 season brought the special talents of veteran Connie Hawkins to Atlanta. With Drew and Lou Hudson and Tom Van Arsdale, they looked good on paper. But Cotton couldn't seem to get anything together on the court. They finished 29-51, last in the Central, nine games behind Maravich and the second-year Jazz.

In eight seasons in Atlanta, the Hawks had gone from champs to chumps. In the end, Maravich was gone, and there was no one else to blame.

Fitzsimmons was replaced by assistant Gene Tormohlen for the final eight games of the 1975-76 season. The Hawks had reached rock bottom and rested there amid rampant rumors that the team would be purchased and moved yet again.

But the future held a new owner, a new coach and a new life, all in Atlanta. What had been torn apart would be built again.

Eddie Johnson scores against Washington in April 1979.

Ted Takes Charge

1976-83

W hat happened next had nothing to do with scouting or drafting or trapping or even basketball. What happened next was about real estate and leverage and solvency and eventually one guy's willingness to do the least reasonable thing when everyone else in town knew better. And for that one senseless act, the Atlanta Hawks not only kept their first name but soon delivered to their city some of its most vivid basketball memories.

The Atlanta of the mid-1970s had struck a shelf in its development, the business boom that heralded the start of the decade slowed as the city slowly caught up with the plans the private sector had drawn out before it. And no one was more hamstrung in that pause than Tom Cousins, his real estate concerns had flattened out like a bad quiche. As 1976 wore down, Cousins' company not only looked hard at what to do with his Omni arena, but the Hawks and Flames hockey team were both imminently dumpable.

Cousins could get no further than the flirting stage with the few buyers who would even consider the purchase of a struggling pro basketball team. The league had just fought off the incursion of the ABA through merger and while it flourished in its older markets, the NBA, having sky-rocketed from 10 to 22 teams in the previous 10 years, still sought its niche in sporting America. In December 1976, only some 5,200 people kept the faith each time the Hawks played at home.

The pot boiled into the last week of 1976: Cousins even tracked down an interested party on a radio-call to the Queen Elizabeth II at sea. But there were simply no takers. The same scenario would play out four years later with the Flames, who would be bought off and summarily shipped out of the country. But not the Hawks.

"It was only after all other avenues failed that Ted finally got into the deal," said Mike Gearon, a huge hoops fan who in the wild years to come would find himself the team's general manager. "I mean, Ted has always been known as a leverage guy, and all his financial people had trouble convincing him this wasn't a good idea. He was a real last resort, literally a 12th-hour deal, but Tom Cousins was not in the position to keep anything. And Ted just was not going to let them leave town."

So it came to be that Ted Turner, still more flake than shake in his hometown in those times, came to assume controlling interest in the Hawks during the final days of 1976. His interest cost him $1.5 million. Six years before, he'd bought a no-count local UHF television station, squeezed an existence from an inherited billboard company and in what would be the finest of many exercises in folly, had just bought the Atlanta Braves—"for nothing down and not much per month," he used to say—the year before. His purchase of the Hawks, which amounted to more of a debt assumption than an actual buy, made sense to no one. The day the sale went through, Turner watched the team snap an eight-game losing streak against Denver, which pleased him so well that he retired to the dressing room and kissed Lou Hudson, his new star guard, flush on the cheek.

"This basketball is great, really great," the new owner said. With an empty hall and a .375 record?

"It's the like pyramids in Egypt. It took a helluva lot of people carrying a few rocks, right? I just want the Hawks to be halfway viable economically."

Which was pure Turner. Never mind the facts; just get a bucket and start bailing. The slack gate that season was generating a league-low $15,114 nightly gross. Against a payroll of $1.4 million, the franchise took in a mere $600,000, and first-year losses of $1.5 million matched Turner's original investment. The team finished 20 games under .500 and Hubie Brown, who was about the only thing bolted down on the management side, filled the arena with trade-mark salty language that echoed around the empty hall like a cave call.

"I don't have a pressing need, just a lot of work in a lot of

Ted Turner with the Hawks' Bill Putnam.

Hubie talks to his charges during a timeout.

areas," said general manager Mike Storen, who had replaced Bud Seretean and would soon be replaced by Gearon, who would be replaced by Lewis Schaffel, who would be replaced by Gearon again. If the Hawks were not the most calamitous franchise in the league, it was not for lack of trying.

But one stone was in place that would bring the boat around. Having won the penultimate ABA championship with the Kentucky Colonels in 1975, Brown was the most lasting property Turner inherited. He was fiercely driven, an ethic he brought to every aspect of his job, and what he did with the Hawks was not rebuilding but more prefabricated refurbishing. Just three seasons later, the Hawks would somehow win the Central Division and rally the city.

But first, Turner took the roster apart, asking Brown to dump the big contracts. Within the first nine months, Lou Hudson, nine years a Hawk, was dealt away while Truck Robinson was acquired and then traded away—the net gain of the transaction being Ron Behagen for compensation. Brown would not rely solely on the college draft, for only three rookies—Armond Hill, Tree Rollins and Eddie Johnson—would ever make the team off his first two drafts.

Instead Brown worked the fledgling free agent market and scoured the bushes seeking whatever talent slipped by league scouts. That was how he found Charlie Criss, the 5-foot-8 pixie the team signed out of the Eastern League. In the first year, Brown pared the team payroll almost in half to $800,000. Dan Roundfield, an uncertain quantity on the Indianapolis Pacers, became a free-agent acquisition, Gearon spending a marathon 12-hour cram session to study Roundfield's career in an Indianapolis motel room before asking Turner to lay out the cash to sign him. Tom McMillen, a Rhodes Scholar with all-world elbows, was obtained from New York for future picks.

In two years, the Hawks made the playoffs, the first post-season appearance in five years. In Brown's first three years, 29 players wore the Hawks uniform. Only four players—John Drew, Steve Hawes, John Brown and Armond Hill—remained from that first group in 1979, when the team went 46-36, a what-hath-god-wrought 15-win improvement.

What was going on might be called the last pure coaching job the NBA would see. Teams of the era, and particularly the Hawks with their modest pay scale, still belonged to the coaches. The day was yet unheard of when a Magic Johnson might force the firing of a Paul Westhead. And no one, with the possible exception of a contemporary Bill Fitch, wielded his power like Brown. With a full 10-man playing rotation, with brutal player criticisms in both the lockerroom and in the media, the Hawks coach never left in question who held the hammer, a style that would gradually yield to the "advisor-coach" in the dawn of the 1980s.

But Brown sold wildly in Atlanta, where attendance more than doubled over his first three years. The underachievers. The blue-collar team. The appeal to a city unaccustomed to victory was undeniable. Stan Kasten, just 27 years old but instrumental in the reformation of the franchise, was named general manager in 1979 and was promptly voted the league's executive of the year, ending once and for all the front office merry-go-round. At no time was the club more steady at all levels.

And something else more remarkable was underway, a

Tree Rollins guards Utah's Maravich.

trip into the future that not even the club's keenest mind first realized. Not long after coming to Atlanta, McMillen was off on a drive with Turner when the owner pulled off into a field that McMillen related "was littered with twisted metal, which (Turner) grandly described as his 'satellite farm'."

And the Hawks, along with the Atlanta Braves, were on the edge with him, the basketball team beamed off the distant corners of the world where the NBA was only a rumor. The writer's personal denouement came on some lost night in some North Carolina college town motel, where I for the first time clicked on a cable-wired television and discovered Steve Hawes taking apart the Houston Rockets from the top of the key. It was 2:30 a.m. It was a taped replay. It made for great late-night TV. And it made such sense, the wonder was why no one had done this before.

This run, the *Mr. Toad's Wild Ride* in sneakers, reached its crescendo in 1980, when the Hawks won the Central Division, finishing off the schedule with a mad 22-9 rush to bring the franchise its first title since 1970. Roundfield blossomed into the league's finest forward; Rollins overcame a penchant for fouling to become a formidable if not notorious defensive presence in the lane; and Eddie Johnson, or "Jet," as the Hawks called him, went from a third-round draft pick two years before to an All-Star. The club won a record 50 games and Brown, who was voted coach of the year after the 1977-78 season, would no doubt have won it again if the Hawks had gone somewhere in the post-season.

But they did not. The Philadelphia 76ers of Julius Erving and Darryl Dawkins dumped Atlanta from the quarterfinals

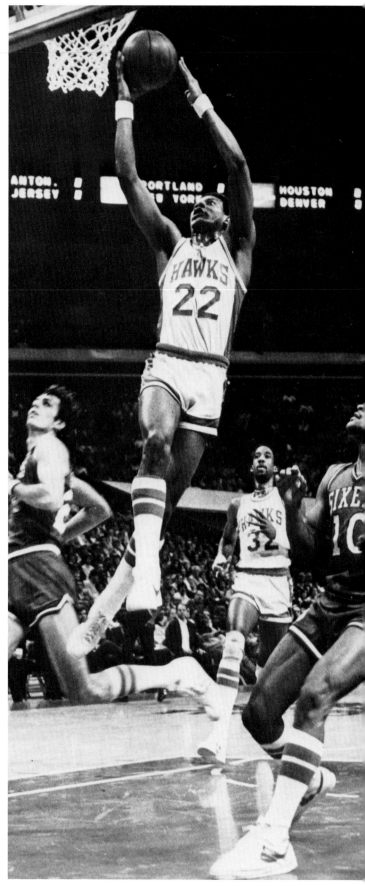

John Drew led the Hawks in scoring for six seasons.

The Hawks Drew Deuces

The rookie started his first NBA game at age 20 (scored 32 too), became the youngest All-Star in league history a year later and declared it was high time someone made the movie of his life. These became the defining moments in the strange career of John Drew, the Hawk who once had it all but never really comprehended what to do with it.

Eight years a Hawk, Drew eight times was the team's leading scorer, doing so for three different coaches. He was Atlanta's bridge at small forward between Lou Hudson and Dominque Wilkins. At 6-foot-6, he owned outstanding range with a genteel jump shot, but it was his ability to create shots off the dribble and draw the foul that caused most opponents problems. Other than Moses Malone, the Atlanta franchise never knew a better offensive rebounder than Drew in his early seasons, no statistic a better indication of hard endeavor.

But Drew soon became a lightning rod for controversy. His defensive skills never evolved and a long-term running battle with Hubie Brown served to polarize the entire franchise. A true manchild, Drew could never deal properly with criticism. That his career would collapse under the weight of a monstrous drug problem did not surprise those who got to know him. That the rookie lobbied for the feature biographical film bespoke of a man with a jumbled shopping list in life.

"I got more talent than Dan Roundfield," Drew said once. "But Roundfield plays on heart and guts."

Because Drew often wouldn't, in the end, it cost him.

No one could have dreamt up a finer high school legend, Drew becoming the nation's top prep scorer in 1972 at J.F. Shields High in Beatrice, Ala. (population: 455). He'd go for 70 a night sometimes, working the ball off the floor like it was on wires. This he owed to playing on dirt courts during the summers.

"They were hard and lumpy," he said, "but they really helped your ball-handling. Once you got in a real gym, you didn't have any trouble at all."

He came into the league after two years at little Gardner-Webb (N.C.) College. Gene Tormohlen was stunned to discover him during a scouting trip and eventually convinced the team to take him with the 25th pick of the 1974 draft. Cotton Fitzsimmons was forced by injuries to immediately start the rookie only a month after his 20th birthday. While Drew slumped and was benched after a wild two-month debut—this unchecked surging and slumping would mark his whole career—he later moved into Hudson's spot when the veteran developed elbow trouble. Drew would become the primary offensive focus in the post-Pete Maravich era.

No first-year player had a more productive season, but Drew would finish second to Golden State's Keith Wilkes in rookie-of-the-year voting. Drew would never be any better than he was that year.

"Some people say I'm a cocky kid, and maybe I do talk a lot of stuff on the floor," he said that season. "But I just have a lot of self-confidence. I don't think about who or what I'm playing against. I just go out and play." (En route to the lockerroom at half time, he'd stop to pick up a bag of popcorn.)

Such laissez-faire would run head-long into the structured philosophies of Brown, who took over the team from Fitzsimmons in 1976. Drew and Brown coexisted for five years, but barely. Drew could score 22 points in 22 minutes, as he did one night, but could never provide the defense Brown's system required. Brown was not one to make allowances for players unsuited for his scheme. There were moments. Like the night against Denver on March 30, 1978 when Drew was three-points shy of breaking

Nate Archibald's then-Omni scoring record of 52 points. Brown put him on the bench the last three minutes.

Yet Drew would not pick up the gauntlet and declined to fight his coach in the media, not even after Brown was fired. Why? Said Drew, "Hey, you can't beat Hubie Brown with words."

Even in his worst Atlanta seasons, Drew would average more than 18 points and, in a different way, could be one of the club's more amusing personalities. As he wore No. 22, he took to calling himself "Deuces" and would sometimes announce to press row that he would be entering the game by holding down two fingers from each hand as he walked down to report to the scorer. Throughout, he remained friendly and could be candid, even if in a kid's way. As he said one day after a practice, "I don't want you to quote me like I'm conceited but, you know, I can do anything."

In the championship season of 1979-80, Drew would lead the Hawks in four offensive categories, made the All-Star team and marveled that he could have turned pro right out of Beatrice. But his productivity began to tail and when the franchise began its overhaul after Brown's departure, Drew was one of the first to go.

Four weeks shy of his 28th birthday, he was traded in one of the most significant moves the franchise made in the 1980s, sent to Utah (with Freeman Williams) on September 3, 1982, for Dominque Wilkins. While Wilkins became a cornerstone of the franchise even into the following decade, Drew quickly degenerated into one of the league's most acute failure stories. Within two years, the Jazz released him and the league subsequently banned him for life after a succession of drug offenses. In 1987, seven years after his last All-Star season, Drew was jailed on a cocaine conviction.

His name is still scattered throughout the record book, even 10 years after his Hawk seasons, including the night in his rookie year he took 25 rebounds from the Los Angeles Lakers and the 50-point game against Denver when he set three Omni records in one half

But John Drew's career will not be remembered strictly for what he did, perhaps more for what might have been. For several bright seasons, his was one of the greatest NBA stories ever told. But in the end, the film rights went unpurchased.

in a mere five games, a numbing conclusion to one of the era's biggest basketball stories. That team, still regarded as one of the league's most innovative for Brown's relentless trap and press strategies, came to represent what was possible in the NBA, how astute planning, opportunism, a pinch of luck and pure endeavor could in a few short seasons make a champion out of derangement.

Yet just as quickly, it was gone. Several factors contributed. Brown's coaching challenge to the Hawks was always a vocal and strident one and gradually their response weakened. His running criticism of Drew, his leading scorer, became legendary around the league but grew wearisome within the club. And drug-related troubles of Drew and Johnson grated further on Brown. The front office became troubled by deteriorated relations between coach and bench while Brown became infuriated over weakened support from the front office.

One year later, with injuries to Roundfield and Rollins compounding the off-court problems, the Hawks collapsed with a 31-51 record. Milwaukee had created a vast talent margin that would dominate the division for years to come and Atlanta management faced another restructuring job. The lightning that had been harnassed with Brown's arrival was now all gone from the bottle. With three games left on the 1980-81 schedule, he was relieved of his job by vote of the team's board of governors.

It would take two coaches five years to duplicate what had been accomplished in Turner's first 2 1/2 years of ownership. The franchise had been saved, a divisional championship had been won, basketball had been successfully reintroduced to the populace and if the end of Brown's time with the team was strained, the public response went to show that Atlanta for the first time in a while cared about its Hawks.

"Those were some of the greatest years of my life," said Gearon.

On the last night he would coach the team, Brown sensed what awaited him as he was chauffeured to the Omni by Mike Fratello, his curly-topped assistant whose bright time with the franchise was yet to come. He whipped the car into a parking place while Brown, peering out at two passers-by, suddenly threw his arms out wide and flashed a huge pair of peace symbols, reminiscent of Richard Nixon's pose at the helicopter steps. Only in the back seat that night, Hubie Brown's smile was so huge so as to take up an entire window.

"Slaprock" shows "McNasty" Mahorn his elbow.

McMillen with Atlanta youth in the 1970s.

From "Slaprock" To Senate Steps

In the relatively brief history of professional sport in Atlanta, the city has never born witness to a sharper mind—or sharper elbows—than when Charles Thomas McMillen came to town in 1977. A Hawk for six of his 11 NBA years, he never averaged double-figures, hardly ever started, could barely hurdle the bench and the prematurely gray hair offered up a deceptive image of an oversized middle-aged man lost in his pursuit of a younger man's game.

Yet these very things may have been his strong point, for McMillen never appeared to excel until the game was reckoned afterwards. In an age of increasing specialization within the league, he could play all three front-line positions, defended his man as if every shot was the last and rebounded with two padded but out-turned elbows that sent a certain qualm throughout the NBA. They earned him the roughshot nickname "Slaprock."

And in between, he would say things like "Economic progress and social justice aren't opposing goals. They are dependent on each other." In a league of divergent personality, Tom McMillen was nothing if not singular.

A Rhodes Scholar, A Phi Beta Kappa and a 6-foot-11 collection of steep angels, he shattered the jock stereotype in the same manner of Bill Bradley a decade before him. Like other kids with the basketball disease, he would break into the gym just to practice, a habit which helped make him the best foul-shooting big man the Hawks have seen, his 47 straight conversions in 1978-79 still a franchise record. After the games, he was a reporter's dream, with just the most casual questions illiciting uncommon analysis which improved any story.

"Basketball is the framework of my life right now," he said one night. "It's what I enjoy doing most. But it's not my whole life. The great thing about sports is the accessibility to people."

That ethic underwrote his whole career.

The ninth pick of the 1974 draft, he had turned his back on the league to attend Oxford on the Rhodes Scholarship. But the financial impact of the NBA-ABA merger convinced him to return after one year, and he finished his studies abroad as a part-time student. He had been in the league two seasons when the Hawks targeted him. Seeking rebounding and front-line aggressiveness, Atlanta offered New York—where McMillen shared the bench with Bradley in his final season—a second-round draft pick for him, and the Knicks snapped it up on Nov. 14, 1977. With the exception of Doc Rivers, never would the Hawks get such service out of a second-round transaction.

McMillen would never be better than his first year in Atlanta, a perfect addition for Hubie Brown's by-the-numbers system. A part-time starter that year, he averaged 12.5 points and almost eight rebounds in 31 starts during Brown's transition year while McMillen's articulated jump shot enabled him to post the team's top shooting percentage. As the team upgraded its talent, McMillen continued to work on his game—had to work on his game, particularly at the defensive end—and within the club's full 10-man playing rotation, his value never tailed off.

McMillen launches a shot in 1983.

"I never was quick and wasn't a very good jumper," he said "Besides having the white man's disease, I have terrible feet. They've always given me trouble. There wasn't much I could do about that, but I could do something about being weak—which I was—and about my defense. I lifted weights. I watched people play defense, thought about it, practiced it."

His work against Washington's Elvin Hayes during the 1979 playoffs earned a spot in Brown lore. As well, during Kevin Loughery's first season, McMillen was the accessory to the robbery of the year in Milwaukee one 1982 night. With the Hawks trailing by one with a second to play, McMillen inbounded the ball from mid court, putting a high lob near the backboard where Dan Reoundfield would jump for the tip-in. But Roundfield was sealed off from the play and as the ball came down tantalizingly close to the hoop, Milwaukee's Harvey Catchings gave a halting attempt to bat it away. Instead, he tipped in the perfect lob and the Hawks ran laughing from the court.

But McMillen's finest hours no doubt came during the 1979 playoffs, when the Hawks trailed defending NBA champion Washington 3-1 in the Eastern Conference semifinals and faced Game 5 at Capital Centre. John Drew had been hurt in Game 4 and Brown shooed McMillen in to play at small forward, a position he had never played before. He had practiced to learn the spot and, paired off against the Bullets' Bobby Dandridge, also drew a critical defensive assignment. But he scored 19 points with six rebounds in just 33 minutes and the Hawks won 107-103 to send the series back to Atlanta.

Through it all, McMillen experienced a gradual gravitation towards politics. The most poignant moment of his young life was the assassination of John Kennedy, and his time at Oxford stirred notions about public service. In the lockerroom, the Hawks were calling him "Senator" long before he intended to run for anything, and he slowly played his cards. After the most serious injury of his career—torn knee ligaments in 1980—he was up and out two weeks after surgery, stumping New Hampshire for Jimmy Carter. By age 29, he was serving on the Democratic National Party's finance committee. He considered running in the 1982 and 1984 Congressional races in Maryland but decided instead to continue playing.

He left the franchise in the summer of 198; the departure was two-purposed. Dealt to the Bullets, he could finish out his career in the shadow of the Capitol and the Hawks picked Randy Wittman in the exchange, who became a three-year starter. After his retirement in 1986, he was elected to the U.S. Congress in Maryland's Fourth District on November 1—the season's opening night—and is now, among other things, the tallest man on the Hill.

"What people don't realize about me is that I've had to fight and scrap for everything I've ever gotten," said Congressman Tom McMillen, who wasn't called Slaprock for nothing.

That Championship Season 1979-80

It was the season of Bird's and Magic's apprenticeship, when the NBA reconsidered the old ABA and adopted the rebel league's three-point shot. Pete Maravich retired, Walter Kennedy went into the Hall of Fame and in Atlanta, a wayward basketball franchise found its way upstairs and into the light.

The Atlanta Hawks of 1979-80 hardly jumped upon the league from hiding, for the team had made the playoffs the previous two years and the spring before had run NBA championship finalist Washington to the limit in the postseason before succumbing. But these Hawks were nevertheless suspicious, the roster stocked with foreign faces, its coach this mad scientist with the huge floor presence that his experience in the ABA fostered and even promoted. The Hawks hadn't placed a player on the All-NBA team since Maravich seven years before and the 46 victories of the previous season had represented the highest total since Richie Gurerin's second season in Atlanta. For the first time in years,

there was a real anticipation come the fall.

"Last year's goal was respect, just earning respect," Hubie Brown said as October wore into November. "This year's goal is getting to the playoffs and then picking it up from there."

Though the major players—Dan Roundfield, Eddie Johnson and John Drew—were in place, this was no static group. The roster would include three new faces (Ronnie Lee, Sam Pellom and James McElroy) and five would be gone within a year (Lee, Terry Furlow, Jack Givens, John Brown and Rick Wilson).

But now in his fourth season, Hubie Brown's mark was embedded deep into the team. In the telling comment by journeyman Andre McCarter before Brown cut him in camp, "When you talk about beating out somebody here," said the guard, "you have to be a superman both intellectually and physically."

The team sprung from the gate like a freed beast, going out

Dan Roundfield, Armond Hill, Jack Givens and Tree Rollins celebrate their last-second victory over Boston that earned Atlanta the 1980 divisional title.

Roundfield was a key.

to a immediate 11-5 record, the finest start since 1969. The Philadelphia 76ers had not lost a game that October but were then swept by the Hawks on back-to-back nights. In the first meeting with the Bullets since the playoffs the previous spring, Atlanta took revenge at 109-104 and stood alone atop the Central Division. And in just a few short days, what appeared to be the franchise's coming-together went another way.

First, Lewis Schaffel, the former New Orleans Jazz general manager (and larcenist behind the Truck Robinson deal) who had been brought in the previous summer as G.M., resigned suddenly, barely a month into the season. A former player agent, Schaffel, the club's 12th general manager in 12 years, never truly meshed with the Atlanta front office and his vacancy again pushed Mike Gearon into the G.M. chair. That Brown's two-year contract extension was announced within 48 hours was hardly coincidental, for he had not been comfortable with Schaffel and the episode reflected oddly on an organization that had been nothing but ascendent the previous two years.

That was how the week of November 18th began and it would not pass without another jolt, the consummation of the Terry Furlow trade. Furlow, a 6-foot-4 guard from Michigan State, had come to the team from Cleveland the previous January in a trade for Butch Lee and had promptly become the club's jump shot off the bench. He was the only player involved in a cash-and-future-options deal with Utah Nov. 23. Without him, the Hawks would become the league's fourth worst shooting team; the loss of a perimeter threat was duly noted in the Hawks' lockerroom.

The team went wild in San Antonio the next week with an Atlanta record 20-for-27 fourth quarter in a 143-120 win, the highest output in eight years. But soon the winning trailed off; the Hawks played sub-.500 basketball into late January after the fast start. The team won the games it was supposed to, but Atlanta was 16-18 against winning teams. While the Hawks never strayed far from the division lead, there would have to be some modification if there was to be any late-season progression.

That progression had its unlikely beginning in the January 24th deal with Detroit, when the team exchanged Butch Lee for James McElroy, Dan Roundfield's old teammate at Central Michigan and a saxophone buff as well. Although McElroy would be just a 39 percent shooter in a Hawks uniform that year, his added jump shot had a beneficial effect. Atlanta ran off a seven-game win streak as soon as he joined the team. And it was that jumpstart that set the tone for the final third of the season. The Hawks finished the schedule on a 22-9 tear, with Brown's 10-man rotation cutting a path through the league in the later stages.

"The fatigue factor hits a lot of teams in February and March," said Steve Hawes, who shared the center position with Tree Rollins throughout the Brown era. "By playing everybody on our roster, we are able to avoid this."

They clinched the division with two weeks to go on an 88-87 win over Boston and a week later (March 23) set an Atlanta record with a 49th victory against San Antonio. As opposed to the claw job in the post-season the year before, Atlanta would draw the first-round bye this time, waiting a week while the 76ers eliminated Washington in the first round. This was not an unwelcomed development, for the Bullets had eliminated Atlanta from the playoffs in the two previous seasons and that winter, the Hawks had gone 4-2 against Philadelphia.

Yet it all broke down quickly. In Game 1 in the Spectrum, John Brown slipped on a Philadelphia inbounds play with 20 seconds left, which gave Bobby Jones an unchallenged break-away layup and a 107-104 victory. The Hawks had led much of the game and were perhaps one play away from taking the Sixers late. But the tone was set for the series.

Philadelphia won Game 2, 99-92, with another late surge. The Hawks made the best of the Game 3 in the Omni, forcing 22 turnovers in a 105-93 win which set up the determining day of the season. On April 14, a Sunday night, Atlanta produced their worst performance of the year, losing a 107-83 blowout, the Sixers' first team shooting 80 percent and running Atlanta off the floor for a 3-1 edge. Game 5, a 105-100 loss back in Philadelphia, was almost an afterthought.

The team had established its first 50-win season since the franchise came from St. Louis and had participated in the playoffs for the third straight season. As well, the club set attendance records that would stand into the mid-1980s and Roundfield became the team's first all-NBA pick in eight seasons. But simultaneously, the underachievement was palpable.

Undressing after Game 5, Eddie Johnson threw both shoes across the room into a garbage can.

"Might as will just start everything over," commented the guard, saying more than he knew.

Eddie Johnson played nine seasons for Atlanta.

Drew came to the big time from a small college.

Armond Hill (24) against Philly.

The Hawks boasted a workmanlike frontcourt.

Brown demanded control from the bench.

Hubie Brown, flanked by assistants Frank Layden and Mike Fratello, wants an answer.

Hubie Took Control

Hubie Brown was a catcher as a kid, which seems perfect now since no man later wanted more to be in on every single, solitary play. But it was during a collision at home plate that Brown's left eye was injured, poked hard with a wayward finger, and the muscles never healed quite right. So he grew up slightly wall-eyed, looking out at a world from two directions. The condition would serve him well, as he developed an unsettling stare—the head tilted back slightly, the eyes black—that could wither a ref at 100 paces.

But the two-way vision in another way also became a coach's perspective, for Hubie Brown always saw his job split into "The Way Things Are" versus "The Way Things Should Be." And he would spend his days on the bench ever trying to convert the first condition into the second.

"The easiest thing is to just say you're going to let the players do their dance and let the talent win it or lose it," he said once. "I want complete control."

Words with official Jack Madden

An NBA coach could still have it in 1976, when Brown—Army vet, former high school economics teacher, once a hot-shot guard at Niagara University—was introduced to Atlanta as the Hawks' third coach since the franchise came to town eight years before. He inherited a team that had lost a record 53 games the year before. So in his first season, Brown brought in 10 new players. After two years, he was voted the league's coach of the year. In four seasons, he won the Central Division. And after five seasons, he was gone, fired after a philosophical drift opened between bench and front office.

But what he accomplished in those frenetic five seasons was to blow life into a listless franchise that the city had all but abandoned. His teams, collections of discards and college nobodies, set attendance records and won against for better talent essentially because of Brown's system. He called every play form the sideline and developed a player rotation unseen in the league, a complete turnover of 10 men determined solely not by ebb and flow of the game but by the clock. The Hawks pressed and trapped and for three straight years were among the three best defensive teams in the league.

And there was never any doubt about where the direction came from, for Brown maintained strict control. In his early seasons with the Omni nearly empty, fans were privy to the NBA's saltiest bench coaching, the coach filling the building with the New Jersey invective that became a trademark. It wasn't that the man was vulgar but that his vocabulary was built around certain optimum phrases that the coach simply could not communicate without. During on East Coast trip, the team was scheduled to practice at a Catholic school and Brown stressed on the bus trip that everyone should watch their language. Yet once out on the court, he summarily blasted the previous night's play with vivid terminology that had cassocks turning all around the grounds.

For a team without stars, it was no surprise that a coach would emerge first as the compelling personality. Brown's Hawks went four seasons before placing someone on the All-Star team and hence, Brown became a primary target of the city's focus. Smitten with his abilities, Ted Turner even approached him about managing his woeful Atlanta Braves, an offer Brown seriously pondered before rejecting as folly.

He was tough on all his players but it would become particularly difficult for the ones he felt let him down. He could tolerate the off-court problems posed by an Eddie Johnson, for he felt Johnson would give everything once the game started. But he never felt that way about John Drew, and the coach's criticisms of his high-scoring forward became legendary. Not that Brown was ever easy on anyone.

"You must make them play to their potential," his creed went. "And you must make them cry for mercy."

It was the only way Brown knew and he knew it well, for sports were far more than a diversion for him as a kid. Charlie Brown, his father, watched every game the son played through grade and high school and the playing field failures carried more significance around their home than the successes. But it sharpened the appreciation for winning, the competitive backbone that served Brown during his years at Niagara when the Purple Eagles fielded some of the best teams in school history.

Coaching came naturally after the Army, starting with New Jersey high school football, baseball and basketball in 1959. Within eight years, he was an assistant basketball coach at William and Mary. By 1972 he joined old Niagara teammate Larry Costello as a Milwaukee Bucks assistant. Two years later, he took over the ABA Kentucky Colonels and won the championship the following season. The Hawks called when the team disbanded.

Throughout, Brown's disciplined method was his signature and ultimately, it caused his departure from the Hawks. As quickly as the championship season came in 1980, it turned around completely the next year and every corner of the front office had its own reasons why. Injuries may have been foremost but Brown, suffering from painful sciatica, recognized what was coming. With three games left on the schedule (and three years left on his contract), the team board of trustees voted to relieve him on March 26, 1981.

Said Charlie Criss, the little guard Brown found in the Eastern League, "It's a hurting thing."

From there, Brown took a turn at trying to remodel the New York Knicks and excelled in his television work as an analyst, which revolutionized the field. He had taken the Hawks to the playoffs three times in five years, revived a plummeting franchise and had shown that name talent was not necessarily the only way to win in the NBA.

And through it all, the catcher had called the whole game.

Roundfield breaks away against Indiana and slams over present Hawks assistant coach Johnny Davis.

Roundfield: The Crucial Component

What became the franchise's most crucial component was an ABA castaway who weighed hardly 205 pounds and played most his career without the benefit of his four front teeth. Basketball had always seemed a sort of secondary pursuit for Dan Roundfield, who happened into the game only through a freakish teenaged growth spurt. But when he happened to Atlanta in 1978 and was given a stage and the script, he was strangely transformed into one of the league's finest, if not underestimated, power forwards.

His superb jumping ability stretched Roundfield far beyond his 6-foot-8 frame, and for six seasons he functioned as the Hawks' primary inside scoring threat against bigger opponents almost every night. The people around the league couldn't say enough.

"A joy to work with as an individual," said Hubie Brown, not one to gush. "He's not only intelligent but a true professional who knows his job as well as everyone else's. He definitely affects the outcome of every game."

"He's Atlanta's best player," said Bill Fitch, then with Boston. "When you scout the Hawks, the first thing you see to do right away is double-team Roundfield."

"He's the best in the league at his position," Utah's Frank Layden said in 1981. "He's by himself right now."

He had been by himself before and plenty, for basketball was barely a life's option. A shy kid growing up in urban Detroit, Roundfield hardly fit the mold for the city game, where personna often exceeds capability. His best friend James McElroy, who would play along side him in college and later join him on the Hawks, recalled that, "You'd have thought the guy was from some little country town like Stick Place, Arkansas. The guy was square. I mean, the guy was so square, he'd cut you with the edges."

Roundfield was naturally inclined toward baseball, or at least believed he was until he grew seven inches between his sophomore and junior years at Chadsey High School and was singled out in a hallway by a basketball coach and asked to try out. For that grand opportunity, he earned a spot at center on what became the worst prep team in Detroit.

"There were two teams in the city that didn't win a game that year," he said. "We played them [the other team] and we were ahead. But a fight broke out in the stands and since it was in our gym, we had to forfeit."

It got no better. Only a handful of colleges offered scholarships and Roundfield turned them all down, taking an academic scholarship at Central Michigan. He made the basketball team as a walk-on, built a reputation as a shot-blocker and became a central cog. By his senior season, the team made the NCAA tournament. After graduation he was ready to walk away to a job with a chemical company when he was drafted by the NBA and ABA. Perhaps more curious than serious, he signed with Indiana where, as at Chadsey, he was often forced to play center for some truly forgettable teams.

He broke his wrist four times and seemed dispensible as a

Roundfield controls the boards with teammate Billy Paultz.

reserve. So after three seasons, the Pacers allowed him to turn free agent. Hubie Brown, seeking to bolster a front line which was the worst rebounding group in the NBA, promptly signed him on June 9, 1978. The Hawks immediately moved from last to ninth in team rebounding. For six years, despite any number of injuries, Roundfield led the Hawks in rebounding each season he was with the team, three times making the All-Star team. In addition, he was a five-time all-defensive team selection. It is not unfair to say that during his time in Atlanta, no one outworked him.

Playing along side Tree Rollins, the pair posed a nasty proposition for opponents who chose to bring the play inside. Roundfield and Rollins together averaged five blocks and 7.5 fouls every game at a time when Atlanta was known best for defensive guile. Roundfield became Atlanta's bellwether; when he went down with a torn thigh muscle in early 1982 and missed 21 games, the Hawks lost 15 of them. The following season, Dominque Wilkins' rookie year, Roundfield delivered his fellow forward a primary lesson on front line service when he led the team in scoring, rebounding and minutes during his most statistically productive period.

The only hole left in Roundfield's portfolio, in fact, was in public recognition. Throughout his career, Roundfield played a muscle position despite weighing only 205 pounds, which hardly marked him as a power forward in the traditional sense. Not a refined offensive player, his points came off the game's angriest work within 10 feet of the basket. All this clashed with popular public perception of what forwards could do—Julius Erving was then in full flight—which was reflected nowhere more than the 1980 All-Star Game, when all four starting forwards were small forwards.

This bothered Brown, whose system funneled the offensive flow toward John Drew and even Eddie Johnson. While the combative coach boasted his prize power forward's abilities around the league, Roundfield was not Marques Johnson or Truck Robinson or even Elvin Hayes, who served up better named recognition and diminished somewhat Roundfield's profile. As Brown griped in 1980, "We can't change our style to get Roundfield or Johnson 25 points a game. But if Danny became a free agent today, there would be 21 teams trying to get him."

Even at age 31, Roundfield was attractive to other teams. Finally in the Hawks' effort to retool, on June 18, 1984 the team made a move that changed the franchise, sending Roundfield home to Detroit for Cliff Levingston and Antoine Carr. In his six Atlanta seasons, Roundfield managed 10.7 rebounds each game, setting team records that lasted well after his retirement. He finished his career with Washington in 1987, when the culmination of leg injuries finally grounded him. But a career that began in reluctance had turned full circle, even if not everybody noticed.

"I don't mind," Roundfield said once. "because basically I am just another professional basketball player. That's what I do for a living." Which was a long, long walk from the hallway at Chadsey.

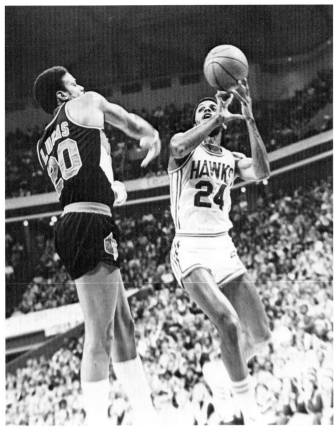

Armond Hill takes on Portland's Maurice Lucas.

Johnson often drove Atlanta's offense.

Roundfield was a warrior.

'Nique soared in the 1988 playoffs.

⮈ Fratello And The Air Force ⮊

Fact: Mike Fratello stood 5-6, weighed in at a hefty 140-something when he played linebacker at Montclair State College. Still, a former owner of the Chicago Bulls, Jonathan Kovler, decided Fratello was too short to coach in the NBA.

Fact: Mike Fratello used an iron will and a clever eye for talent to rescue an aging team by turning over all but two of its key components in a bare two years, thereby establishing the Hawks as models for renovation across the NBA.

Like Budd Schulberg's title character in "What Makes Sammy Run?", Fratello burned his candles at a ferocious pace in seven years as head coach of the Hawks. He burned to win, burned to be a star. And he kept company with successful and the celebrated; from Tommy Lasorda to Frank Sinatra.

Fratello's first Hawks team collapsed around him after starting 28-21, finishing 40-42. It was a bricks-in-the-head wake up call that cried for change. Fratello had engineered a successful draft day that produced Doc Rivers and Randy Wittman in 1983. A year later he and general manager Stan Kasten did it even better, swapping veteran forward Dan Roundfield to Detroit for Antoine Carr, Cliff Levingston and two second-round draft picks. It was one of the best trades in franchise history. But they weren't finished, taking Michigan State center Kevin Willis with the 11th pick of the draft.

The Hawks only won 34 games in 1984-85, but there were mitigating circumstances. Offered a guarantee of $100,000 a game to play in New Orleans, they went there for 12 "home" games. Looking to the future, they worked in sometimes puzzling combinations. They wound up in the first NBA lottery, their first of three lottery appearances in eight years, and the result in June, 1985, was the fifth pick—Jon Koncak.

But the Hawks were on the way. They went to camp terribly short-handed in the back court with Doc Rivers nursing a broken wrist and Eddie Johnson and Mike Glenn in free agency. But rookies Spud Webb, a free pickup, and John Battle, a fourth-rounder, saw the door open for them and found jobs they would keep for six years. Levingston won a role in the forward rotation, Koncak alternated with Tree Rollins, Willis stepped up at big forward and Dominque Wilkins became a star.

But first there was a struggle. The Hawks opened the 1985-86 season Oct. 15 at home, with the 5-7 Webb

Hawks coach Mike Fratello.

making his debut as NBA's smallest player ever, his friend Manute Bol, 7-7, stepping out as the league's tallest. The Hawks lost by nine. One night later, they played in Milwaukee and lost by 26.

The next morning Kasten received a frantic phone call from owner Ted Turner. "It was the first—and the last—time Ted ever called me at home," Kasten recalled. "He asked me if we'd done the right thing by making the team over. He asked, 'Can we win a game?' I told Ted not to worry, but, yeah, I was a little worried myself."

The Hawks beat the Knicks three nights later, and the fledgling Air Force was born. Two significant events gave them flight. The first was the return of Rivers on Dec. 4, 1985. The Hawks beat Portland that night to be 9-11. On Dec. 27 they lost in Washington. At the airport the next morning, as the Hawks waited for a flight to New York, Levingston told Fratello he had a sore thumb and could not play against the Knicks. Sensing the chance to make a statement, Fratello pointed to a gate that said: Atlanta. Fratello told Levingston to go home, that the Hawks could survive without him. He was right. That night Koncak grabbed 20 rebounds and his team battered the Knicks 100-80 to square their record at 15-15. It was the beginning.

Growing with every game, Fratello's team won 35 of its last 52 games to finish second in the Central Division. A year later, the Hawks set a franchise record with 57 victories, winning 50 the following season, despite an injury-induced second-half slump.

The Hawks lacked firepower from the perimeter and in the low post, but they did it with defense, team defense. From Nov. 4, 1986 through Jan. 26, 1988, the Hawks held their opponents under 100 points in 62 of 120 games; under 90 points in 18 games, two of these in the 70s.

In a league that glorified the scoring average, the Hawks gave the game a twist: they used their smothering defense to start their offense. Fratello once explained that "the nature of offense is that it comes and goes. But defense can be a constant weapon if you want to work and think. Defense is mental preparation and physical effort. That's what you need, those two things."

The Hawks played defense from the inside out, trapping on the interior, attempting to take the first and

Criss Again

The Atlanta Hawks were staggering, nearly 10 games under .500 in the winter of 1985. Orphaned to New Orleans for 12 home games, they privately called this their "Season in Hell." And it was never more lonely or frustrating than in early February after a loss in Philadelphia.

The Hawks' next "home" date, the only one in a span of eight games, was to be played the next night in New Orleans against Dallas. The itinerary called for a one-hour stopover in Atlanta to change planes. During the brief respite the wives of Eddie Johnson and Tree Rollins brought infants to Hartsfield International Airport to celebrate first birthdays with their fathers.

By season's end, the team had lost seven of its 12 "home" games, but the franchise had earned $1.2 million for their trouble. Only one had sold out, putting promoter Barry Mendelson in a deep financial hole. That one sellout of 10.079 at the University of New Orleans gym, was a gem in the wreckage of the season. On March 12, 1985, Larry Bird set a Boston Celtics single game scoring record with 60 points, sinking 22 of 36 shots from the field, 14 of 15 from the line. His greatest shot of the game, made as he was knocked into the Hawks' bench, did not count, but was so spectacular the Hawks' Doc Rivers pleaded with referee Hugh Evans, "You got to count it, Hugh. You got to allow a shot that good."

But in February matters were bleak. Johnson had sprained an ankle in the 76ers game, put him on the sideline along with fellow guards Mike Glenn and Rivers for a game against the Mavericks and others to follow. Coach Mike Fratello decided to seek help. It was sitting in the back of the plane in the person of former Hawks guard Charlie Criss, who now served as analyst on Hawks telecasts. Criss' career formally ended in 1982, but he played nine games in emergency duty in 1983-84 and now Fratello needed him again. That made Criss perhaps the only man in modern NBA history to work in the TV booth one night and play an NBA game the next.

A gym rat, 5-8 Charlie Criss was always ready. Against Dallas he played 29 minutes as a reserve, dealing 11 assists. Against Milwaukee on Feb. 7, Fratello decided to start Criss against the likes of Craig Hodges, Sidney Moncrief and Ricky Pierce. He was superb as the Hawks rallied from 17 points down in the third quarter to win with Criss playing 45 of the game's 53 minutes. He scored just two points, but had seven assists and did not commit a turnover while working the entire fourth quarter and overtime. In all, he played four games before going back to the booth. The Hawks won two of them.

That marked the end of a career that started in 1977. But, had Fratello ever called again, Charlie Criss would have been ready. New Orleans, on the other hand, never recovered.

second options away from the offensive team, content to gamble that few clubs could defeat them with the third and fourth calls in their system. These schemes were born in the fertile minds of John Wooden and Dean Smith. They had not flourished in the NBA.

Ron Rothstein, once an assistant with the Hawks before going on to Detroit and Miami, said the secrets to success were commitment and unselfishness. "They cover each other's backs. On the Hawks, a guy knows when he gives help, he gets help, so they aren't reluctant to respond and that is a subtle mental aspect of the game. A lot of NBA players are selfish. When a guy knows his back is not covered, he won't make the first move."

But all the defensive help in the world could not make the Hawks consistent shooters and that deficiency was their downfall each spring when they arrived at the playoffs. Although they won 157 games, losing 91 in three years, the Air Force always crashed in the second-round of the playoffs, where they were 14-16. In 1986 they were routed by Boston; in 1987 dispatched in five games by Detroit. In '88 they made their stand but could not overcome Boston in an historic seven-game set.

Kasten, who had become the Hawks' president, decided his team could never reach the championship round with its individual components, and in the summer of '88 he took a calculated gamble to raise the Hawks to the top of the NBA with two bold, calculated moves. With the first, he traded Randy Wittman to Sacramento for guard Reggie Theus, a consistent 20-point-a-game scorer. Later that summer, he allowed Rollins, a free agent, to sign with Cleveland so the Hawks could bring in another free agent, Moses Malone.

Theus, a handsome, dapper man, gave the Hawks the perimeter threat to complement Wilkins' inside game. Malone, three times MVP and a member of Philadelphia's championship team in 1983, brought relentless rebounding and a low-post game. Wilkins averaged 26.2, Theus 15.8.

Randy Wittman works the ball.

Tree bites Bird's shot.

Antoine Carr provided offense off the bench.

It turned out to be too much of a good thing.

Lacking the commitment to defense of earlier Hawks teams, this one struggled and was only 31-20 when it lost a road game to first-year expansion team Miami on Feb.19,1989. The Hawks were 40-28 when they lost at New Jersey on March 28. Abruptly, the team took off, winning 12 of its last 14, including nine in a row, to finish 52-30.

At last the team appeared to have come together, but what glittered was fool's gold. During the season, the Hawks dominated Milwaukee, beating the Bucks all six times they played. But in the playoffs it was a different story. Milwaukee's role players did their jobs. The Hawks stars fragmented, each trying to carry the load. The result was an infamous first-round ouster in five games.

Fratello's relationships with his holdover players had become increasingly difficult as they tasted success and became resentful of his authoritarian style. But Fratello had other problems with Theus and Malone, neither of whom shared his commitment to the basics of the game. In one revealing interview, Malone dismissed Fratello's call to do those things not reflected in the box score. "That's Tree Rollins basketball," Malone said. "If that's what they want, bring back Tree Rollins."

That summer, the Hawks left Theus exposed to the expansion draft and he went to Orlando. Malone remained, but his relationship with Fratello dissolved completely. Rivers' back gave out and Antoine Carr was dealt to Sacramento. Point guard Kenny Smith joined the Hawks, but only for a half-season before he would in turn move on. The team crashed to 35-39 with only two weeks remaining in the season. A late surge—seven victories in the final eight games—brought the Hawks to 41-41, not good enough to be a winner, not good enough to make the playoffs.

Just three victories shy of Richie Guerin's franchise-record 327 wins as coach, Fratello had come to the end of his seven-year road as head coach of the Hawks. Fratello indicated that it was time to leave, to give the Hawks another voice.

It had been a good run.

Air Force One

On June 9, 1983, the Atlanta Hawks took a step back to the future, and hired former assistant coach Mike Fratello to be head coach, handing him the reins of an aging and cranky team that begged to be made over.

The franchise was reeling and some connected however loosely with the NBA marked Atlanta as one of several fringe cities that did not belong if the league was to gain prominence of the major leagues of baseball and football.

The argument was not wholly invalid. The divisive tenure and departure of coach Hubie Brown had fractured the town's loyalties to the team. Subsequent mediocre performance under Kevin Loughery created a condition of ennui. Attendance dropped by more than 3,700 to 7,138 a game, not half the capacity of the Omni.

In strode Fratello, looking like a choir boy with a salon perm, and anything but. Too much like Hubie, some said. But Fratello took what he needed from Brown, his long time friend and boss, to build a consistent winner.

In time, the Atlanta Air Force was born, the hearts of the fans soaring with the flying circus that became Hawks basketball. Attendance swelled.

The league took note, and the Atlanta way of doing things became the model for the reconstruction of teams in Cleveland and Chicago and Phoenix. Careful drafting. Judicious trading.

That formula carried the Hawks to the most successful regular season in the 42-year history of the franchise, including a quarter-century in Atlanta.

Not coincidentally, it is the formula by which the franchise operates today.

"Tree"

If he ever had a talent for scoring, it was verbally beaten out of him by Hubie Brown, his first Hawks coach, he used to say. Then again, he was slower than mud. Bad feet committed him to a side-to-side, rocking action as he ran, rather like that of a freight train on a hard pull. But Tree Rollins could rebound and he could block shots. Best of all, Tree Rollins was a leader.

When he was a Hawks assistant coach, Willis Reed recalled how Rollins, then a young player from Clemson, worked summers as a counselor at Reed's basketball camp for boys. "We always invited the best young players and most all of them had bigger reputations than Tree. But Tree was always the favorite of the kids. Part of it might have been his name, but mostly it was his personality. He was the Pied Piper as far as these kids were concerned."

By time the Hawks were remade in 1985, Rollins was a veteran NBA center, wise in the ways of the league. As the young Hawks established a reputation for impeccable defense, they revolved around their Tree. More than that, all basketball life revolved around the team captain. It was notat all unusual on a bus ride from an airport to a road hotel to hear young Hawks squabbling good-naturedly but with some heat over where they would eat and what movie they would attend. Inevitably, opposing forces turned to Rollins for disposition and his word was law.

On the court he also enforced the law. When Rollins and the Hawks separated in 1988, he had played in more games and blocked more shots than anyone in franchise history.

Rollins slams the 'Sixers.

Rivers on a roll.

The Good Doctor

Doc Rivers remembers sitting in a Chicago hotel room on draft day 1983, secure in the knowledge that he would be selected in the first round as a junior out of Marquette. He was wrong. He lasted until the Hawks made him the 31st pick of the draft. Rivers remembers that he wept with disappointment. It was his last display of basketball self-pity.

Strong-willed, Rivers pushed himself through a two-year apprenticeship with Randy Wittman as his partner. By strict definition Wittman was not drafted by the Hawks. He was acquired from Washington in a trade for Tom McMillen, but the pick was orchestrated by Atlanta management. Together. Rivers and Wittman were to become the starting back court tandem in the fall of 1985, at the precise moment the young Hawks were learning to fly.

But there was a delay. Rivers broke his right wrist days before training camp. He missed the first 19 games of the season, the team struggling to 8-11 before meeting Portland Dec. 4, 1985. Rivers was activated that morning after two days of practice, insisting he was ready. And he was. In 33 minutes, he scored 16 points, dealt 10 assists, had a team record-equalling eight steals as the Hawks whipped Portland, 109-98

There was no turning back after that. With Rivers at the point, the Hawks finished the season winning 42 of their remaining 62 games, starting a run of four consecutive seasons with at least 50 victories. At the end of an eight-year run as a Hawk, Rivers held the franchise records for assists and steals. What more could you ask of a point guard?

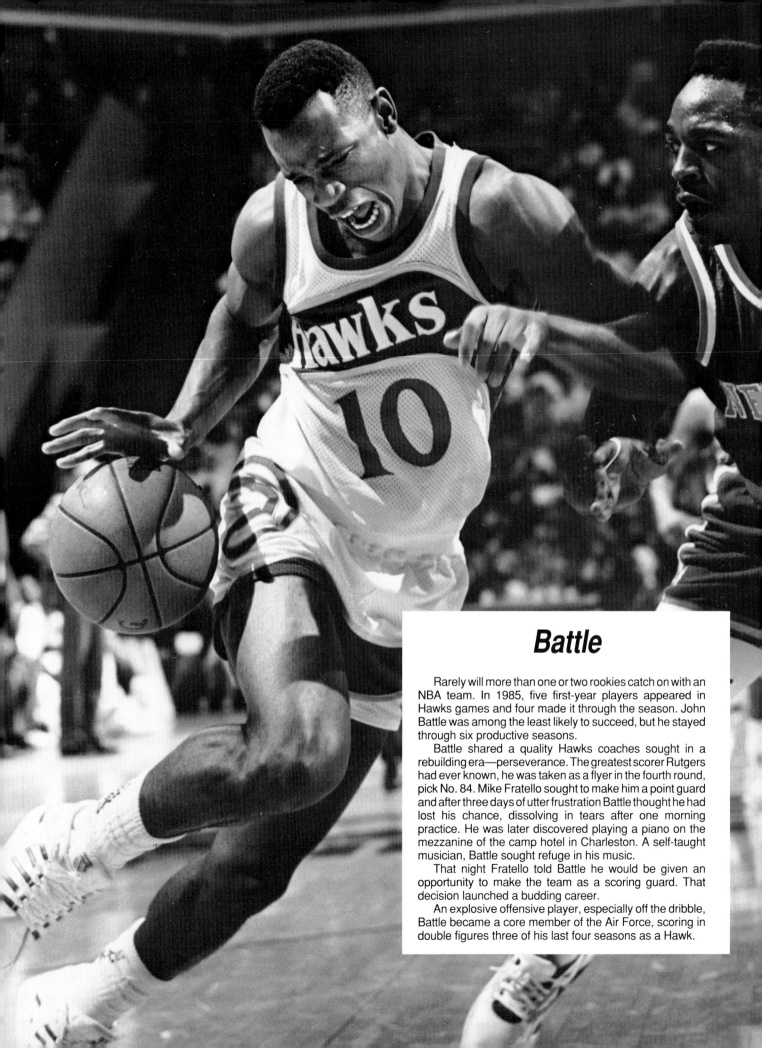

Battle

Rarely will more than one or two rookies catch on with an NBA team. In 1985, five first-year players appeared in Hawks games and four made it through the season. John Battle was among the least likely to succeed, but he stayed through six productive seasons.

Battle shared a quality Hawks coaches sought in a rebuilding era—perseverance. The greatest scorer Rutgers had ever known, he was taken as a flyer in the fourth round, pick No. 84. Mike Fratello sought to make him a point guard and after three days of utter frustration Battle thought he had lost his chance, dissolving in tears after one morning practice. He was later discovered playing a piano on the mezzanine of the camp hotel in Charleston. A self-taught musician, Battle sought refuge in his music.

That night Fratello told Battle he would be given an opportunity to make the team as a scoring guard. That decision launched a budding career.

An explosive offensive player, especially off the dribble, Battle became a core member of the Air Force, scoring in double figures three of his last four seasons as a Hawk.

Carr and Cliff

At Wichita State, they were known as The Bookends. One powerful, the other swift, they were destined to be successful NBA players. Detroit drafted both; Cliff Levingston as the ninth pick in 1982, Antoine Carr as the eighth pick in 1983. They traded to the Hawks for Dan Roundfield in June, 1984.

They were otherwise dissimilar in personality and in their style of play. Levingston was known as "the social director." He wore a gold medallion that read Good News. And forever after he was known as News. His game was hustle. Levingston was a marginal shooter and a ball handler. But he had been a 9.6 sprinter in his high school days. He played his game above the rim in six-and eight-minute bursts that energized his teammates. Carr, on the other hand, was muscular and given to being overweight. While Levingston missed only three games in one four-year stretch, Carr battled a series of injuries that included stress fractures of his shin bone, a broken thumb and severe burns on his leg suffered in a therapy pool accident. But Carr possessed refined low post skills that must have made his old college pal jealous.

When they could play together, Carr and Levingston gave the Hawks the most feared second unit forward tandem in the business. Ironically, they also left Atlanta a bare half-season apart; Carr in one of the Hawks' annual deals with Sacramento on Feb. 13, 1989, and Levingston as a free agent to Chicago the following summer.

Above, Carr soars against the Celtics. Right, Levingston on the move.

Slam Bam.

The U-Nique Factor

I f there is such a thing as pre-determination, then Dominique Wilkins was destined to become an Atlanta Hawk. Every turn of fortune shepherded that outcome in 1982.

It was a year in which the Los Angeles Lakers had the first pick, the San Diego Clippers the second, the Utah Jazz the third. It was a year in which three stellar juniors, all forwards, elected to come out for the draft.

Unquestionably, these three—James Worthy of North Carolina, Terry Cummings of Depaul and Wilkins of Georgia—would be the top three selections in the draft. Lakers general manager Jerry West wavered between Worthy and Wilkins; the Clippers let it be known they would select Cummings. When West chose Worthy, that left Wilkins to Utah and opened the door for the Hawks.

As club president Stan Kasten recalls, "We had already had a top-10 pick in Keith Edmonson. We already had all-stars in John Drew, Eddie Johnson and Dan Roundfield. But we had not had an elite player, a box office draw, not since Pete Maravich. Wilkins was interesting to us for all those reasons and he was from Georgia. It made sense. But it was hard to do."

In the weeks following the '82 Draft the Hawks learned of circumstances that conspired against the Jazz. They had struggled in New Orleans and they were not doing big business in their new home, Salt Lake City. Owner Sam Battistone, strapped for cash, already had a premier scorer in Adrian Dantley and could not stand another large payout. In fact, the Jazz selected Wilkins only because the draft had very little depth. After preliminary negotiations the Hawks knew they had a chance for a major coup.

"Late in August I got impression this kid could be had for a package, plus cash," Kasten relates. "Mike Gearon was the club president then. He loved the idea. We attended a Turner board meeting and told them we could take a huge amount of money, maybe a million, and get Wilkins or we could invest in Darryl Dawkins. We laid out the options and advocated getting Wilkins. I vividly recall that Ted turned to his business guy and asked him, 'Can we get a million?' The guy says, 'No, we can't.' Ted turns to me and says, 'Go do it; do it now.'"

Kasten made the deal contingent upon signing Wilkins, flew to Boston and struck a preliminary agreement with agent Bob Woolf. Gearon then flew Wilkins and his mother, Mrs. Gertrude Baker, to Boston to sign a six-year contract worth $2.6 million, at the time the second-highest ever paid an NBA rookie. That done, the Hawks sent Battistone his much-needed infusion of cash, $1 million, plus Drew and Freeman Williams.

The deal was not as one-sided as it seems, Kasten says. "We got a great player, but they got the money that helped them stay in business, helped to retain the franchise there. Drew had drug problems, but he also was an important contributor for them and they won a division title."

The Hawks also won a divisional title with Wilkins. In that marvelous era when they were known as Atlanta's Air Force, Wilkins was the wing commander. Truly, he has been a franchise in Atlanta. His credentials: All-NBA first team once, all-NBA second team three times; league scoring champion in 1986 (the last one not named Michael Jordan); seven times an all-star; eight straight years his team's leading scorer.

He enters the 1992-93 season with the sixth-highest

Wilkins has been more than a superstar in Atlanta.

career scoring average in NBA history (26.2) and he will be only the 17th player to reach 20,000 points in his career.

Until Wilkins went down with a torn right Achilles tendon Jan. 28, 1992, he had missed only 16 games in 9 1/2 seasons. He has never worked fewer than the 32.8 minutes a game he averaged as a rookie. No matter the price—this season Wilkins will earn $3.5 million—he is worth it by NBA standards.

Check out these testimonials:

"He is a great player who has never been fully appreciated," Indiana general manager Donnie Walsh said a few years ago. "There are simply very few people in this world who can do the things he can do. If there is Bird and Magic and Michael (as the very best players), then he's the next guy. He's unstoppable. You double-team him and he finds ways to beat you. When he came into the league, he was a backward-type kid socially and on the court. Now, he's always gracious when he wins. He never makes excuses when he loses. I tell you, without him I think Atlanta would be just an average team. He's the only player they have who goes out every night and scores."

Kevin Loughery was Wilkins' first head coach in Atlanta. Later, as an analyst on Hawks' cable, Loughery saw him often, and still later he spent a year under coach Bob Weiss as an assistant, observing Wilkins under a microscope again. Loughery says, "Guys like him are so rare because he comes to play every night. He doesn't take a night off, ever. He gives you everything he has in every game. Plus, he's a very coachable guy. He listens to his coaches. You can't say that about every star player."

To see Wilkins dressed in silks and skin shoes, wearing metal spectacles, hair careful pomaded, greeting total strangers with ease and grace is to see a man who has grown marvelously in his first decade out of college.

To see Wilkins perform on the court is to admire the product of hard work. His second Hawks coach, Mike Fratello, remembers vividly the limitations of the kid known as " The Human Highlight Film" when he came out of Georgia. "He couldn't shoot and he couldn't dribble. He was a terrific athlete with tremendous natural athletic talent but he wasn't a basketball player yet. He had his choices. He could grow or he could stay the same. He wanted to grow and it took a lot of hard work, but he was willing to pay the price."

At the All-Star level, Wilkins cannot afford to stop working. His Achilles shredded on a simple foot plant during a game against Philadelphia, he has worked harder to prepare for the 1992-93 season than he ever thought possible. "They told me if I wanted to get back to where I was I would have to pay a price. I was willing to do that," he said. "The payoff is I will be back and I'm convinced as good as ever. But this also could extend my career because I'll be in the best condition of my career at the age of 32."

After 10 years in the league, Wilkins not only runs harder to get in shape, he is caught up in the race for endorsement dollars. He has the United States and Europe to promote Reebok. He does spots for Coca-Cola's Minute Maid soft drink. He is featured in TV spots for McDonald's. He makes appearances on behalf of Pro Line hair products. He is paid to endorse firms that sell meats, wallpaper, trading cards and a breakfast cereal, Cheerios.

There is a Wilkins all-star basketball game and a golf and tennis event, both for charity. He is involved in a downtown night club called Dominique's.

But the focus for the onetime dunking machine is basketball "because that's where it all starts and where it all ends. Everything I have I owe to the game."

Truly, Wilkins is capable in the most extraordinary things. Take this spurt midway during the 1987-88 season: over an 11-game span Wilkins averaged 40.5 points a night, shooting .503 from the field, sinking 14 of 30 three-point shots. That season he averaged 30.7 ppg.

Under Fratello, Wilkins played his regular position, small forward, but also doubled up at big guard. Under present coach Bob Weiss he has worked at both slots, plus taken his turn as a power forward when Weiss goes to his small lineup. One night in an Omni game against Chicago, Wilkins played eight minutes of the fourth quarter at center. The Hawks out scored the Bulls by 11 in that span. Not as exciting as the night Wilkins outscored Jordan 57-41, but the result was the same—the Hawks won.

One night against Indiana, Wilkins threw up a series of high bank shots that defied defense and beat the Pacers. This was a new assortment for him and then-Pacers coach Jack Ramsay had difficulty accepting the result. "Throw enough stuff against the wall and some of it sticks," Ramsay said rather ungraciously. Wilkins smiled when he heard that. Next time the teams met he did it again. Ramsay just shook his head this time.

Since joining the league as a raw 22-year-old Wilkins has sought acceptance as an equal by the best players in the game. After reaching their level, he never forgot the man to whom he owed the greatest debt.

It was Magic Johnson who first embraced Wilkins as a fellow superstar. Johnson, Wilkins says, who helped him gain legitimacy, who saw that he was invited to all the summertime all-star games. "He always said, 'Hey, what about 'Nique?' He always made sure I was included. I played in every game he had in (L.A.). It was Magic's idea that I would have my game in Atlanta. He went to the people and helped me get it started. I wouldn't have a game in Atlanta if it weren't for Magic. He did it all."

Although Wilkins had often spoken of marriage someday, it was Johnson's illness that made him realize his bachelor days were truly dangerous. Within a few months he became engaged to Nicole Berry. "I'd found what I needed in a woman," he said. "And I knew when Magic became ill that it was time for me to face up to my responsibilities. I'd learned there are a lot of people out there who want to take advantage of you. You have to accept certain responsibilities for yourself, to your family, to your team, and conduct your life in a certain way. My mother has always stressed the importance of family to me. I've always been close with my brothers and sisters. It was time for me to settle down."

Settled does not mean settling for second best. At age 32, Wilkins may no longer be slam-dunk king of the NBA (a title he held twice), but what his game may have lost in pure athleticism it has gained in maturity.

And Kasten can look back over the decade since he gave up two players and paid $1 million for the rights to Dominque Wilkins and say, "It was the greatest personnel move we ever made."

His big challenge will be to regain form after heel surgery during the 1991-92 season.

Webb won the 1989 slam dunk championship.

Webb Was Enough

In the career of every athlete there comes a moment of truth against heavy odds in which he learns if he is good enough. In Spud Webb's case, that moment came during his first week of training camp in 1985 as he attempted to catch on with the Hawks as a rookie free agent. Webb had been a fifth-round pick of Detroit, released after summer camp. The Pistons decided he could not shoot well enough to compensate for his slight 5-7 frame.

The Hawks needed guards when they went to came in Charleston, S.C., and they saw Webb as a kid who could push the ball in scrimmage and activate the fast break. But on the fourth day of camp, Webb reached in for a steal and was struck in the mouth by Sedric Toney's elbow, requiring 22 stitches in his upper lip. He missed that night's session and could not practice the next two days.

Hawks coaches made a fateful decision on Friday morning before a Sunday game with New York that would open the exhibition season. Webb would either practice or be replaced. The guard corps already in tatters with an injury to Doc Rivers and the free agency of Eddie Johnson and Mike Glenn, the team could wait no longer.

Webb understood. With stitches bristling from his lip, he practiced. On Sunday he started and answered questions dealing with skill and courage. On the Hawks' first possession of the game, the tiny player sped into the foul lane already packed with Knicks, including a rookie named Patrick Ewing. Webb literally disappeared in a sea of arms and legs as though swallowed whole. Like a great porpoise, Dominique Wilkins came out of the swell of athletes to dunk the ball with Spud Webb's first assist nicely done.

By January, Webb had established himself as a useful NBA player, possessing terrific speed and with a knack for finding the right man on the break—usually Wilkins. His teammates took his basketball skills seriously, but they were quite amused with the notion that Webb would compete in the NBA Slam-Dunk contest during All-Star Game weekend in his home town of Dallas. Tree Rollins suggested Webb come out like Mighty Mouse. He suggested Webb wear a cape and offered to buy one. Wilkins wanted Webb to use a ladder. Webb complained, "Ya'll trying to make a joke out of this."

The joke was Webb's. He soared to the dunking championship, beating Wilkins in the finals, then averaged 10 point a game the rest of the season. Never again was there a question about his talent.

More Force

Jon Koncak was the fifth pick of the 1985 Draft, a product of the NBA's first lottery, a player the Hawks believed would provide a solid foundation for their team as Rollins' eventual replacement. While Koncak was a good shooter at SMU, it was hoped his sturdy 7-footer's body and long arms would enable him to become a fine defender. In time, his defensive skills improved while his offensive game atrophied. Koncak had one magnificent series of games at the end of the 1988-89 season and became the recipient of a six-year, $13.2 million contract that startled the basketball world. That contract forever altered Koncak's life and not always for the better.

Scott Hastings had skills comparable to those of Koncak, but not the body. A second-round pick by the Knicks, Hastings was dealt to the Hawks after a half-season. Only once allowed to play as many as 1,000 minutes in a season, he became the consummate role player, the class clown. That was enough to provide him with a 10-year NBA career. But when they began to disassemble the Air Force, he was the first to go as part of the 1988 expansion draft to Miami.

Jon on the block.

Scott Hastings and Jon Koncak get advice from a fan.

Rebounder Extraordinaire

Five years before his benchmark season as the greatest rebounder in Atlanta Hawks history, Kevin Willis was considered to be the best young power forward in the business. That came with a season of 16.1 points, 10.5 rebounds, .536 shooting that included awesome games of 30 or more points and 20-plus rebounds.

The irony of Willis' career is that while he needed five more years to reach his peak, his strong-arming tactics had a profound and very quick impact on the Detroit Pistons' championship seasons. After seeing his team bullied by Willis one night in the Silverdome, Detroit coach Chuck Daly decried the absence of "manhood" on his team's front line.The following summer, the Pistons dumped their own power forwards, acquired Rick Mahorn form Washington and became a dominant team.

But Willis' career took a little more time. A track man who did not play high school basketball until his junior year, Willis was an emerging player at Michigan State when the Hawks made him the 11th pick of the 1984 Draft. Hawks President Stan Kasten remembers Willis seemed impervious to the ravings of his college coach, Jud Heathcote. "I knew if he could shrug that off, he could play for Mike," Kasten once said.

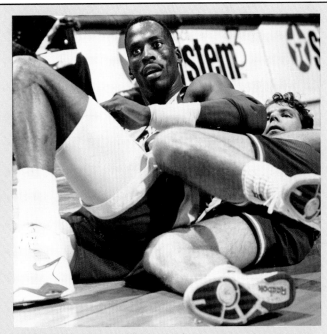

Willis has always been willing to tangle.

Battling Moses.

Boxing the Chief

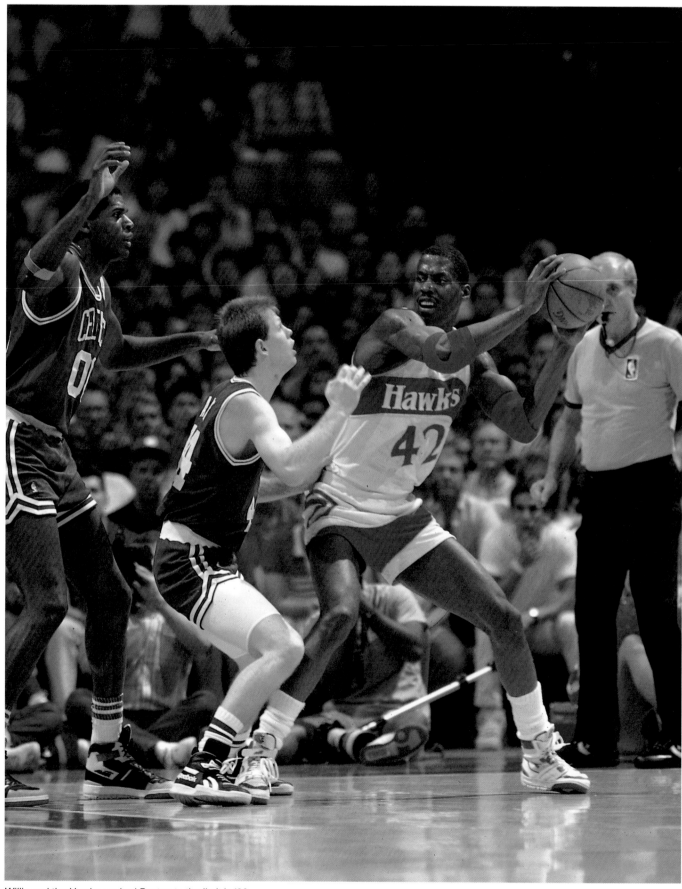

Willis and the Hawks pushed Boston to the limit in '88

Rattling The Garden Ghosts

With one fateful play, its original scheme forever lost in controversy, its execution terribly flawed, the direction and purpose of the Atlanta Hawks was forever changed, all but one of its principal components scattered to the four corners of the nation over the next three seasons.

The fateful day was May 20. 1988, the Hawks needing one victory to eliminate Boston in the second round of the playoffs.

The 1986-87 Hawks had achieved a franchise-record 57 victories, but were smashed by Detroit in five quick second-round games after dropping home court advantage in Game 1 of the series. A year later, the team broke through a late-season slump in which it lost six of its last nine to finish 50-32. The Hawks of 1985-86 had won their last three to achieve 50 victories. But in the spring of '88 with Kevin Willis slumping far below his '87 level of performance, John Battle debilitated after a long bout with serious hepatitis, and Jon

Carr challenged Bird.

Koncak absent the final two months with a knee injury, 50 became a symbol of dissatisfaction. Only a strong post-season could save the season.

The Hawks were extended the full five games before beating Milwaukee in the opening round of the playoffs, compounding questions about them. The Boston series that followed provided an astonishing emotional rollercoaster ride. As expected, the Hawks lost the first two games played at Boston Garden. They had not beaten the Celtics on their home court in nine straight regular-season games over three seasons, and none of these games were particularly close. Since the Celtics had only shown slight signs of slippage, what followed was entirely unexpected.

The Hawks came back to win Game 3 at home. Benefitting a schedule that called for back-to-back games, they won again to square the series before heading back to the Garden. At that point it was academic. If need be, the Celtics knew they could prevail in the full seven games, simply by holding service at home.

Including playoff games, the Hawks had been beaten 13 straight in the Garden. In Game 5 of the 1986 Playoffs they had been eliminated by a whopping 132-99. The other Eastern contenders, Chicago and Detroit, had dropped a combined 30 straight in Boston. Certainly, there is a natural order of things in this world and losing in Boston was part of it, expecially when the stakes are high. The Celtics had won 18 straight playoff games at home when they sought to break the two-all series tie.

This night all proceeded according to plan as the Hawks trailed 48-43 at the half. Midway of the third quarter, they were down 64-53 and Dominique Wilkins was only 5-of-19 from the field, a certain sign of disaster. Heading into the fourth quarter it was only 77-69.

Here, K.C. Jones made a critical decision to rest three starters and insert rookie Reggie Lewis at guard. Hawks coach Mike Fratello countered, shifting Wilkins to guard. The response from Wilkins was 11 points in six minutes, his first field goal of the second half tying it at 86-all. Wilkins sank two foul shots for 99-98 and the Hawks, about to launch a 10-0 run, never trailed again and

prevailed 112-104 with a shocking 43-27 fourth quarter that gave them the series lead, 3-2, and put them on the threshold of glorious achievement.

In retrospect, Fratello believes that his team was unable to retain its sense of purpose when the series moved back to Atlanta for Game 6; that the Hawks were seduced by the unbounded joy of the Atlanta community into believing they had already won the series.

In any event, the Hawks shot poorly, saw their advantages in rebounding and shot-blocking go for naught. Still, they were in the game and with bare seconds remaining had the ball on an out-of-bounds play at mid-court. It was a play never to be forgotten. Cliff Levingston took the pass because he was the player least likely to be closely guarded. Levingston then committed himself, driving at Robert Parish in the lane, Parish unyielding and Levingston throwing up an awkward left-handed hook shot that had no chance, the game ending 102-100... Boston, the series again tied, home court advantage relinquished.

The result was predictable: heart break. The manner in which it was suffered however, was hardly anticipated, for the Hawks played one of the most extraordinary games in franchise history before yielding 118-116. "The greatest NBA game I've ever seen," Fratello said.

"A game to pull out the tapes in the future, watch them and say, 'that was quite a game,' said Boston's Danny Ainge.

On his way to 47 points, Wilkins put his team ahead seven times in the fourth quarter. On his way to 34 points, Larry Bird put the Celtics in the lead five times. Caught in the middle, Kevin McHale gave this description of the action that swirled around him: "It was like two gunfighters standing blink-to-blink seeing which one would draw first and which one would drop first. Dominique would make one; Larry would make one: Dominique would make one; Larry would make one. There was a stretch of about four minutes in there that was some of the purest basketball you'll ever see. It was the hardest I've worked on defense and had 47 points scored on me."

K.C. Jones called it "some of the best basketball" he had ever seen. The action broke with the Celtics leading 114-111. It came on a goal tending call of Ainge's breakaway layup bid. Rivers swore he did not touch the ball as he flew by the hoop, out of bounds, but conceded he could not have prevented Ainge from rebounding and scoring.

So the Hawks were beaten in perhaps their finest hour. Wilkins with his 47 points, Randy Wittman 22, Doc Rivers 18 assists. Not enough. It was not something to build on. When training camp opened five months later, Tree Rollins was gone. Wittman and Scott Hastings were gone. Antoine Carr and Levingston had two more seasons as Hawks, as did Fratello. Spud Webb and John Battle had three more and they would leave. The stage was set for Moses Malone, Reggie Theus and others.

All from one fateful play.

Other Flyers

Throughout the Air Force years, there were other players who came, briefly filled a role and quickly drifted away. Mike McGee was one, a shooter whose 10.4 ppg. helped the Hawks win 57 games in 1986-87. Early the following season he was shipped to Sacramento. Johnny Davis, now an assistant coach , spent the last half-season of his career—actually his second term as a Hawk—helping the young birds win 50 for the first time in 1986. Gus Williams ended his career as a role player with the '87 Hawks. His brother Ray preceded him. Lorenzo Charles was too low-key, Roy Marble too high-strung. Each lasted a year. Saddest of all was Chris Washburn, incapable of self-discipline, hooked on drugs, a distraction to his teammates, a disaster to himself.

From Russia With Spud

As they say, it seemed like a good idea at the time. Actually, sending the Atlanta Hawks to the Soviet Union for two weeks in 1988 was Bob Wussler's idea. Bob Wussler was the executive vice-president of TBS, a man so important he had once been thrown out of the president's chair at CBS.

Bob Wussler had been to the Soviet Union so often he was eligible for dual citizenship. Wussler should have known better, but he painted this rosy picture of a two-week good-will mission/summer vacation for players, coaches, executives, and their families and assorted media types. The reality of abject poverty and hopelessness the Hawks encountered was painful.

The seeds of revolt that officially deposed the Communist system on New Year's Day 1992 began to sprout that summer of 1988. The amenities enjoyed in the West were virtually nonexistent, the American party learned early on their tour as they flew from Atlanta to Moscow, to the Black Sea "resort" community of Sukhumi, to Tblisi in Soviet Georgia. The dated arena where the first game was played became headquarters for Soviet Army troops who bloodily suppressed protests later that summer.

In Vilnius, Lithuania, there was more basketball and the promise of more insurrection. In Moscow for a stay of three days on the final official stop there was another game and the group learned that U.S. currency could buy items forbidden to Soviet citizens in hotel shops.

Some players had unique individual experiences.

Dominique Wilkins skipped Sukhumi and Tiblisi and planned to meet the team in Vilnius. Only when he landed hours late in Moscow on a flight from Frankfurt, Germany—all planes entering the USSR had to land in Moscow—he was abandoned by a Soviet sports committeeman who did not want to be late for his dinner. He was allowed on the Aeroflot's last plane to Vilnius, four hours later, wedged into a middle seat, chin to knee. Soviet forward Sergi Tarakanov later told Wilkins, "If your players always take Aeroflot, their careers end at age 25."

Spud Webb flew in with his agent and refused to leave his hotel room except to attend games and practices. When the Hawks toured the Kremlin he, Kevin Willis and Willis' companion remained in the hotel. Webb's representative, Robin Blakely, explained: "Spud doesn't trust the Russians."

The Hawks' party, totalling 69 people, learned some interesting facts about Soviet air travel: The term "charter flight" only means you board first. No food is served; only a thin yellow liquid is distributed in small plastic bowls which are re-filled and passed out again. Toilets come equipped with one cloth towel. All Soviet airliners have bubble noses for bomb sites and thick clouds of vapor that pour from air vents.

As for the resort of Sukhumi, promised beaches were rock-strewn and unwalkable. Promised tennis courts lacked nets. Tiles floated in the one swimming pool. Promised horseback riding, water skiing and yachting were nonexistent.

One night, the electricity failed completely. One night after an hours-long dinner at an outdoor Georgian restaurant that lacked toilet facilities, the local who drove the group bus encountered five fire trucks, sirens wailing, lights flashing, and passed them all on a two-lane winding road.

Sometimes, there weren't enough seats on busses or rooms in the hotels. Minor inconveniences.

Upon arrival in Sukhumi the leader of the Soviet delegation announced there were no porters to unload the baggage. "I think they are all ill or busy." One afternoon, while posing for a photo in front of St. Basil's cathedral in Moscow's Red Square, the team broke into a spontaneous rendition of "God Bless America." The singers were stopped by police who insisted this unlawful assembly would disrupt traffic, although autos are not allowed in the square.

In a separate effort to cheer up the travel party, Fratello had tins of spaghetti and sauce flown in for an Italian dinner to break up the constant diet of cucumber, tomato and small pieces of meat served at every meal.

At the farewell party at the Hotel Cosmos, Soviet security allowed a large number of questionable foreigners and local prostitutes to join in bringing the festivities to an early end.

When members of the travel party complained of broken promises to a guide named Sergei he responded this way: "Everything is as it seems only no one knows what that is."

It seemed a fitting epitaph.

O'Toole in the early years, with Lou Hudson.

Joe's view from the bench.

"Hey, Joe..."

The Hawks beat Joe O'Toole to town by one year. They've been together ever since.

For nearly a quarter-century Joe O'Toole has been a healer, father confessor, traveling secretary, social adviser, critic, fan, part-time assistant coach and friend to players and coaches in the organization. At once, he keeps track of time outs, personal fouls, the scissors and tape and every man on the roster.

In the locker room his name is "Hey, Joe..."

He's worked for six coaches—Richie Guerin, Cotton Fitzsimmons, Hubie Brown, Kevin Loughery, Mike Fratello and Bob Weiss—and gotten along with all of them, modified his schedule and his style to suit.

But there were favorites. A man doesn't work a job for nearly a quarter-century and not have favorites. "I guess I could try to be diplomatic and hedge a bit, but I think everybody knows Tree Rollins has always been special to me," O'Toole confesses. "We were together a long, long time and I never knew a finer person or a nicer person than Tree."

O'Toole can give you an all-star team of nice guys who could also play the game pretty well when they were Hawks. "Tree is my center. Tom McMillen my power forward. Dominique Wilkins my small forward and Pistol Pete Maravich and Lou Hudson would be my guards. But there were also guys like John Wetzel and Butch Beard, friends, who may not have been great players but were great people."

Rollins may have been his best friend on the team and McMillen, now a U.S. Representative from Maryland, may be among the favorites, but everyone got equal treatment in the training room. Eddie Johnson and John Drew, who gave into their personal demons, always received help from O'Toole whether it was in the hours prior to just after a game on in the middle of the night when the cries for help were too personal.

In terms of NBA seniority, O'Toole ranks second. Joe Proski of Phoenix beat him to the NBA by two years.

After that, O'Toole is second to no one. He was among the founders of the National Basketball Trainers Association, author of its constitution and ethics in 1972, chairman for four years, member of the board for 10 and the first recipient of the NBA Athletic Trainer of the Year Award in 1983.

Thanks to Joe O'Toole and his trusty personal computer there is now ia record of illness and injury in the NBA that aids physicians in determining patterns that produce problems for players. In 1988 he became the first NBA trainer to receive the NBA Society of Physicians Association's Irwin E. Vinnick Award for contributions to the game.

All this is part of a pattern. O'Toole has never been able to do only one thing at a time. At Cortland State University he ran track and played on the football team's offensive line. He was a student football coach for two years, student trainer three years. He has a B.S. from Cortland, a masters from Indiana and is a graduate of the Mayo Clinic's School of Physical Therapy.

In his spare time, O'Toole can sit in his boat on an Alabama lake, eat ice cream and fish at the same time.

Stacey Augmon was the only NBA rookie to start in 82 games during the 1991-92 season.

Hawks coach Bob Weiss.

What Lies In The Future?

When the Hawks finished their first full season under the stewardship of general manager Pete Babcock and his new head coach Bobby Weiss, Atlanta fans were promised a younger, more exciting team. Certainly, they've taken steps in that direction. Only three players—Dominique Wilkins, Kevin Willis and Jon Koncak—remain from the group that strung together four 50-or-more victory seasons from 1984-86 to 1988-89.

The Hawks went to training camp in 1991 with five players who had no more than a season of experience. They won 38 games and may have reached 50 had they not lost Wilkins to a torn Achilles tendon in the 42nd game and Travis Mays to a torn tendons in the second game of the season.

The good news is that Mays appears better than new and Wilkins has shown enough so the Hawks know he will at least be a very effective player again. That should be good enough to put the Hawks back in the playoff hunt again. More importantly, Wilkins and Mays form part of the foundation for a team that is building for the rest of the '90s.

This is a roster lacking in two important areas: The Hawks do not have an established point guard and they do not have a shot-blocker. These are problems that will prevent this team from ranking with the very best. Still, the Hawks offer solid credentials as they try to rekindle the excitement that rocked the Omni in the late '80s.

In their third seasons, Babcock and Weiss are assembling the players who can fit their system of motion and speed-up offense. Consider the nucleus:

* Mays, 24, averaged 14.3 ppg and ranked 13th in the league in three-point shooting in his only full NBA season at Sacramento. He was the 14th pick of the 1990 draft.

* Stacey Augmon, 24, averaged 13.3 ppg. as a rookie last season, playing guad for the first time in his career. He was the ninth pick in 1991.

* Rumeal Robinson, 26, averaged 13 ppg in his first full season as point guard. The 10th pick in 1990, he may be used on both sides this season.

* Snoop Graham, 25, averaged 10.1 ppg and ranked 15th in the NBA in three-point shooting after being signed as a rookie free agent.

* Duane Ferrell, 27, got his first chance to play significant NBA minutes and responded with 12.7 ppg and a team-best .524 shooting percentage.

* Morlon Wiley, 26, joined the team as a free agent guard on New Year's Day and showed a unique talent for distributing the ball. With a team that has plenty of scorers, he may be the point guard who fits best.

* Adam Keefe, 22, ninth pick of the 1992 draft, gives the Hawks a young power player with passing skills and the ability to run the floor.

Mix this group with Wilkins, who was second in the NBA in scoring with 28.1 ppg. when he went down last January. Add newly assertive power forward Kevin Willis, who averaged 18.3 ppg. and an astonishing 15.5 rebounds. Include Blair Rasmussen, a high-post center whose skills complement the others on the front court. Blend it all together; it's a pretty nice team.

Chief among Hawks' assets is versatility. Nearly every player on the roster can work at two positions and Wilkins has played four—including center—in his 10-year career. That's an enticing menu for Weiss, a coach who likes to taunt opponents with unorthodox lineups. It may also be pleasing to the palate of those who like entertaining basketball.

Hawks' Records

1968-92

1968-69

Player	G.	Min.	FGA	FGM	Pct.	FTA	FTM	Pct.	Reb.	Ast.	PF	Disq.	Pts.	Avg.
Lou Hudson	81	2869	1455	716	.492	435	338	.777	533	216	248	0	1770	21.9
Zelmo Beaty	72	2578	1251	586	.470	506	370	.731	798	131	272	7	1546	21.5
Joe Caldwell	81	2720	1106	561	.507	296	159	.537	303	320	231	1	1281	15.8
Bill Bridges	80	2930	775	351	.453	353	239	.677	1132	298	290	3	941	11.8
Don Ohl	76	1995	901	385	.427	208	147	.707	170	221	232	5	917	12.1
Walt Hazzard	80	2420	869	345	.397	294	208	,707	266	474	264	6	898	11.2
Paul Silas	79	1853	575	241	.419	333	204	.613	745	140	166	0	686	8.7
Jim Davis	78	1367	568	265	.467	231	154	.677	529	97	239	6	684	8.8
Richie Guerin	27	472	111	47	.423	74	57	.770	59	99	66	0	151	5.6
Skip Harlicka	26	218	90	41	.456	31	24	.774	16	37	29	0	106	4.1
Dennis Hamilton	25	141	67	37	.552	5	2	.400	29	8	19	0	76	3.0
George Lehman	11	138	67	26	.388	12	8	.667	9	27	18	0	60	3.5
Dwight Waller	11	29	9	2	.222	7	3	.429	10	1	8	0	7	0.6

1969-70

Player	G.	Min.	Fga	FGM	Pct.	FTA	FTM	Pct.	Reb.	Ast.	PF	Disq.	Pts.	Avg.
Lou Hudson	80	3091	1564	830	.531	450	371	.824	373	276	225	1	2031	25.4
Joe Caldwell	82	2857	1329	674	.507	551	379	.688	407	287	255	3	1727	21.1
Walt Hazzard	82	2757	1056	493	.467	330	267	.809	329	561	264	3	1253	15.3
Bill Bridges	82	3269	932	443	475	451	331	.734	1181	3545	292	6	1217	14.8
Jim Davis	82	2623	943	438	.464	318	240	.755	796	238	335	5	1116	13.6
Walt Bellamy	23	855	287	141	.491	124	75	.605	310	88	97	2	357	15.5
Gary Gregor	81	1603	661	286	.433	113	88	.779	397	63	159	5	660	8.1
Al Beard	72	941	392	183	.467	163	135	.828	140	121	124	0	501	7.0
Don Ohl	66	984	372	176	.473	72	58	.806	71	98	113	1	410	6.2
Dave Newmark	64	612	296	127	.429	77	59	.766	174	42	128	3	313	4.9
Grady O'Malley	24	113	60	21	.350	19	8	.421	26	10	12	0	50	2.1
Gene Tormohlen	2	11	4	2	.500	0	0	.000	4	1	3	0	4	2.0
Richie Guerin	8	64	11	3	.273	1	1	1.000	2	12	9	0	7	0.9

1970-71

Player	G.	Min.	FGA	FGM	Pct.	FTA	FTM	Pct.	Reb.	Ast.	PF	Disq.	Pts.	Avg.
Lou Hudson	76	3113	1713	829	.484	502	381	759.	386	257	186	0	2039	26.8
Pete Maravich	81	2926	1613	738	.458	505	404	.800	298	355	238	1	1880	23.2
Walt Hazzard	82	2877	1126	517	.459	415	315	.759	300	514	276	2	1349	16.5
Walt Bellamy	82	2908	879	433	.493	556	336	.604	1060	230	271	4	1202	14.7
Bill Bridges	82	3140	834	382	.458	330	211	.639	1233	240	317	7	975	11.9
Jerry Chambers	65	1168	526	237	.451	134	106	.791	245	61	119	0	580	8.9
Jim Davis	82	1864	503	241	.479	288	195	.677	546	108	253	5	677	8.3
Len Chappell	42	451	161	71	.441	74	60	.811	133	16	63	2	202	4.8
John Vallely	51	430	204	73	.358	59	45	.763	34	47	50	0	191	3.7
Bob Christian	54	524	127	55	.433	64	40	.625	177	30	118	0	150	2.8
Herb White	38	315	84	34	.405	39	22	.564	48	47	62	2	90	2.4
Bob Riley	7	39	9	4	.444	9	5	.556	12	1	5	0	13	1.9

Left—Lou Hudson scores against the Jazz.

1971-72

Player	G.	Min.	FGA	FGM	Pct.	FTA	FTM	Pct.	Reb.	Ast.	PF	Disq.	Pts.	Avg.
Lou Hudson	77	3042	1540	775	.503	430	349	.812	385	309	225	0	1899	24.7
Pete Maravich	66	2302	1077	460	.427	438	355	.811	256	393	207	0	1275	19.3
Walt Bellamy	82	3187	1089	593	.545	581	340	.585	1049	262	255	2	1526	18.6
Jim Washington	67	2416	729	325	.446	256	201	.785	601	121	217	0	851	12.7
Don Adams	70	2030	779	307	.394	273	204	.747	494	137	259	5	818	11.7
Herm Gilliam	82	2337	774	345	.446	173	145	.838	335	377	232	3	835	10.2
Bill Bridges	14	546	134	51	.381	44	31	.705	190	40	50	1	133	9.5
Don May	75	1285	476	234	.492	164	126	.768	217	55	133	0	594	7.9
Milt Williams	10	127	53	23	.434	29	21	.724	4	20	18	0	67	6.7
George Trapp	60	890	388	144	.371	139	105	.755	183	51	144	2	393	6.6
John Vallely*	9	110	43	20	.465	20	13	.650	11	9	13	0	53	5.9
Tom Payne	29	227	103	45	.437	46	29	.630	69	15	40	0	119	4.1
Jeff Halliburton	37	288	133	61	.459	30	25	.833	37	20	50	1	147	4.0
Larry Sidegfried	21	335	77	25	.325	23	20	.870	32	52	32	0	70	3.3
Bob Christian	56	485	142	66	.465	61	44	.721	181	28	77	0	176	3.1
Jim Davis	11	119	33	8	.242	18	10	.556	36	8	14	0	26	2.4
Shaler Hamilton	1	4	0	0	.000	0	0	.000	0	0	1	0	0	0.0

1972-73

Player	G.	Min.	FGA	FGM	Pct.	FTA	FTM	Pct.	Reb.	Ast.	PF	Disq.	Pts.	Avg.
Lou Hudson	75	3027	1710	816	.477	481	397	.825	467	258	197	1	2029	27.1
Pete Maravich	79	3089	1788	789	.441	606	485	.800	346	546	245	1	2063	26.1
Walt Bellamy	74	2802	901	455	.505	526	283	.538	964	179	244	1	1193	16.1
Herm Gilliam	76	2741	1007	471	.468	150	123	.820	399	482	257	8	1065	14.0
George Trapp	77	1853	824	359	.436	194	150	.773	455	127	274	11	868	11.3
Jim Washington	75	2833	713	308	.432	224	163	.728	801	174	252	5	779	10.4
Steve Bracey	70	1050	395	192	.486	110	73	.664	107	125	125	0	457	6.5
Don Adams	4	76	38	8	.211	8	7	.875	22	5	11	0	23	5.8
Jeff Halliburton	24	238	116	50	.431	22	21	.955	26	28	29	0	121	5.0
Don May	32	317	134	61	.455	31	22	.710	67	21	55	0	144	4.5
Bob Christian	55	759	155	85	.548	79	60	.759	305	47	111	2	230	4.2
John Wetzel	28	504	94	42	.447	17	14	.824	58	39	41	1	98	3.5
John Tschogl	10	94	40	14	.350	4	2	.500	21	6	25	0	30	3.0
Eddie Mast	42	447	118	50	.424	30	19	.633	136	37	50	0	119	2.8

1973-74

Player	G.	Min.	FGA	FGM	Pct.	FTA	FTM	Pct.	Off. Reb.	Def. Reb.	Tot. Reb..	Ast.	PF	Disq	Stl.	Blk. Sh.	Pts.	Avg.	Hi
Maravich	76	2903	1791	819	.457	568	469	.826	98	276	374	396	261	4	111	13	2107	27.7	42
Hudson	65	2588	1356	678	.500	353	295	.836	126	224	350	213	205	3	160	29	1651	25.4	44
Gilliam	62	2003	846	384	.454	134	106	.791	61	206	267	355	190	5	134	18	874	14.1	35
Bellamy	77	2440	801	389	.486	383	233	.608	264	476	740	189	232	2	52	48	1011	13.1	34
J. Washington	73	12519	612	297	.485	196	134	.684	207	528	735	156	249	5	49	74	728	10.0	23
J. Brown	77	1715	632	277	.438	217	163	.751	177	264	441	114	239	10	29	16	717	9.3	25
D. Jones	74	1448	502	238	.474	156	116	.744	145	309	454	86	197	3	29	64	592	8.0	33
Bracey	75	1463	520	241	.463	96	69	.719	26	120	146	231	157	0	60	5	551	7.3	25
Wetzel	70	1232	252	107	.425	57	41	.719	39	131	170	138	147	1	73	19	255	3.6	17
Schlueter	57	547	135	63	.467	50	38	.760	54	101	155	45	84	0	25	22	164	2.9	12
Ingelsby	48	398	131	50	.382	37	29	.784	10	34	44	37	43	0	19	4	129	2.7	10
Tschogl	64	499	166	59	.355	17	10	.588	33	43	76	33	69	0	17	20	128	2.0	14

1974-75

Player	G.	Min.	FGA	FGM	Pct..	FTA	FTM	Pct..	Off. Reb.	Def. Reb.	Tot. Reb	Ast..	PF	Disq	Stl.	Blk. Sh.	Pts.	Avg.	Hi
Hudson	11	380	225	97	.431	57	48	.842	14	33	47	40	33	1	13	2	242	22.0	36
Drew	78	2289	1230	527	.428	544	388	.713	357	479	836	138	274	4	119	39	1442	18.5	44
Arsdale	73	2570	1269	544	.429	383	294	.768	70	179	249	207	231	5	78	3	1382	18.0	35
Gilliam	60	1393	736	314	.427	113	94	.832	76	128	204	170	124	1	77	13	722	12.0	26
Sojourner	73	2129	775	378	.488	146	95	.651	196	446	642	93	217	10	35	57	851	11.7	29
Henderson	79	2131	893	367	.411	241	168	.697	51	161	212	314	149	0	105	7	902	11.4	32
J. Brown	73	1986	684	315	.461	250	185	.740	180	254	434	133	228	7	54	15	815	11.2	28
Meminger	80	2177	500	233	.466	263	168	.639	84	130	214	397	160	0	118	11	634	7.9	26
J. Washington	38	905	259	114	.440	55	41	.745	52	141	193	68	86	2	23	13	269	7.1	19
Lee	9	177	36	12	.333	39	32	.821	24	46	70	8	25	0	1	4	56	6.2	16
Kauffman	73	797	261	113	.433	84	59	.702	67	115	182	81	103	1	19	4	285	3.9	17
Wetzel	63	785	205	87	.426	77	68	.883	34	80	114	77	108	1	51	8	242	3.8	14

1975-76

Player	G.	Min.	FGA	FGM	Pct..	FTA	FTM	Pct..	Off. Reb.	Def. Reb.	Tot. Reb	Ast..	PF	Disq	Stl.	Blk. Sh.	Pts.	Avg.	Hii
Drew	77	2351	1168	568	.502	656	488	.744	286	374	660	150	261	11	138	30	1660	21.6	42
Hudson	81	2558	1205	569	.472	291	237	.814	104	196	300	214	241	3	124	17	1375	17.0	42
Henderson	81	2900	1136	469	.413	305	216	.708	58	207	265	374	195	1	137	10	1154	14.2	33
Van Arsdale	75	2026	785	346	.441	166	126	.759	35	1521	186	146	202	5	57	7	818	10.9	26
D. Jones	66	1762	542	251	.463	219	163	.744	171	353	524	83	214	8	52	61	665	10.1	24
Sojourner	67	1602	524	248	.473	119	80	.672	126	323	449	58	174	2	38	40	576	8.6	22
C. Hawkins	74	1907	530	237	.447	191	136	.712	102	343	445	212	172	2	80	46	610	8.2	22
J. Brown	75	1758	486	215	.442	209	162	.775	146	257	403	126	235	7	45	16	592	7.9	22
Meminger	68	1418	379	155	.409	152	100	.658	65	86	151	222	116	0	54	8	410	6.0	27
Holland	33	351	213	85	.399	34	22	.647	15	26	41	26	48	0	20	2	192	5.8	21
Willoughby	62	870	284	113	.398	100	66	.660	103	185	288	31	87	0	37	29	292	4.7	20
DuVal	13	130	43	15	.349	9	6	.667	1	7	8	20	15	0	6	2	36	2.8	10
Creighton	32	172	43	12	.279	16	7	.438	13	32	45	4	23	0	2	9	31	1.0	5

1976-77

Player	G.	Min.	FGA	FGM	Pct..	FTA	FTM	Pct..	Off. Reb.	Def. Reb.	Tot. Reb	Ast..	PF	Disq	Stl.	Blk. Sh.	Pts.	Avg.	Hi
Drew	74	2688	1416	689	.487	577	412	.714	280	395	675	133	275	9	102	29	1790	24.2	42
Robinson	36	1449	648	310	.478	241	186	.772	133	329	462	97	130	3	38	20	806	22.4	34
Hudson	58	1745	905	413	.456	169	142	.840	48	81	129	155	160	2	67	19	968	16.7	39
Henderson	46	1568	453	196	.433	168	126	.750	18	106	124	386	74	0	79	8	518	11.3	27
Charles	82	2487	855	354	.414	256	205	.801	41	127	168	295	240	4	141	45	913	11.1	27
Meriweather	74	2068	607	319	.526	255	182	.714	216	380	596	82	324	21	41	82	820	11.1	27
Hawes	44	945	305	147	.480	88	67	.761	78	183	261	63	141	4	36	24	361	8.2	19
Barker	59	1354	436	182	.417	164	112	.683	111	290	401	60	223	11	33	41	476	8.1	21
Hill	81	1825	439	175	.399	174	139	.799	39	104	143	403	245	8	85	6	489	6.0	26
Brown	77	1405	350	160	.457	150	212	.807	75	161	236	103	217	7	46	7	441	5.7	20
Denton	45	700	256	103	.402	47	33	.702	81	137	218	33	100	1	14	16	239	5.3	25
Terry	12	241	87	47	.540	21	18	.857	8	10	18	25	21	0	9	1	112	9.3	22
Willoughby	39	549	169	75	.444	63	43	.683	65	105	170	13	64	1	19	23	193	4.9	16
Sojourner	51	551	203	95	.468	57	41	.719	49	97	146	21	66	0	15	9	231	4.5	18
Davis	7	67	35	8	.229	13	4	.308	2	5	7	2	9	0	7	0	20	2.9	6
Dickerson	6	63	12	6	.500	8	5	.625	0	2	2	11	13	0	1	0	17	2.8	6

1977-78

Player	G.	Min.	FGA	FGM	Pct..	FTA	FTM	Pct..	Off. Reb.	Def. Reb.	Tot. Reb	Ast..	PF	Disq	Stl.	Blk. Sh.	Pts.	Avg.	Hi
Drew	70	2203	1236	593	.480	575	437	.760	213	298	511	141	247	8	119	27	1623	23.2	48
Hawes	75	2325	854	387	.453	214	175	.818	180	510	690	190	230	4	78	57	949	12.7	27
Criss	77	1935	751	319	.425	296	236	.797	24	97	121	294	143	0	108	5	874	11.4	30
Behagen	26	571	249	117	.470	70	51	.729	53	120	173	34	97	3	30	12	285	11.0	22
E. Johnson	79	1875	686	332	.484	201	164	.816	51	102	153	235	232	4	100	4	828	10.5	29
McMillen	68	1683	568	280	.493	145	116	.800	151	265	416	84	233	8	33	16	676	9.9	23
Hill	82	2530	732	304	.415	223	189	.848	59	172	231	427	302	15	151	15	797	9.7	21
Charles	21	520	184	73	.397	50	42	.840	6	18	24	82	53	0	25	5	188	9.0	17
O. Johnson	82	1704	619	292	.472	130	111	.854	89	171	260	120	180	2	80	36	695	8.5	22
Rollins	80	1795	520	253	.487	148	104	.703	179	373	552	79	326	16	57	218	610	7.6	21
Brown	75	1594	405	192	.474	200	165	.825	137	166	303	105	280	18	55	8	549	7.3	27
Robertson	63	929	381	168	.441	53	37	.698	15	55	70	103	133	2	74	5	373	5.9	18
Terry	27	166	68	25	.368	11	9	.818	3	12	15	7	14	0	6	0	59	2.2	6

1978-79

Player	G.	Min.	FGA	FGM	Pct..	FTA	FTM	Pct..	Off. Reb.	Def. Reb.	Tot. Reb	Ast..	PF	Disq	Stl.	Blk. Sh.	Pts.	Avg.	Hi
Drew	79	2410	1375	650	.473	677	495	.731	225	297	522	119	332	19	128	16	1795	22.7	50
Johnson	78	2413	982	501	.510	292	243	.832	65	105	170	360	241	6	121	11	1245	16.0	30
Roundfield	80	2539	916	462	.504	420	300	.714	326	539	865	131	358	16	87	176	1224	15.3	38
Furlow	29	576	235	113	.481	70	60	.857	32	39	71	81	42	0	18	13	286	9.9	30
Hawes	81	2205	756	372	.492	132	108	.818	190	401	591	184	264	1	79	47	852	10.5	27
Hill	82	2527	682	296	.434	288	246	.854	41	123	164	480	292	8	102	16	838	10.2	26
Rollins	81	1900	555	297	.535	141	89	.631	219	369	588	49	328	19	46	254	683	8.4	24
Givens	74	1347	564	234	.415	135	102	.756	98	116	214	83	121	0	72	17	570	7.7	22
Lee	49	997	313	144	.460	117	88	.752	11	48	59	169	88	0	56	1	376	7.7	21
McMillen	82	1392	498	232	.466	119	106	.891	131	201	332	69	211	2	15	32	570	7.0	22
Criss	54	879	289	109	.377	86	67	.779	19	41	60	138	70	0	41	3	285	5.3	17
Wilson	61	589	197	81	.411	44	24	.545	20	56	76	72	66	1	30	8	186	3.0	10
Herron	14	81	48	14	.292	13	12	.923	4	6	10	3	11	0	6	2	40	2.9	7

1979-80

Player	G.	Min.	FGA	FGM	Pct.	FTA	FTM	Pct.	Off. Reb.	Def. Reb.	Tot. Reb.	Ast.	PF	Dsq.	Stl.	Blk. Sh.	Pts.	Avg.	Hi
Drew	80	2306	1182	535	.453	646	489	.757	203	268	471	101	313	10	91	23	1559	19.5	40
Johnson	79	2622	1212	590	.487	338	280	.828	95	105	200	370	216	2	120	24	1465	18.5	36
Roundfield	81	2588	1007	502	.499	465	330	.710	293	544	837	184	317	6	101	139	1334	16.5	31
Hawes	82	1885	605	304	.502	182	150	.824	148	348	496	144	205	4	74	29	761	9.3	24
Rollins	82	2123	514	287	.558	220	157	.714	283	491	774	76	322	12	54	244	731	8.9	20
McElroy	31	516	171	66	.386	53	37	.698	20	29	49	65	45	1	21	5	171	5.5	20
McMillen	53	1071	382	191	.500	107	81	.757	70	150	220	62	126	2	36	14	463	8.7	24
Furlow	21	404	161	66	.410	51	44	.863	23	19	42	72	19	0	19	9	177	8.4	22
Criss	81	1794	578	249	.431	212	172	.811	27	89	116	246	133	0	74	4	671	8.3	26
Hill	79	2092	431	177	.411	146	124	.849	31	107	138	424	261	7	107	8	479	6.1	17
Givens	82	1254	473	182	.385	128	106	.828	114	128	242	59	132	1	51	19	470	5.7	20
Brown	28	361	98	37	.378	44	34	.773	21	41	62	14	66	0	3	4	108	3.9	12
Pellom	44	373	108	44	.407	30	21	.700	28	64	92	18	70	0	12	12	109	2.5	10
Lee	30	364	91	29	.319	17	9	.529	11	22	33	67	65	1	15	4	67	2.2	8
Wilson	5	59	14	2	.143	6	4	.667	2	1	3	11	3	0	4	1	8	1.6	3

1980-81

Player	G.	Min.	FGA	FGM	Pct.	FTA	FTM	Pct.	Off. Reb.	Def. Reb.	Tot. Reb.	Ast.	PF	Dsq.	Stl.	Blk. Sh.	Pts.	Avg.	Hi
Drew	67	2075	1096	500	.456	577	454	.787	145	238	383	79	264	9	98	15	1454	21.7	47
Johnson	75	2693	1136	573	.504	356	279	.784	60	119	179	407	188	2	126	11	1431	19.1	40
Roundfield	63	2128	808	426	.527	355	256	.721	231	403	634	161	258	8	76	119	1108	17.6	29
Matthews)	34	1105	330	161	.488	123	103	.837	16	56	72	212	122	1	61	7	425	12.5	26
Hawes	74	2309	637	333	.523	278	222	.799	165	396	561	168	289	13	73	32	889	12.0	32
Criss	66	1708	485	220	.454	214	185	.864	26	74	100	283	87	0	61	3	626	9.5	21
McMillen	79	1564	519	253	.487	108	80	.741	96	199	295	72	165	0	23	25	587	7.4	21
Rollins	40	1044	210	116	.552	57	46	.807	102	184	286	35	151	7	29	117	278	7.0	13
Pellom	77	1472	380	186	.489	116	81	.698	122	234	356	48	228	6	50	92	453	5.9	20
Shelton	55	586	219	100	.457	58	35	.603	59	79	138	27	128	1	18	5	235	4.3	22
McElroy	54	680	202	78	.386	59	48	.814	10	38	48	84	62	0	20	9	205	3.8	12
Burleson	31	363	99	41	.414	41	20	.488	44	50	94	12	73	2	8	19	102	3.3	12
A. Collins	29	395	99	35	.354	36	24	.667	19	22	41	25	35	0	11	1	94	3.2	15
D. Collins	47	1184	530	230	.434	162	137	.846	96	91	187	115	166	5	69	11	597	12.7	25
Hill	24	624	116	39	.336	50	42	.840	10	41	51	118	60	0	26	3	120	5.0	14

1981-82

Player	G.	Min.	FGA	FGM	Pct.	FTA	FTM	Pct.	Off. Reb.	Def. Reb.	Tot. Reb.	Ast.	PF	Dsq.	Stl.	Blk. Sh.	Pts.	Avg.	Hi
Roundfield	61	2217	910	424	.466	375	285	.760	227	494	721	162	210	3	64	93	1134	18.6	35
Drew	70	2040	957	465	.486	491	364	.741	169	206	375	96	250	6	64	3	1298	18.5	35
Johnson	68	2314	1011	455	.450	385	294	.764	63	128	191	358	188	1	102	16	1211	17.8	35
Williams	23	189	110	42	.382	26	22	.846	2	10	12	19	18	0	6	0	110	4.8	15
Sparrow	82	2610	730	366	.501	148	124	.838	53	171	224	424	240	2	87	13	857	10.5	22
Hawes	49	1317	370	178	.481	126	96	.762	89	231	320	142	156	4	36	34	456	9.3	19
Criss	27	552	210	84	.400	73	65	.890	6	32	38	75	40	0	23	2	235	8.7	31
Glenn	49	833	291	158	.543	67	59	.881	5	56	61	87	80	0	26	3	376	7.7	26
Macklin	79	1516	484	210	.434	173	134	.775	113	150	263	47	225	5	40	20	554	7.0	30
Matthews	47	837	298	131	.440	79	60	.759	19	39	58	139	129	3	53	2	324	6.9	27
McElroy	20	349	125	52	.416	36	29	.806	6	11	17	39	44	0	8	3	134	6.7	16
Rollins	79	2018	346	202	.584	129	79	.612	168	443	611	59	285	4	35	224	483	6.1	26
Wood	19	238	105	36	.343	28	20	.714	22	22	44	11	34	0	9	1	92	4.8	17
Pellom	69	1037	251	114	.454	79	61	.772	90	139	229	28	164	0	29	47	289	4.2	17
Shelton	4	21	6	2	.333	2	1	.500	1	2	3	0	3	0	1	0	5	1.3	4

1982-83

Player	G.	Min.	FGA	FGM	Pct.	FTA	FTM	Pct.	Off. Reb.	Def. Reb.	Tot. Reb.	Ast.	PF	Dsq.	Stl.	Blk. Sh.	Pts.	Avg.	Hi
Roundfield	77	2811	1193	561	.470	450	337	.749	259	621	880	225	239	1	60	115	1464	19.0	36
Wilkins	82	2697	1220	601	.493	337	230	.682	226	252	478	129	210	1	84	63	1434	17.5	34
E.Johnson	61	1813	858	389	.453	237	186	.785	26	98	124	318	138	2	61	6	978	16.0	32
Davis	53	1465	567	258	.455	206	164	.796	37	91	128	315	100	0	43	7	685	12.9	31
Sparrow	49	1548	512	264	.516	113	84	.743	39	102	141	238	162	2	70	1	615	12.6	30
Smith	15	142	66	29	.439	14	13	.929	2	6	8	14	17	0	2	0	71	4.7	18
McMillen	61	1364	424	198	.467	133	108	.812	57	160	217	76	143	2	17	24	504	8.3	26
Rollins	80	2472	512	261	.510	135	98	.726	210	533	743	75	294	7	49	343	620	7.8	22
Glenn	73	1124	444	230	.518	89	74	.831	16	74	90	125	132	0	30	9	534	7.3	25
Matthews	64	1187	424	171	.403	112	86	.768	25	66	91	249	129	0	60	8	442	6.9	26
Macklin	73	1171	360	170	.472	131	101	.771	85	105	190	71	189	4	41	10	441	6.0	19
Brown)	26	305	104	49	.471	40	25	.625	35	53	88	9	46	1	5	5	123	4.7	16
Hawes	46	860	244	91	.373	62	46	.742	53	175	228	59	110	2	29	8	230	5.0	20
Edmonson	32	309	139	48	.345	27	16	.593	20	19	39	22	41	0	11	6	112	3.5	14
Pellom	2	9	6	2	.333	0	0	.000	0	0	0	1	0	0	0	0	4	2.0	4
G.Johnson	37	461	57	25	.439	19	14	.737	44	73	117	17	69	0	10	59	64	1.7	6
Hastings	10	42	16	5	.313	6	4	.667	5	5	10	2	3	0	1	1	14	1.4	4

1983-84

Player	G.	Min.	FGA	FGM	Pct.	FTA	FTM	Pct.	Off. Reb.	Def. Reb.	Tot. Reb.	Ast.	PF	Dsq.	Stl.	Blk. Sh.	Pts.	Avg.	Hi
Wilkins	81	2961	1429	684	.479	496	382	.770	254	328	582	126	197	1	117	87	1750	21.6	39
Roundfield	73	2610	1038	503	.485	486	374	.770	206	515	721	184	221	2	61	74	1380	18.9	37
Johnson	67	1893	798	353	.442	213	164	.770	31	115	146	374	155	2	58	7	886	13.2	29
Davis	75	2079	800	354	.443	256	217	.848	53	86	139	326	146	0	62	6	925	12.3	29
Rivers	81	1938	541	250	.462	325	255	.785	72	148	220	314	286	8	127	30	757	9.3	21
Rollins	77	2351	529	274	.518	190	118	.621	200	393	593	62	297	9	35	277	666	8.6	22
Glenn	81	1503	554	312	.563	70	56	.800	17	87	104	171	146	1	46	5	681	8.4	24
Matthews	6	96	30	16	.533	22	18	.818	1	3	4	21	13	0	5	1	50	8.3	15
Williams	13	258	114	34	.298	46	36	.783	19	31	50	16	33	0	14	1	105	8.1	16
Wittman	78	1071	318	160	.503	46	28	.609	14	57	71	71	82	0	17	0	350	4.5	14
Hastings	68	1135	237	111	.468	104	82	.788	96	174	270	46	220	7	40	36	305	4.5	16
Criss	9	108	22	9	.409	5	51	.000	3	8	11	21	4	0	3	0	23	2.6	6
Brown	68	785	201	94	.468	65	48	.738	67	114	181	29	161	4	18	23	236	3.5	11
Hill	15	181	46	14	.304	21	17	.810	2	8	10	35	30	1	7	0	45	3.0	8
Pinone	7	65	13	7	.538	10	6	.600	0	10	10	3	11	0	2	1	20	2.9	6
Paultz	40	486	88	36	.409	33	17	.515	35	78	113	18	57	0	8	7	89	2.2	9
Landsberger	35	335	51	19	.373	26	15	.577	42	77	119	10	32	0	6	3	53	1.5	7

1984-85

Player	G.	Min.	FGA	FGM	Pct.	FTA	FTM	Pct.	Off. Reb.	Def. Reb.	Tot. Reb.	Ast.	PF	Dsq.	Stl.	Blk. Sh.	Pts.	Avg.	Hi
Wilkins	81	3023	1891	853	.451	603	486	.806	226	331	557	200	170	0	135	54	2217	27.4	48
Johnson	73	2367	946	453	.479	332	265	.798	38	154	192	566	184	1	43	7	1193	16.3	34
Rivers	69	2126	701	334	.476	378	291	.770	66	148	214	410	250	7	163	53	974	14.1	30
Williams	34	867	380	176	.439	123	79	.642	45	123	168	94	83	1	28	8	417	12.3	22
Wittman	41	1168	352	187	.531	41	30	.732	16	57	73	125	58	0	28	7	406	9.9	28
Levingston	74	2017	552	291	.527	222	145	.653	230	336	566	104	231	3	70	69	727	9.8	22
Willis	82	1785	690	322	.467	181	119	.657	177	345	522	36	226	4	31	49	765	9.3	24
Glenn	60	1126	388	228	.588	76	62	.816	20	61	81	122	74	0	27	0	518	8.6	21
Carr	62	1195	375	198	.528	128	101	.789	79	153	232	80	219	4	29	78	499	8.0	17
Rollins	70	1750	339	186	.549	93	67	.720	113	329	442	52	213	6	35	167	439	6.3	19
Criss	4	115	17	7	.412	6	4	.667	2	12	14	22	5	0	3	0	18	4.5	8
Russell	21	377	63	34	.540	17	14	.824	8	32	40	66	37	1	17	4	83	4.0	10
Hastings	64	825	188	89	.473	81	63	.778	59	100	159	46	135	1	24	23	241	3.8	16
Eaves	3	37	6	3	.500	6	5	.833	0	0	0	4	6	0	0	0	11	3.7	6
Brown	69	814	192	78	.406	68	39	.574	76	147	223	25	117	0	19	22	195	2.8	12
Granger	9	92	17	6	.353	8	4	.500	1	5	6	12	13	0	2	0	16	1.8	5
Lowe	15	159	20	8	.400	8	81	.000	4	11	15	42	23	0	11	0	24	1.6	6
Rautins	4	12	2	0	.000	0	0	—	1	1	2	3	3	0	0	0	0	0.0	0

1985-86

Player	G.	Min.	FGA	FGM	Pct.	FTA	FTM	Pct.	Off. Reb.	Def. Reb.	Tot Reb.	Ast.	PF	Disq.	Stl.	Blk. Sh.	Pts.	Avg.	Hi
Wilkins	78	3049	1897	888	.468	705	577	.818	261	357	618	206	170	0	138	49	2366	30.3	57
Witman	81	2760	881	467	/530	135	104	.770	51	119	170	306	118	0	81	14	1043	12.9	24
Willis	82	2300	811	419	.517	263	172	.654	243	461	704	45	294	6	66	44	1010	12.3	39
Rivers	53	1571	464	220	.474	283	172	.608	49	113	162	443	185	2	120	13	612	11.5	29
Johnson	39	862	328	155	.473	110	79	.718	17	58	75	219	72	1	10	1	394	10.1	24
Levingston	81	1945	551	294	.534	242	164	.678	193	341	534	72	260	5	76	39	752	9.3	25
Williams	19	367	143	57	.399	48	41	.854	19	26	45	67	48	1	28	1	159	8.4	20
Koncak	82	1695	519	263	.507	257	156	.607	171	296	467	55	296	10	37	69	682	8.3	21
Webb	79	1229	412	199	,483	275	216	.785	27	96	123	337	164	1	82	5	616	7.8	23
Carr	17	258	93	49	.527	27	18	.667	16	36	52	14	51	1	7	15	116	6.8	14
Davis	27	402	107	46	.430	59	51	.864	2	17	19	112	32	0	13	0	144	5.3	17
Rollins	74	1781	347	173	.499	90	69	.767	131	327	458	41	239	5	38	167	415	5.6	14
Battle	64	639	222	101	.455	103	75	.728	12	50	62	74	80	0	23	3	277	4.3	22
Charles	36	273	88	49	.557	36	24	.667	13	26	39	8	37	0	2	6	122	3.4	12
Hastings	62	650	159	65	.409	70	60	.857	44	80	124	26	118	2	14	8	193	3.1	12
Toney	3	24	7	2	.286	1	1	1.000	0	2	2	0	6	0	1	0	5	1.7	5

1986-87

Player	G.	Min.	FGA	FGM	Pct.	FTA	FTM	Pct.	Off. Reb.	Def. Reb.	Tot Reb.	Ast.	PF	Disq.	Stl.	Blk. Sh.	Pts.	Avg.	Hi
Wilkins	79	2969	1787	828	.463	742	607	.818	210	284	494	261	149	0	117	51	2294	29.0	57
Willis	81	2626	1003	538	.536	320	227	.709	321	528	849	62	313	4	65	61	1304	16.1	35
Rivers	82	2590	758	342	.451	441	365	.828	83	216	299	823	287	5	171	30	1053	12.8	27
Wittman	71	2049	792	398	.503	127	100	,787	30	94	124	211	107	0	39	16	900	12.7	30
McGee	76	1420	677	311	.459	137	80	.584	71	88	159	149	159	1	61	2	788	10.4	31
Levingston	82	1848	496	251	.506	212	155	.731	219	314	533	40	261	4	48	68	657	8.0	19
Webb	33	532	162	71	.438	105	80	.762	6	54	60	167	65	1	34	2	223	6.8	17
Battle	64	804	315	144	.457	126	93	.738	16	44	60	124	76	0	29	5	381	6.0	27
Koncak	82	1684	352	169	.480	191	125	.654	153	340	493	31	262	2	52	76	463	5.6	15
Rollins	75	1764	313	171	.546	87	63	.724	155	333	488	22	240	1	43	140	405	5.4	14
Carr	65	695	265	134	.506	103	73	.709	60	96	156	34	146	1	14	48	342	5.3	20
Williams	33	481	146	53	.363	40	27	.675	8	32	40	139	53	0	17	5	138	4.2	12
Hastings	40	256	68	23	.338	29	23	.7993	16	54	70	13	35	0	10	7	71	1.8	7
Wilson	2	2	2	0	.000	0	0	...	0	0	0	1	1	0	0	0	0	0.0	0
Henderson	6	10	5	2	.400	1	1	1.000	2	1	3	0	1	0	0	0	5	0.8	3

1987-88

Player	G.	Min.	FGA	FGM	Pct.	FTA	FTM	Pct.	Off. Reb.	Def. Reb.	Tot Reb.	Ast.	PF	Disq.	Stl.	Blk. Sh.	Pts.	Avg.	Hii
Wilkins	78	2948	1957	909	.464	655	541	.826	211	291	502	224	162	0	103	47	2397	30.7	51
Rivers	80	2502	890	403	.453	421	319	.758	83	283	366	747	272	3	140	41	1134	14.2	37
Battle	67	1227	613	278	.454	188	141	.750	26	87	113	158	84	0	31	5	713	10.6	27
Wittman	82	2412	787	376	.478	89	71	.798	39	131	170	302	117	0	50	18	823	10.0	20
Levingston	82	2135	564	314	.557	246	190	.772	228	276	504	71	287	5	52	84	819	10.0	29
Carr	80	1483	517	281	.544	182	142	.780	94	195	289	103	272	7	38	83	705	8.8	24
Wood	14	79	30	16	.533	8	7	.875	1	5	6	19	6	0	4	0	48	3.4	10
Webb	82	1347	402	191	.475	131	107	.817	16	130	146	337	125	0	63	12	490	6.0	14
Koncak	49	1073	203	98	.483	136	83	.610	103	230	333	19	161	1	36	56	279	5.7	25
McGee	11	117	52	22	.423	6	2	.333	4	12	16	13	6	0	5	0	51	4.6	18
Rollins	76	1765	260	133	.512	80	70	.875	142	317	459	20	229	2	31	132	336	4.4	20
Washburn	29	174	49	22	.449	23	13	.565	19	36	55	3	19	0	4	8	57	2.0	8
Whatley	5	24	9	4	.444	4	3	.750	0	4	4	2	3	0	2	0	11	2.2	3
Hastings	55	403	82	40	.488	27	25	.926	27	70	97	16	67	1	8	10	110	2.0	10

1988-89

Player	G.	Min.	FGA	FGM	Pct.	FTA	FTM	Pct.	Off. Reb.	Def. Reb.	Tot Reb.	Ast.	PF	Disq.	Stl.	Blk. Sh.	Pts.	Avg.	Hi
Wilkins	80	2997	1756	814	.464	524	442	.844	256	297	553	211	138	0	117	52	2099	26.2	41
Malone	81	2878	1096	538	,491	711	561	.789	386	570	956	112	154	0	79	100	1637	20.2	37
Theus	82	2517	1067	497	.466	335	285	.851	86	156	242	387	236	0	108	16	1296	15.8	32
Rivers	76	2462	816	371	,455	287	247	,861	89	197	286	525	263	6	181	40	1032	13.6	32
Battle	82	1672	628	287	.457	238	194	.815	30	110	140	197	125	0	42	9	779	9.5	21
Levingston	80	2184	568	300	,528	191	133	.696	194	304	498	75	270	4	97	70	734	9.2	23
Carr	78	1488	471	226	.480	152	130	.855	106	168	274	91	221	0	31	62	582	7.5	22
Koncak	74	1531	269	141	.524	114	63	.553	147	306	453	56	238	4	54	98	345	4.7	16
Webb	81	1219	290	133	.459	60	52	.867	21	102	123	284	104	0	70	6	319	3.9	21
Ferrell	41	231	83	35	.422	44	30	.682	19	22	41	10	33	0	7	6	100	2.4	16
Tolbert	50	341	94	40	.426	37	23	.622	31	57	88	16	55	0	13	113	103	2.1	9
Bradley	38	267	86	28	.326	16	8	500	7	25	32	24	41	0	16	2	72	1.9	8
Mannion)	5	18	6	2	.333	0	0		0	2	2	2	2	0	2	0	4	.8	2

1989-90

Player	G.	Min.	FGA	FGM	Pct.	FTA	FTM	Pct.	Off. Reb.	Def. Reb.	Tot Reb.	Ast.	PF	Disq.	Stl.	Blk. Sh.	Pts.	Avg.	Hi
Wilkins	80	2888	1672	810	.484	569	459	.807	217	304	521	200	141	0	126	47	2138	26.7	44
Malone	81	2735	1077	517	.480	631	493	.781	364	448	812	130	158	0	47	84	1528	18.9	31
Rivers	48	1526	480	218	.454	170	138	.812	47	153	200	264	151	2	116	22	598	12.5	24
Willis	81	2273	805	418	.519	246	168	.683	253	392	645	57	259	4	63	47	1006	12.4	30
Smith	33	674	204	98	.480	65	55	.846	7	30	37	142	45	0	22	1	255	7.7	22
Battle	60	1477	544	275	.506	135	102	.756	27	72	99	154	115	0	28	3	654	10.9	27
Webb	82	2184	616	294	.477	186	162	.871	38	163	201	477	185	0	105	12	751	9.2	26
Long	48	1030	384	174	.453	55	46	.836	26	57	83	85	66	0	45	5	404	8.4	20
Carr	44	803	248	128	.516	102	79	.775	50	99	149	53	128	4	15	34	335	7.6	21
Levingston	75	1706	424	216	.509	122	83	.680	113	206	319	80	216	2	55	41	516	6.9	21
Volkov	72	937	284	137	.482	120	70	.583	52	67	119	83	166	3	36	22	357	5.0	17
Matthews	1	13	3	1	.333	2	2	1.000	0	0	0	5	0	0	0	0	4	4.0	4
Koncak	54	977	127	78	.614	79	42	.532	58	168	226	23	182	4	38	34	198	3.7	12
Toney	32	286	72	30	.417	25	21	.840	3	11	14	52	35	0	10	0	88	2.8	11
Marble	24	162	58	16	.276	29	19	.655	15	9	24	11	16	0	7	1	51	2.1	7
Workman	6	16	3	2	.667	2	2	1.000	0	3	3	2	3	0	3	0	6	1.0	4
Ferrell	14	29	14	5	.357	6	2	.333	3	4	7	2	3	0	1	0	12	0.9	4
Williams	5	14	4	0	.000	0	0	...	0	1	1	0	2	0	0	0	0	0.0	0

1990-91

Player	G.	Min.	FGA	FGM	Pct.	FTA	FTM	Pct.	Off. Reb.	Def. Reb.	Tot Reb.	Ast.	PF	Disq.	Stl.	Blk. Sh.	Pts.	Avg.	Hi
Wilkins	81	3078	1640	770	.470	574	476	.829	261	471	732	265	156	0	123	65	2101	25.9	45
Rivers	79	2586	1020	444	.435	262	221	.844	47	206	253	340	216	2	148	47	1197	15.2	36
Battle	79	1863	862	397	.461	316	270	.854	34	125	159	217	145	0	45	6	1078	13.6	28
Webb	75	2197	803	359	.447	266	231	.868	41	133	174	417	180	0	118	6	1003	13.4	32
Willis	80	2373	881	444	.504	238	159	.668	259	445	704	99	235	2	60	40	1051	13.1	29
Malone	82	1912	598	280	.468	372	309	.831	271	396	667	68	134	0	30	74	869	10.6	25
Ferrell	78	1165	356	174	.489	156	125	.801	97	82	179	55	151	3	33	27	475	6.1	20
Robinson	47	674	242	108	.446	80	47	.588	20	51	71	132	65	0	32	8	265	5.6	19
Moncrief	72	1096	240	117	.488	105	82	.781	31	97	128	104	112	0	50	9	337	4.7	16
McCormick	56	689	187	93	.497	90	66	.733	56	109	165	32	91	1	11	14	252	4.5	12
Koncak	77	1931	321	140	.436	54	32	.593	101	274	375	124	265	6	74	76	313	4.1	20
Wilson	25	162	70	21	.300	26	13	.500	16	24	40	11	13	0	5	1	55	2.2	8
Wright	4	20	3	2	.667	1	1	1.000	1	5	6	0	3	0	0	0	5	1.3	3
Leonard	4	9	0	0	...	4	2	.500	0	2	2	0	2	0	0	1	2	0.5	2

1991-92

Player	G	MIN	FG	FGA	PCT	FG	FGA	PCT	FT	FTA	PCT	OFF	DEF	TOT	AST	PF	DQ	STL	TO	BLK	PTS	AVG
Wilkins	42	1601	424	914	.464	37	128	..289	294	352	.835	103	192	295	158	77	0	52	122	24	1179	28.1
Willis	81	2962	591	1224	.483	6	37	.162	292	363	.804	418	840	1258	173	223	0	72	197	54	1480	18.3
Augmon	82	2505	440	899	.489	1	6	.167	213	320	.666	191	229	420	201	161	0	124	181	27	1094	13.3
Robinson	81	2220	423	928	.456	34	104	.327	175	275	.636	64	155	219	446	178	0	105	206	24	1055	13.0
Ferrell	66	1598	331	632	.524	11	33	.333	166	218	.761	105	105	210	92	134	0	49	99	17	839	12.7
Graham	78	1718	305	682	.447	55	141	.390	126	170	.741	72	159	231	175	193	3	96	91	21	791	10.1
Rasmussen	81	1968	347	726	.478	5	23	.217	30	40	.750	94	299	393	107	233	1	35	51	48	729	9.0
Volkov	77	1516	251	569	.441	35	110	.318	125	198	.631	103	162	265	250	178	2	66	102	30	662	8.6
Mays	2	32	6	14	.429	3	6	.500	2	2	1.000	1	1	2	1	4	0	0	3	0	17	8.5
Cheeks	56	1086	115	249	.462	3	6	.500	26	43	.605	29	66	95	185	73	0	83	36	0	259	4.6
Sanders	12	117	20	45	.444	0	0	---	7	9	.778	9	17	26	9	15	0	5	5	3	47	3.9
Wiley	41	767	71	160	.444	14	38	.368	21	30	.700	22	51	73	166	73	0	43	52	3	177	4.3
Monroe	38	313	53	144	.368	6	27	.222	19	23	.826	12	21	33	27	19	0	12	23	2	131	3.4
Koncak	77	1489	111	284	.391	0	12	.000	19	29	.655	62	199	261	132	207	2	50	54	67	241	3.1
Leonard	5	13	4	6	.667	0	0	---	2	2	1.000	3	2	5	1	3	0	1	1	0	10	2.0

In perhaps the Easterns Conference's most competitive series in the late 1980s, Doc Revers guards Isiah Thomas.

All-Time Career Leaders

GAMES PLAYED

	Wayne Rollins	814	1977-88
*	Bob Pettit	792	1954-65
	Dominique Wilkins	762	1982-
*	Cliff Hagan	746	1956-66
	Lou Hudson	730	1968-77
@	Bill Bridges	683	1962-71
	Eddie Johnson	619	1977-86
	John Drew	595	1974-82
	Glenn Rivers	568	1983-91
	Kevin Willis	562	1984-
*	Lenny Wilkens	555	1960-68
@	Zelmo Beaty	501	1962-69

MINUTES PLAYED

*	Bob Pettit	30,590	1954-65
	Dominique Wilkins	28,211	1982-
	Lou Hudson	25,825	1968-77
@	Bill Bridges	23,574	1962-71
*	Cliff Hagan	21,731	1956-66
	Wayne Rollins	20,763	1977-88
*	Lenny Wilkens	19,566	1960-68
	Eddie Johnson	18,852	1977-86
	John Drew	18,362	1974-82
	Glenn Rivers	17,301	1983-91
@	Zelmo Beaty	17,159	1962-69

AVERAGE MINUTES

*	Bob Pettit	38.6	1954-65
	Pete Maravich	37.2	1970-74
	Dominique Wilkins	37.0	1982-
	Walt Bellamy	36.1	1969-74
	Lou Hudson	35.4	1968-77
*	Lenny Wilkens	35.3	1960-68
@	Bill Bridges	34.5	1962-71
@	Zelmo Beaty	34.2	1962-69
	Dan Roundfield	34.2	1978-84
*	Slater Martin	33.6	1956-60

TOTAL POINTS

*	Bob Pettit	20,880	1954-65
	Dominique Wilkins	19,975	1982-
	Lou Hudson	16,049	1968-77
*	Cliff Hagan	13,447	1956-66
	John Drew	12,621	1974-82
	Eddie Johnson	9,631	1977-86
@	Zelmo Beaty	8,717	1962-69
@	Bill Bridges	8,698	1962-71
*	Lenny Wilkens	8,601	1960-68
	Dan Roundfield	7,644	1978-84

FREE THROWS MADE

*	Bob Pettit	6,182	1954-65
	Dominique Wilkins	4,494	1982-
	John Drew	3,527	1974-82
*	Cliff Hagan	2,969	1956-66
	Lou Hudson	2,909	1968-77
*	Lenny Wilkens	2,639	1960-68
*	Zelmo Beaty	2,207	1962-69
@	Bill Bridges	2,147	1962-71
	Eddie Johnson	1,954	1977-86
	Dan Roundfield	1,882	1978-84

SCORING AVERAGE

*	Bob Pettit	26.4	1954-65
	Dominique Wilkins	26.2	1982-
	Pete Maravich	24.3	1970-74
	Lou Hudson	22.0	1968-77
	John Drew	21.2	1974-82
	John Drew	21.2	1974-82
*	Clyde Lovellette	19.3	1958-62
*	Cliff Hagan	18.3	1956-66
	Dan Roundfield	17.6	1978-84
@	Zelmo Beaty	17.4	1962-69
@	Joe Caldwell	16.5	1965-70

MOST FIELD GOALS MADE

	Dominique Wilkins	7,581	1982-
*	Bob Pettit	7,349	1954-65
	Lou Hudson	6,570	1968-77
*	Cliff Hagan	5,239	1956-66
	John Drew	4,545	1974-82
	Eddie Johnson	3,801	1977-86
@	Bill Bridges	3,352	1962-71
@	Zelmo Beaty	3,260	1962-69
	Kevin Willis	3,088	1984-
*	Lenny Wilkens	2,981	1960-68
	Dan Roundfield	2,878	1978-84

MOST FIELD GOALS ATTEMPTED

*	Bob Pettit	16,872	1954-65
	Dominique Wilkins	16,163	1982-
	Lou Hudson	13,501	1968-77
*	Cliff Hagan	11,630	1956-66
	John Drew	9,660	1974-82
	Eddie Johnson	8,157	1977-86
@	Bill Bridges	7,408	1962-71
*	Lenny Wilkens	7,081	1960-68
*	Zelmo Beaty	6,927	1962-69
	Pete Maravich	6,269	1970-74

FIELD GOAL PERCENTAGE

	Mike Glenn	.553	1981-85
	Wayne Rollins	.529	1977-88
	Cliff Levingston	.528	1984-90
	Antoine Carr	.516	1984-90
	Walt Bellamy	.508	1969-74
	Randy Wittman	.507	1983-88
	Kevin Willis	.506	1984-
	Duane Ferrell	.500	1988-
	Dan Roundfield	.498	1978-84
	Tom McMillen	.488	1977-83

TOTAL REBOUNDS

*	Bob Pettit	12,851	1954-65
@	Bill Bridges	8,656	1962-71
	Wayne Rollins	5,994	1977-88
@	Zelmo Beaty	5,622	1962-69
	Dominique Wilkins	5,332	1982-
	Devin Willis	5,229	1984-
*	Cliff Hagan	5,019	1956-66
	Dan Roundfield	4,658	1978-84
	John Drew	4,433	1974-82
	Walt Bellamy	4,123	1969-74
*	Charles Share	4,061	1953-60

*all St. Louis years; @ years spent in St. Louis/Atlanta

MOST FREE THROWS ATTEMPTED
```
*   Bob Pettit ..................... 8,119 ..................... 1954-65
    Dominique Wilkins ......... 5,557 ..................... 1982-
    John Drew ..................... 4,743 ..................... 1974-82
*   Cliff Hagan .................... 3,722 ..................... 1956-66
    Lou Hudson ................... 3,659 ..................... 1968-77
*   Lenny Wilkens ............... 3,486 ..................... 1960-68
@   Bill Bridges ................... 3,099 ..................... 1962-71
@   Zelmo Beaty .................. 2,954 ..................... 1962-69
    Glenn Rivers ................. 2,567 ..................... 1983-91
    Dan Roundfield ............. 2,551 ..................... 1978-84
    Eddie Johnson ............. 2,464 ..................... 1977-86
```

FREE THROW PERCENTAGE
```
*   Clyde Lovellette ............. .832 ..................... 1958-62
    Mike Glenn ..................... .831 ..................... 1981-85
    Herm Gilliam ................. .830 ..................... 1971-75
    Anthony Webb ................ .829 ..................... 1985-91
    Johnny Davis ................. .829 ..................... 1982-86
    Armond Hill ................... .824 ..................... 1976-84
    Charlie Criss ................. .823 ..................... 1977-85
    Tom McMillen ................. .811 ..................... 1977-83
    Scott Hastings ............... .811 ..................... 1982-88
    Pete Maravich ............... .809 ..................... 1970-74
    Dominique Wilkins ......... .809 ..................... 1982-
```

MOST ASSISTS
```
    Glenn Rivers ................. 3,866 ..................... 1983-91
    Eddie Johnson ............. 3,207 ..................... 1977-86
*   Lenny Wilkens ............... 3,048 ..................... 1960-68
*   Bob Pettit ..................... 2,369 ..................... 1954-65
*   Cliff Hagan .................... 2,236 ..................... 1956-66
    Lou Hudson ................... 2,098 ..................... 1968-77
    Anthony Webb ................ 2,019 ..................... 1985-91
@   Bill Bridges ................... 1,997 ..................... 1962-71
    Dominique Wilkins ......... 1,980 ..................... 1982-00
    Armond Hill ................... 1,887 ..................... 1976-84
    Pete Maravich ............... 1,690 ..................... 1970-74
    Walt Hazzard ................. 1,549 ..................... 1968-71
```

MOST BLOCKED SHOTS
```
    Wayne Rollins ............... 2,283 ..................... 1977-88
    Dan Roundfield ............. 716 ..................... 1978-84
    Dominique Wilkins ......... 539 ..................... 1982-00
    Jon Koncak ................... 476 ..................... 1985-00
    Cliff Levingston ............. 371 ..................... 1984-90
    Kevin Willis ................... 337 ..................... 1984-00
    Antoine Carr ................. 286 ..................... 1984-90
    Steve Hawes ................. 243 ..................... 1976-83
    Moses Malone ............... 258 ..................... 1988-91
    John Drew ..................... 182 ..................... 1974-82
    Dwight Jones ................. 176 ..................... 1973-76
```

MOST PERSONAL FOULS
```
    Wayne Rollins ............... 2,924 ..................... 1977-88
@   Bill Bridges ................... 2,575 ..................... 1962-71
*   Cliff Hagan .................... 2,547 ..................... 1956-66
*   Bob Pettit ..................... 2,526 ..................... 1954-65
    John Drew ..................... 2,216 ..................... 1974-82
    Lou Hudson ................... 2,110 ..................... 1968-77
@   Zelmo Beaty .................. 2,002 ..................... 1962-69
    Glenn Rivers ................. 1,910 ..................... 1983-91
*   Lenny Wilkens ............... 1,888 ..................... 1960-68
    Kevin Willis ................... 1,790 ..................... 1984-00
```

REBOUNDING AVERAGE
```
*   Bob Pettit ..................... 16.2 ..................... 1954-65
@   Bill Bridges ................... 12.7 ..................... 1962-71
    Walt Bellamy ................. 12.2 ..................... 1969-74
@   Zelmo Beaty .................. 11.2 ..................... 1962-69
    Dan Roundfield ............. 10.7 ..................... 1978-84
    Moses Malone ............... 9.9 ..................... 1988-91
*   Clyde Lovellette ............. 9.6 ..................... 1958-62
*   Charles Share ............... 9.6 ..................... 1953-60
    Jim Washington ............. 9.4 ..................... 1971-75
    Kevin Willis ................... 9.3 ..................... 1984-00
@   Paul Silas ..................... 8.8 ..................... 1964-69
```

MOST OFFENSIVE REBOUNDS
```
    Dominique Wilkins ......... 2,225 ..................... 1982-00
    Kevin Willis ................... 1,906 ..................... 1984-00
    Wayne Rollins ............... 1,902 ..................... 1977-88
    John Drew ..................... 1,878 ..................... 1974-82
    Dan Roundfield ............. 1,452 ..................... 1978-84
    Cliff Levingston ............. 1,177 ..................... 1984-90
    Moses Malone ............... 1,021 ..................... 1988-91
    Steve Hawes ................. 903 ..................... 1976-83
    Jon Koncak ................... 795 ..................... 1985-00
    John Brown ................... 736 ..................... 1973-80
    Tom McMillen ................. 607 ..................... 1977-83
```

MOST DEFENSIVE REBOUNDS
```
    Wayne Rollins ............... 4,092 ..................... 1977-88
    Kevin Willis ................... 3,323 ..................... 1984-00
    Dan Roundfield ............. 3,116 ..................... 1978-84
    Dominique Wilkins ......... 3,107 ..................... 1982-00
    John Drew ..................... 2,555 ..................... 1974-82
    Steve Hawes ................. 2,244 ..................... 1976-83
    Jon Koncak ................... 1,813 ..................... 1985-00
    Cliff Levingston ............. 1,777 ..................... 1984-90
    Glenn Rivers ................. 1,464 ..................... 1983-91
    Moses Malone ............... 1,414 ..................... 1988-91
    Tom McMillen ................. 1,209 ..................... 1977-83
    John Brown ................... 1,143 ..................... 1973-80
```

MOST STEALS
```
    Glenn Rivers ................. 1,166 ..................... 1983-91
    Dominique Wilkins ......... 1,112 ..................... 1982-00
    John Drew ..................... 859 ..................... 1974-82
    Eddie Johnson ............. 741 ..................... 1977-86
    Armond Hill ................... 478 ..................... 1976-84
    Anthony Webb ................ 472 ..................... 1985-91
    Wayne Rollins ............... 452 ..................... 1977-88
    Dan Roundfield ............. 449 ..................... 1978-84
    Steve Hawes ................. 405 ..................... 1976-83
    Cliff Levingston ............. 398 ..................... 1984-90
    Lou Hudson ................... 364 ..................... 1968-77
```

MOST DISQUALIFICATIONS
```
    Wayne Rollins ............... 88 ..................... 1977-88
    John Drew ..................... 76 ..................... 1974-82
*   Charles Share ............... 74 ..................... 1953-60
@   Zelmo Beaty .................. 65 ..................... 1962-69
@   Bill Bridges ................... 61 ..................... 1962-71
    John Brown ................... 49 ..................... 1973-80
    Armond Hill ................... 39 ..................... 1976-84
*   Lenny Wilkens ............... 38 ..................... 1960-68
    Dan Roundfield ............. 36 ..................... 1978-84
*   Bob Pettit ..................... 33 ..................... 1954-65
```

All-Time Season Leaders

Games Played

* Zelmo Beaty	82	1967-68
Bill Bridges	82	1969-70
Joe Caldwell	82	1969-70
Walt Hazzard	82	1969-70
Jim Davis	82	1969-70
Walt Hazzard	82	1970-71
Walt Bellamy	82	1970-71
Bill Bridges	82	1970-71
Walt Bellamy	82	1971-72
Herm Gilliam	82	1971-72
Ken Charles	82	1976-77
Armond Hill	82	1977-78
Ollie Johnson	82	1977-78
Armond Hill	82	1978-79
Tom McMillen	82	1978-79
Steve Hawes	82	1979-80
Wayne Rollins	82	1979-80
Jack Givens	82	1979-80
Rory Sparrow	82	1981-82
Dominique Wilkins	82	1982-83
Kevin Willis	82	1984-85
Kevin Willis	82	1985-86
Jon Koncak	82	1985-86
Jon Koncak	82	1986-87
Cliff Levingston	82	1986-87
Glenn Rivers	82	1986-87
Cliff Levingston	82	1987-88
Anthony Webb	82	1987-88
Randy Wittman	82	1987-88
John Battle	82	1988-89
Reggie Theus	82	1988-89
Anthony Webb	82	1989-90
Moses Malone	82	1990-91
Stacey Augmon	82	1991-92

MOST MINUTES PLAYED

* Bob Pettit	3,296	1963-64
* Bob Pettit	3,282	1961-62
Bill Bridges	3,269	1969-70
*Bill Bridges	3,197	1967-68
Walt Bellamy	3,187	1971-72
Bill Bridges	3,140	1970-71
*Bill Bridges	3,130	1966-67
Lou Hudson	3,113	1970-71
Lou Hudson	3,091	1969-70
Pete Maravich	3,089	1972-73
Dominique Wilkins	3,078	1990-91
Dominique Wilkins	3,049	1985-86
Lou Hudson	3,042	1971-72
Lou Hudson	3,027	1972-73
Dominique Wilkins	3,023	1984-85

TOTAL POINTS

* Bob Pettit	2,429	1961-62
Dominique Wilkins	2,397	1987-88
Dominique Wilkins	2,366	1985-86
Dominique Wilkins	2,294	1986-87
* Bob Pettit	2,241	1962-63
Dominique Wilkins	2,217	1984-85
* Bob Pettit	2,190	1963-64
Dominique Wilkins	2,138	1989-90
* Bob Pettit	2,120	1960-61
Pete Maravich	2,107	1973-74
* Bob Pettit	2,105	1958-59
Dominique Wilkins	2,101	1990-91
Dominique Wilkins	2,099	1988-89
Pete Maravich	2,063	1972-73
Lou Hudson	2,039	1970-71
Lou Hudson	2,031	1969-70
Lou Hudson	2,029	1972-73

SCORING AVERAGE

* Bob Pettit	31.1	1961-62
Dominique Wilkins	30.7	1987-88
Dominique Wilkins	30.3	1985-86
* Bob Pettit	29.2	1958-59
Dominique Wilkins	29.0	1986-87
* Bob Pettit	28.4	1962-63
Dominique Wilkins	28.1	1991-92
* Bob Pettit	27.9	1960-61
Pete Maravich	27.7	1973-74
Dominique Wilkins	27.4	1984-85
* Bob Pettit	27.4	1963-64
Lou Hudson	27.1	1972-73
Lou Hudson	26.8	1970-71
Dominique Wilkins	26.7	1989-90
Dominique Wilkins	26.2	1988-89
Pete Maravich	26.1	1972-73
* Bob Pettit	26.1	1959-60
Dominique Wilkins	25.9	1990-91
* Bob Pettit	25.7	1955-56
Lou Hudson	25.4	1973-74

MOST FIELD GOALS MADE

Dominique Wilkins	909	1987-88
Dominique Wilkins	888	1985-86
* Bob Pettit	867	1961-62
Dominique Wilkins	853	1984-85
Lou Hudson	830	1969-70
Lou Hudson	829	1970-71
Dominique Wilkins	828	1986-87
Pete Maravich	819	1973-74
Lou Hudson	816	1972-73
Dominique Wilkins	814	1988-89
Dominique Wilkins	810	1989-90
* Bob Pettit	791	1963-64
Pete Maravich	789	1972-73

MOST FIELD GOALS ATTEMPTED

Dominique Wilkins	1,957	1987-88
* Bob Pettit	1,928	1961-62
Dominique Wilkins	1,897	1985-86
Dominique Wilkins	1,891	1984-85
Pete Maravich	1,791	1973-74
Pete Maravich	1,788	1972-73
Dominique Wilkins	1,787	1986-87
Dominique Wilkins	1,756	1988-89
* Bob Pettit	1,720	1960-61
Lou Hudson	1,713	1970-71
Lou Hudson	1,710	1972-73
* Bob Pettit	1,708	1963-64
Dominique Wilkins	1,672	1989-90
Dominique Wilkins	1,640	1990-91
Pete Maravich	1,613	1970-71

FIELD GOAL PERCENTAGE

Mike Glenn	.588	1984-85
Wayne Rollins	.584	1981-82
Mike Glenn	.563	1983-84
Wayne Rollins	.558	1979-80
Cliff Levingston	.557	1987-88
Wayne Rollins	.549	1984-85
Bob Christian	.548	1972-73
Wayne Rollins	.546	1986-87
Walt Bellamy	.545	1971-72
Mike Glenn	.543	1981-82

MOST FREE THROWS MADE

* Bob Pettit	695	1961-62
* Bob Pettit	685	1962-63
* Bob Pettit	667	1958-59
* Bob Pettit	608	1963-64

MOST FIELD GOALS MADE
(continued)

Dominique Wilkins	607	1986-87
* Bob Pettit	582	1960-61
Dominique Wilkins	577	1985-86
Moses Malone	561	1988-89
* Bob Pettit	557	1957-58
* Bob Pettit	557	1955-56
Dominique Wilkins	541	1987-88
* Cliff Hagan	536	1958-59
John Drew	495	1978-79
Moses Malone	493	1989-90
John Drew	489	1979-80
John Drew	488	1975-76
Dominique Wilkins	486	1984-85
Pete Maravich	485	1972-73
Dominique Wilkins	476	1990-91
Pete Maravich	469	1973-74

MOST FREE THROWS ATTEMPTED

* Bob Pettit	901	1961-62
* Bob Pettit	885	1962-63
* Bob Pettit	879	1958-59
* Bob Pettit	771	1963-64
* Bob Pettit	757	1955-56
* Bob Pettit	744	1957-58
Dominique Wilkins	742	1986-87
* Bob Pettit	722	1959-60
Moses Malone	711	1988-89
Dominique Wilkins	705	1985-86
John Drew	677	1978-79
John Drew	656	1975-76
Dominique Wilkins	655	1987-88
John Drew	646	1979-80
Moses Malone	631	1989-90
Pete Maravich	606	1972-73
Dominique Wilkins	603	1984-85
* Lenny Wilkens	583	1966-67
Walt Bellamy	581	1971-72

FREE THROW PERCENTAGE

Tom McMillen	.891	1978-79
Charlie Criss	.890	1981-82
John Wetzel	.883	1974-75
Mike Glenn	.881	1981-82
Wayne Rollins	.875	1987-88
Anthony Webb	.871	1989-90
Anthony Webb	.868	1990-91
Anthony Webb	.867	1988-89
Charlie Criss	.865	1980-81
Glenn Rivers	.861	1988-89
Scott Hastings	.857	1985-86
* Clyde Lovellette	.856	1960-61
Ollie Johnson	.854	1977-78
* Cliff Hagan	.854	1965-66

MOST ASSISTS

Glenn Rivers	823	1986-87
Glenn Rivers	747	1987-88
* Lenny Wilkens	679	1967-68
Eddie Johnson	566	1984-85
Walt Hazzard	561	1969-70
Pete Maravich	546	1972-73
Glenn Rivers	525	1988-89
Walt Hazzard	514	1970-71
Herm Gilliam	482	1972-73
Armond Hill	480	1978-79
Anthony Webb	477	1989-90
Rumeal Robinson	446	1991-92
Glenn Rivers	443	1985-86

MOST BLOCKED SHOTS

Wayne Rollins	343	1982-83
Wayne Rollins	277	1983-84
Wayne Rollins	254	1978-79
Wayne Rollins	244	1979-80
Wayne Rollins	224	1981-82
Wayne Rollins	218	1977-78

Dan Roundfield	176	1978-79
Wayne Rollins	167	1985-86
Wayne Rollins	167	1984-85
Wayne Rollins	140	1986-87

MOST REBOUNDS

* Bob Pettit	1,540	1960-61
* Bob Pettit	1,457	1961-62
Kevin Willis	1,258	1991-92
Bill Bridges	1,233	1970-71
* Bob Pettit	1,224	1963-64
* Bob Pettit	1,221	1959-60
* Bob Pettit	1,216	1957-58
* Bob Pettit	1,195	1962-63
* Bill Bridges	1,190	1966-67
* Bob Pettit	1,182	1958-59
Bill Bridges	1,181	1969-70
* Bob Pettit	1,164	1955-56
Bill Bridges	1,132	1968-69
* Bill Bridges	1,102	1967-68
* Zelmo Beaty	1,086	1965-66
Walt Bellamy	1,060	1970-71
Walt Bellamy	1,049	1971-72
* Bob Pettit	1,037	1956-57
* Zelmo Beaty	966	1964-65
Walt Bellamy	964	1972-73
Zelmo Beaty	959	1967-68
Paul Silas	958	1967-68
Moses Malone	956	1988-89
* Bill Bridges	951	1965-66
Dan Roundfield	880	1982-83
Dan Roundfield	865	1978-79

REBOUND AVERAGE

* Bob Pettit	20.3	1960-61
* Bob Pettit	18.7	1961-62
* Bob Pettit	17.4	1957-58
* Bob Pettit	17.0	1959-60
* Bob Pettit	16.4	1958-59
* Bob Pettit	16.1	1955-56
Kevin Willis	15.5	1991-92
Bill Bridges	15.0	1970-71
Bill Bridges	14.4	1969-70
Bill Bridges	14.2	1968-69
Walt Bellamy	13.2	1972-73
Walt Bellamy	12.9	1970-71
Walt Bellamy	12.8	1971-72
Moses Malone	11.8	1988-89
Dan Roundfield	11.8	1981-82
Jim Washington	11.7	1972-73
Dan Roundfield	11.4	1982-83

MOST OFFENSIVE REBOUNDS

Kevin Willis	418	1991-92
Moses Malone	386	1988-89
Moses Malone	364	1989-90
John Drew	357	1974-75
Dan Roundfield	326	1978-79
Kevin Willis	321	1986-87
Dan Roundfield	293	1979-80
John Drew	286	1975-76
Wayne Rollins	283	1979-80
John Drew	280	1976-77
Moses Malone	271	1990-91
Walt Bellamy	264	1973-74
Dominique Wilkins	261	1990-91
Dominique Wilkins	261	1985-86

MOST DEFENSIVE REBOUNDS

Kevin Willis	840	1991-92
Dan Roundfield	621	1982-83
Moses Malone	570	1988-89
Dan Roundfield	544	1979-80
Dan Roundfield	539	1978-79
Wayne Rollins	533	1982-83
Kevin Willis	528	1986-87
Jim Washington	528	1973-74
Dan Roundfield	515	1983-84
Steve Hawes	510	1977-78
Dan Roundfield	494	1981-82

MOST STEALS
Glenn Rivers	181	1988-89
Glenn Rivers	171	1986-87
Glenn Rivers	163	1984-85
Lou Hudson	160	1973-74
Armond Hill	151	1977-78
Glenn Rivers	148	1990-91
Ken Charles	141	1976-77
Glenn Rivers	140	1987-88
Dominique Wilkins	138	1985-86
John Drew	138	1975-76
Tom Henderson	137	1975-76

MOST PERSONAL FOULS
* Bill Bridges	366	1967-68
Dan Roundfield	358	1978-79
* Zelmo Beaty	344	1965-66
Jim Davis	335	1969-70
* Bill Bridges	333	1965-66
John Drew	332	1978-79
Wayne Rollins	328	1978-79
* Zelmo Beaty	328	1964-65

Wayne Rollins	326	1977-78
* Bill Bridges	325	1966-67
Joe C. Meriweather	324	1976-77
Wayne Rollins	322	1979-80
* Charles Shore	318	1955-56
Dan Roundfield	317	1979-80
Bill Bridges	317	1970-71
Kevin Willis	313	1986-87
John Drew	313	1979-80

MOST DISQUALIFICATIONS
Joe C. Meriweather	21	1976-77
Wayne Rollins	19	1978-79
John Drew	19	1978-79
John Brown	18	1977-78
Wayne Rollins	16	1977-78
Dan Roundfield	16	1978-79
Armond Hill	15	1977-78
Steve Hawes	13	1980-81
Wayne Rollins	12	1979-80
* Bill Bridges	12	1967-68
* Bill Bridges	12	1966-67

Juluis Erving guards John Drew.

1968-92 ATLANTA HAWKS ALL-TIME ROSTER

NAME	HT	WT	COLLEGE	NAME	HT	WT	COLLEGE
DON ADAMS	6-7	210	Northwestern '70	MOSES MALONE	6-10	255	Petersburg High (VA) '74
STACEY AUGMON	6-8	205	UNLV '91	PACE MANNION	6-7	190	Utah '83
TOM BARKER	6-11	230	Hawaii '76	PETE MARAVICH	6-5	200	LSU '70
JOHN BATTLE	6-2	175	Rutgers '85	ROY MARBLE	6-6	190	Iowa '89
ALFRED "Butch" BEARD	6-3	185	Louisville '69	EDDIE MAST	6-9	220	Temple '69
ZELMO "Big Z" BEATY	6-9	235	Prairie View '62	WES MATTHEWS	6-1	165	Wisconsin '81
RON BEHAGEN	6-9	235	Minnesota '73	DON MAY	6-4	200	Dayton '68
WALT "Big Bells" BELLAMY	6-11	245	Indiana '61	TRAVIS MAYS	6-2	190	Texas '90
STEVE BRACEY	6-1	175	Tulsa '72	JAMES McELROY	6-3	185	Central Michigan '81
DUDLEY BRADLEY	6-6	195	North Carolina '79	MIKE McGEE	6-5	207	Michigan '81
CLYDE BRADSHAW	6-0	170	DePaul '81	TOM McMILLEN	6-11	215	Maryland '74
BILL BRIDGES	6-6	235	Kansas '61	DEAN "The Dream" MEMINGER	6-1	170	Marquette '71
JOHN BROWN	6-7	220	Missouri '73	JOE C. MERIWEATHER	6-10	218	So. Illinois '75
RICKEY BROWN	6-10	235	Mississippi State '80	RODNEY MONROE	6-3	185	North Carolina State '91
TOM BURLESON	7-3	256	North Carolina State '74	DAVID NEWMARK	7-0	240	Columbia '68
JOE "Pogo" CALDWELL	6-5	210	Arizona State '64	DON OHL	6-3	190	Illinois '58
ANTOINE CARR	6-9	235	Wichita State '83	GRADY O'MALLEY	6-5	205	Manhattan '69
JERRY CHAMBERS	6-5	185	Utah '66	BILLY PAULTZ	6-11	225	St. John's '70
LEN CHAPPELL	6-8	240	Fordham '73	TOM PAYNE	6-11	225	Kentucky '73
LORENZO CHARLES	6-7	255	N.C. State '85	SAM PELLOM	6-9	225	Buffalo '78
MAURICE CHEEKS	6-1	180	West Texas State '78	JOHN PINONE	6-8	230	Villanova '83
BOB CHRISTIAN	7-0	265	Grambling '69	BLAIR RASMUSSEN	7-0	260	Oregon '85
ART COLLINS	6-4	200	Biscayne '76	LEO RAUTINS	6-8	215	Syracuse '83
DON COLLINS	6-6	190	Washington State '80	BOB RILEY	6-4	235	Mt. St. Mary's '70
JIM CREIGHTON	6-8	200	Colorado '72	GLENN "Doc" RIVERS	6-4	185	Marquette '84
CHARLIE CRISS	5-8	165	New Mexico State '70	TONY ROBERTSON	6-4	170	West Virginia '76
JIM DAVIS	6-9	224	Colorado '64	LEN "Truck" ROBINSON	6-7	225	Tennessee '74
JOHNNY DAVIS	6-2	180	Dayton '77	RUMEAL ROBINSON	6-2	200	Michigan '90
RON DAVIS	6-2	195	Washington State '76	WAYNE "Tree" ROLLINS	7-1	240	Clemson '77
RANDY DENTON	6-10	245	Duke '71	DAN ROUNDFIELD	6-8	205	Central Michigan '75
HENRY DICKERSON	6-4	190	Morris Harvey '73	WALKER D. RUSSELL	6-4	210	Western Michigan '82
JOHN DREW	6-6	205	Gardner-Webb '76	JEFF SANDERS	6-8	240	Georgia Southern '89
DENNIS DUVAL	6-3	175	Syracuse '74	DALE SHCLUETER	6-10	235	Colorado State '67
JERRY EAVES	6-4	185	Louisville '82	CRAIG SHELTON	6-7	205	Georgetown '80
KEITH EDMONSON	6-5	203	Purdue '82	LARRY SIEGFRIED	6-3	190	Ohio State '61
DUANE FERRELL	6-7	215	Georgia Tech '88	PAUL SILAS	6-7	235	Creighton '64
TERRY FURLOW	6-4	190	Michigan State '76	KENNY SMITH	6-3	235	North Carolina '87
HERM GILLIAM	6-3	190	Purdue '69	RANDY SMITH	6-3	180	Buffalo State '71
JACK GIVENS	6-5	205	Kentucky '78	MIKE SOJOURNER	6-8	225	Utah '76
MIKE GLENN	6-3	185	So. Illinois '77	RORY SPARROW	6-2	190	Villanova '80
PAUL GRAHAM	6-6	200	Ohio '89	CLAUDE TERRY	6-5	195	Stanford '72
STEWART GRANGER	6-3	195	Villanova '83	REGGIE THEUS	6-7	213	UNLV '79
GARY GREGOR	6-7	235	South Carolina '68	RAY TOLBERT	6-9	240	Indiana '81
RICHIE GUERIN	6-4	210	Iona '54	SEDRIC TONEY	6-2	180	Dayton '85
SHALER HALIMON	6-6	220	Utah '68	GENE "Bumper" TORMOHLEN	6-9	245	Tennessee '59
JEFF HALIBURTON	6-5	190	Drake '71	GEORGE TRAPP	6-8	215	Long Beach State '71
DENNIS HAMILTON	6-8	210	Arizona State '66	JOHN TSCHOGL	6-6	206	UCSB '72
SKIP HARLICKA	6-1	185	South Carolina '68	TOM VAN ARSDALE	6-5	200	Indiana '65
SCOTT HASTINGS	6-10	235	Arkansas '82	JOHN VALLEY	6-3	185	UCLA '70
STEVE HAWES	6-9	220	Washington '72	ALEXANDER VOLKOV	6-10	235	Kiev Institute '89
CONNIE "The Hawk" HAWKINS	6-8	210	Iowa '60	DWIGHT WALLER	6-7	230	Tennessee State '68
WALT HAZZARD	6-3	185	UCLA '64	CHRIS WASHBURN	6-11	255	North Carolina State '86
CEDRIC HENDERSON	6-9	215	Georgia '88	JIM WASHINGTON	6-7	215	Villanova '65
TOM HENERSON	6-3	190	Hawaii '74	ANTHONY "Spud" WEBB	5-7	133	North Carolina State '85
KEITH HERRON	6-6	190	Villanova '78	JOHN WETZEL	6-5	192	Virginia Tech '67
ARMOND HILL	6-4	190	Princeton '76	ENNIS WHATLEY	6-3	177	Alabama '85
WILBUR HOLLAND	6-0	175	New Orleans '75	HERB WHITE	6-2	195	Georgia '70
LOU "Super Lou" HUDSON	6-5	205	Minnesota '66	MORLON WILEY	6-4	192	Long Beach State '88
TOM INGLESBY	6-3	185	Villanova '73	DOMINIQUE WILKINS	6-8	215	Georgia '83
EDDIE JOHNSON	6-2	190	Auburn '77	FREEMAN WILLIAMS	6-4	195	Portland State '78
GEORGE JOHNSON	6-11	220	Dillard '70	GUS WILLIAMS	6-3	180	USC '75
OLLIE JOHNSON	6-6	200	Temple '72	MIKE WILLIAMS	6-8	255	Cincinnati '83
DWIGHT JONES	6-10	230	Houston '73	MILT WILLIAMS	6-2	185	Lincoln '68
BOB KAUFFMAN	6-8	240	Guilford '68	RAY WILLIAMS	6-3	195	Minnesota '77
JON KONCAK	7-0	250	SMU '85	SLY WILLIAMS	6-7	215	Rhode Island '80
MARK LANDSBERGER	6-8	230	Arizona State '78	KEVIN WILLIS	7-0	240	Michigan State '84
ALFRED "Butch" LEE	6-0	185	Marquette '78	BILL "Poodles" WILLOUGHBY	6-8	210	Dwight Morrow HS (NJ) '75
CLYDE LEE	6-10	230	Vanderbilt '66	MIKE WILSON	6-4	180	Marquette '82
RON LEE	6-4	193	Oregon '76	RICK WILSON	6-5	200	Louisville '78
GEORGE LEHMANN	6-3	190	Campbell '61	TREVOR WILSON	6-8	211	UCLA '90
CLIFF LEVINGSTON	6-8	220	Wichita State '82	RANDY WITTMAN	6-6	210	Indiana '83
JOHN LONG	6-5	195	Detroit '78	AL WOOD	6-6	195	North Carolina '81
SIDNEY LOWE	6-0	195	North Carolina State '83	LEON WOOD	6-2	200	Cal State Fullerton '84
DURAND "Rudy" MACKLIN	6-7	205	LSU '81	HAYWOODE WORKMAN	6-2	180	Oral Roberts '89
				HOWARD WRIGHT	6-8	245	Stanford '89

ATLANTA HAWKS ALL-TIME FRONT OFFICE STAFF

OWNERS
Thomas G. Cousins (1968-77)
Carl E. Sanders (1968-72)
Bill Putnam (1972-77)
R.E. "Ted" Turner (1977-present)

CHAIRMAN OF BOARD
Thomas G. Cousins (1970-72)
Dillard Munford (1972-74)
Michael Gearon (1986-present)

BOARD OF DIRECTORS
Robert Pettit (1971-72)
Herb Dickson (1971-72)
Jack Ashmore, Jr. (1971-72)
Robert W. Cousins (1971-78)
Lew Woodruff (1971-72)
Thomas G. Cousins (1971-72)
Robert Hunter (1971-72)
Paul A. Duke (1972-74)
William K. Hohlstein (1972-75)
Robert Ledbetter (1972-74)
Charles Loudermilk (1972-74)
Herman J. Russell (1972-78)
John W. Wilcox, Jr. (1972-77)
M.B. "Bud" Seretean (1975-present)
Michael Gearon (1977-present)
R.E. "Ted" Turner (1977-present)
Bruce B. Wilson (1978-present)
Lewis Schaffel (1979-80)
Stan Kasten (1980-present)
Michael Fratello (1986-90)
Robert Wussler (1988-90)
Terence F. McGuirk (1991-present)

PRESIDENT
Thomas G. Cousins (1968-69)
James A. Calkin (1969-70)
Robert W. Cousins (1970-72)
William R. Putnam (1972-73)
John W. Wilcox, Jr. (1973-75)
M.B. "Bud" Seretean (1975-77)
Michael Gearon (1977-86)
Stan Kasten (1987-present)

PRESIDENT/GENERAL MANAGER
Stan Kasten (1987-90)

VICE PRESIDENT/GENERAL MANAGER
Stan Kasten (1980-87)
Pete Babcock (1990-present)

GENERAL MANAGER
Marty Blake (1968-70)
Richie Guerin (1972-73)
Pat Williams (1973-74)
M.B. "Bud" Seretean (1975-77)
Mike Storen (1977)
Michael Gearon (1977-79)

EXECUTIVE VICE PRESIDENT
Lewis Woodruff (1968-70)
Lee Douglas (1990-present)

EXECUTIVE VICE PRESIDENT/ GENERAL MANAGER
Lewis Schaffel (1979-80)

VICE PRESIDENT
Carl Sanders (1968-70)

VICE PRESIDENT/MARKETING
Bob Hope (1978-79)
Lee Douglas (1985-87)

VICE PRESIDENT/BUSINESS MANAGER
Steven Funk (1980-82)
Bob Wolfe (1988-92)

VICE PRESIDENT/ASST. GENERAL MANAGER
Stan Kasten (1978-80)
Steven Funk (1982-84)
Lee Douglas (1988-90)

VICE PRESIDENT/ASST. GM/MARKETING
Lee Douglas (1987-88)

VICE PRESIDENT/FINANCE
Stan Humphries (1975-78)
Steven Funk (1985-present)

ASSISTANT GENERAL MANAGER
Bob Kauffman (1975-77)
Stan Kasten (1979-80)

ASST. GM/DIRECTOR OF SCOUTING
Brendan Suhr (1988-89)

TEAM SECRETARY
Jack P. Ashmore (1968-72)

ASSISTANT SECRETARY
Robert P. Hunter (1970-72)

TEAM DIRECTOR
Herbert J. Dixon (1968-69)

CONSULTANT
Robert H. Kent (1970-71)
Rich Buckelew (1981-present)

HEAD COACH
Richie Guerin (1968-72)
Cotton Fitzsimmons (1972-76)
Hubie Brown (1976-81)
Kevin Loughery (1981-83)
Mike Fratello (1983-90)
Bob Weiss (1990-present)

ASSISTANT COACH/DIRECTOR OF SCOUTING
Gene Tormohlen (1968-76)
Frank Layden (1976-79)
Ed Badger (1990-92)

ASSISTANT COACH
Michael Fratello (1978-82, 1983-84)
Brendan Suhr (1979-88)
Fred Carter (1981-83)
Bob Reinhart (1983-84)
Ron Rothstein (1983-86)
Willis Reed (1985-87)
Brian Hill (1986-90)
Don Chaney (1987-88)
Cazzie Russell (1988-90)
Kevin Loughery (1990-91)
Johnny Davis (1990-present)
Bob Weinhauer (1991-present)

TRAINER
Skip Franz (1968-69)
Joe O'Toole (1969-present)

EQUIPMENT MANAGER
Louis Funkenstein (1968-70)

STRENGTH/CONDITIONING COACH
Roger Hinds (1992-present)

SCOUTS
Rich Buckelew (1978-81)
Richie Adubato (1980-81)
Ron Rothstein (1980-81)
Richard Kaner (1986-present)
Rex Hughes (1989-90)
Jack Nolan (1989-present)

BUSINESS MANAGER
Irv Gack (1968-73)
Joel Bobo (1983-85)
Bob Wolfe (1985-88)

CONTROLLER
Alvan Herring (1972-75)
Chuck Duncan (1975-78)
Steven Funk (1978-80)
Greg Clements (1981-83)

TREASURER
Thomas G. Cousins (1969-70)

DIRECTOR OF MARKETING/ BROADCASTING
Leo Ornest (1972-75)

DIRECTOR OF BROADCASTING
Skip Caray (1968-73)
Wayne Long (1977-87)

DIRECTOR OF COMMUNICATIONS
John P. Culver (1969-70)

DIRECTOR OF PUBLIC RELATIONS
Tom McCollister (1969-74)
Jim Schultz (1974-77)
John Marshall (1977-78)
Chet Wright (1978-81)
Bill Needle (1981-89)
Arthur Triche (1989-present)

DIRECTOR OF PUBLICATIONS
Wayne Minshew (1978-79)

DIRECTOR OF MARKETING
Bob Longmire (1979-80)
Lee Douglas (1981-85)

DIRECTOR OF SALES
Pres Judy (1968-69)
James Pepper (1968-70)
Alex Gaines (1971-72)
Gabe Meadows (1972-73)
Dick Dorfman (1973-74)
Lee Douglas (1979-80)
Frank Timmerman (1979-88)
Cheryl Dukes (1988-present)

DIRECTOR OF CORPORATE SALES/PUBLIC RELATIONS
Lee Walburn (1974-75)

DIRECTOR OF CORPORATE SALES AND PROMOTIONS
Lee Stepancik (1975-81)
Frank Timmerman (1988-present)

DIRECTOR OF CORPORATE RELATIONS
William Paullin (1980-81)

DIRECTOR OF COMMUNITY RELATIONS
Johnny Davis (1987-90)
Mel Pender (1990-present)

ADVERTISING SALES AND PROMOTION
Susan Hock (1969-71)

TICKET DIRECTOR
Virgil Martin (1969-73)
Bob Farrell (1974-75)

DIRECTOR OF TICKET OPERATIONS
Lee Douglas (1980-81)

TEAM CHAPLAIN
Rev. David W. Smith (1971-72)
Bill Alexson (1981)
Marty Kennedy (1981-present)

VOICE OF THE HAWKS
Skip Caray (WSB-AM, 1968-69), (WSB-TV, 1968-70), (WGST-AM, 1977-78) (WTCG TV, 1978-79), (WTBS-TV, 1979-80)
Skip Caray and Larry Munson (WSB-AM, 1969-70)
Skip Caray and Phil Schaefer (WSB-AM, 1970-75)
Pete Van Wieren and Skip Caray (WQXI-TV, 1977-78
Skip Caray and Pete Van Wieren (WSB AM, 1978-79)
Skip Caray and Chet Wright (WSB-AM, 1979-81)
Skip Caray and John Washington (WTBS-TV, 1980-81)
Skip Caray and John Sterling (WSB-AM, 1981-83), (WTBS-TV, 1982-83)
Skip Caray and Fred Hickman (WTBS-TV, 1981-82)
John Sterling, Lou Hudson, Pete Van Wieren and Dennis Dumler (WCNN-AM, 1983-84)
John Sterling and Lou Hudson (TBS Sports, 1983-84)
John Sterling (WCNN-AM, 1984-85)
John Sterling and Charlie Criss (WVEU-TV, 1984-86)
John Sterling (WSB-AM, 1985-86)
John Sterling and Steve Holman (TBS Sports, 1986-89)
John Sterling and Charlie Criss (WGNX-TV, 1986-87)
John Sterling (WGNX-TV, 1987-89)
Steve Holman (WGST-AM, 1989-present)
Skip Caray and Rick Barry (TBS Sports, 1989-91)
John Sterling and Mike Glenn (SportSouth/ WGNX-TV, 1990-91)
Skip Caray and Dick Versace (TBS Sports, 1991-92)
Art Eckman and Mike Glenn (SportSouth/ WGNX-TV, 1991-92)

TEAM PHYSICIANS
Dr. Joseph Dimon (1968-74)
Dr. William Stone (1968-69)
Dr. Charles Harrison (1969-76)
Dr. David Apple (1974-present)
Dr. Louis Freedman (1978-present)
Dr. Milton Frank (1985-present)
Dr. Robert Marmer (1990-present)

ADMINISTRATIVE STAFF
Mike Bentley (1971-72)
Connie Smith (1974-76)
Jean Johnson (1975-77)
Diane Bercegeay (1976-79)
Mary Godleski (1977-78)
Frank Timmerman (1977-79)
Chet Wright (1977-78)
Chuck Herendeen (1977-78, 1985-89)
Mark Gettleson (1977-78)
Lee Douglas (1978-79)
Bill Lellyett (1978-79)
Phil Caudill (1978-80)
Jerome Haley (1978-79)
Jim Pate (1978-79)
Harold Cohn (1978-80)
Nancy Hansen (1978-79)
Andre DeLorenzo (1978-79)
Robert DeLong (1978-79)
Patti Hardiman (1978-83)
Candy Alger (1978-79)
Bethe Howison (1979-80)
Mary Darnall (1979-81)
Hilli Fick (1979-80)
Earl Cambron (1979-81)
Mark Cella (1979-80)
Tammy Pearson (1979-80)
Katharine Herring (1980-88)
Gerald Alford (1980-82)
Lu Ann Cline (1980-84)
Annie Rushin (1980-82)
Debi Irving (1980-81)
Stephen Dell (1980-81)
Ed Ganem (1980-81)
Jay Goizueta (1980-81)
Greg Wait (1980-81)
Randy Smith (1981-84)
Ann Leatherwood (1981-82)
Denise Dickson (1981-82)
Penny Wright-Barber (1981-83)
Rex Hussman (1981-82)
Ron Johnson (1981-82)
Denny Harmon (1981-82)
Don Jones (1981-82)
Dennis Pugh (1981-82)
Amy McClure (1982-83)
Kerry Adcock (1982-83)
George McLain (1982-84)
Mark Sellers (1982-83)
Jeff Unger (1982-84)
Chris Smith (1982-83)
Charley Smith (1982-present)
Beth Futral (1983-86)
Wendy Stauffer (1983-84)
Tracy Ziebarth (1983-84)
Debbie Maxwell (1983-85)
Frank Parks (1983-91)
Danielle Brown (1984-86)
Scott Wiggins (1984-87)
Jane Goldsmith (1984-85)
Hugh Lombardi (1984-87)
Mike Hundley (1984-86)
Gregg Suhr (1984-85)
Derryl Zimmerman (1984-87)

Pete Coratti (1985-86)
Frank Schwarzer (1985-89)
Karen Latimer (1985-86)
Becky Kram (1986-87)
Donna Ivester-Feazell (1985-present)
Teresa Hurd (1986-87)
Patti Anderson (1986-89)
David Bevans (1986-87)
David Couch (1986-87)
Randy Duffin (1986-87)
Cheryl Dukes (1986-88)
Dale Hendricks (1986-present)
Teresa Jones (1986-87)
Judy Stevens (1986-88)
Ron Williamson (1986-89)
Hollye Hodges (1987-90)
Scott Scoggins (1987-88)
Matt Williams (1987-88)
Susan McKown (1987-89)
R.J. Bonds (1987-88)
Scott Bowers (1987-present)
Tom Brown (1987-88)
Herb Gilchrist (1987-88)
Hugh Hudson (1987-89)
Harriette Jackson (1987-89)
Ramona Lewis (1987-89)
Greg Minton (1987-88)
Carolyn Vason (1987-88)
Anil Vaswani (1987-90)
Tracy White (1987-present)
Margie Smith-Sikes (1988-present)
Whitney Grant (1988-present)
Tom Ordover (1988-89)
Dan Taylor (1988-present)
Warnette Zanders (1989-present)
Tyler Barnes (1989-90)
Kris Villilo (1989-91)
Joe Corbino (1989-90)
Sherman Wheeler (1989-92)
Kay Smith (1990-91)
Darrin May (1990-present)
Lawrence Bacon (1990-91)
Carla Boyd (1990-91)
Kim Coleman (1990-present)
Sally Green (1990-91)
Jim Loucks (1990-91)
Kenneth Kokinda (1990-91)
Todd Thomas (1990-91)
Lynda Breeden (1990-91)
Nell Merkle (1990-91)
Tracey Griffin-Hammaren (1990-present)
Amanda Wimbush (1990-present)
John Carey (1991-present)
Barrie Cohn (1991-present)
Michael Epps (1991-present)
Don Hensley (1991-present)
K.C. Link (1991-92)
Stephanie McNeal (1991-92)
Deborah Rubin (1991-92)
Lisa Schroeder (1991-92)
Travis Smith (1991-92)
Chuck Washington (1991-present)
Hannah-Catherine Allport (1991-present)
Mike Adams (1991-present)
Jeff Crawford (1991-present)
Louis Artiaga (1992-present)
Bryan Bartley (1992-present)
Sharon Bradley (1992-present)
Belinda Johnson (1992-present)
David Lawrence (1992-present)
Teyon McCoy (1992-present)
Katherine Ingram (1992-present)

TEAM MASCOT
Rob Cleveland
Harry Nixon (1985-86)
Wayne Pee (1986-90)
Wayne Jordan (1990-present)

HOME COURT
Alexander Memorial Coliseum (1968-72)
The Omni (1972-present)

TEAM COLORS
Columbia Blue, White and Red (1968-70)
Royal Blue, White and Lime Green (1971-72)
Red and White (1972-78)
Red, White and Gold (1978-present)

Spud Webb and Reggie Theus.

DATES OF IMPORTANCE COVERING THE HAWKS 25 YEARS IN ATLANTA

May 3, 1968	It is announced that the St. Louis Hawks would move South to the city of Atlanta for the 1968-69 season, under the guidance of new owners Tom Cousins and former Georgia Governor Carl Sanders.
October 15, 1968	Hawks drop regular season opener 125-110 to Cincinnati at Georgia Tech's Alexander Memorial Coliseum.
October 19, 1968	Atlanta beats Milwaukee for the franchise's first win, 125-107.
1968-69 Season	In their first Atlanta season under Richie Guerin, the Hawks finish 48-34 ... After beating San Diego 4-2 in the Western Division semi-finals, Atlanta loses 4-1 in the Western Division finals to the L.A. Lakers ... Zelmo Beaty, Lenny Wilkens and Bill Bridges become the first Hawks players to appear in the All-Star Game.
1969-70 Season	Hawks win first Division (Western Division) title, conclude season with a 48-34 record ... The Lakers beat Atlanta for the second straight year in the Western Division finals, 4-0 ... Lou Hudson and Joe Caldwell are selected to appear in the All-Star Game.
1970-71 Season	Hawks make the playoffs again after finishing 36-46, but New York halts their postseason run in the Eastern Conference semi finals, 4-1 ... Pete Maravich named NBA All-Rookie ... Bill Bridges, Lou Hudson and Joe Caldwell are selected to appear in the All Star Game.
1971-72 Season	In Richie Guerin's final season as head coach, Atlanta concludes the season at 36-46, and is eliminated in the playoffs (Eastern Conference semi-finals) by the Boston Celtics, 4-2 ... Lou Hudson makes his third straight All-Star Game appearance.
October 15, 1972	Hawks play first regular season game at The Omni.
1972-73 Season	Making their fifth straight playoff appearance - and first under rookie coach Cotton Fitzsimmons (46-36 record) - Atlanta i stopped for the second year in a row by the Celtics, 4-2 ... Lou Hudson and Pete Maravich represent the Hawks in the All-Star Game ... Maravich and Hudson each score 2,000 or more points during the regular season - a feat matched only in NBA history by the Lakers' Jerry West and Elgin Baylor.
1973-74 Season	Atlanta's record falls to 35-47, as the Hawks miss the playoffs for the first time in franchise history ... First-year players John Drew and John Brown make the NBA All-Rookie Team ... Lou Hudson and Pete Maravich again earn All-Star Game selections.
May 4, 1974	Pete Maravich traded to New Orleans (Jazz) in exchange for Dean Meminger, Bob Kauffman and future draft choices.
1974-75 Season	Atlanta struggles to their worst record since moving from St. Louis, 31-51.
1975-76 Season	Cotton Fitzsimmons is released after posting a 30-44 record, and Gene Tormohlen is named interim coach as the Hawks end the regular season at 31-51 ... John Drew plays in the 1976 All-Star Game.
July 17, 1976	Hubie Brown named head coach.
1976-77 Season	Ted Turner purchases the team (January 3, 1977) ... Hawks finish in sixth place with a 31-51 record.
Sept. 30, 1977	Lou Hudson traded to L.A. Lakers for Ollie Johnson.
1977-78 Season	Hubie Brown named NBA Coach of the Year after leading Atlanta to a 41-41 record and their first playoff berth in five years.
1978-79 Season	The rebuilding process continues under Hubie Brown, as Atlanta goes 46-36 ... Washington beats the Hawks in the Western Conference semi-finals, 4-3.
1979-80 Season	Hawks win second Division (Central Division) title, conclude season with a 50-31 record ... Philadelphia cruises to a 4-1 series win in the Eastern Conference semi-finals ... John Drew, Eddie Johnson and Dan Roundfield are Atlanta's representa tives in the All-Star Game ... Roundfield becomes the first Hawk to earn First Team All-Defensive Team mention.
1980-81 Season	Atlanta falls 20 games under the .500 mark (31-51) and out of the playoffs for the first time in five years ... Dan Roundfield and Eddie Johnson make the All-Star Game team for the second straight year.
May 21, 1981	Hawks name Kevin Loughery head coach.
1981-82 Season	After posting a 42-40 record, Atlanta returns to the playoffs, but is eliminated in the first round by Philadelphia, 2-0 ... Dan Roundfield makes his third consecutive All-Star Game appearance.
Sept. 3, 1982	Hawks acquire Dominique Wilkins from Utah in exchange for John Drew, Freeman Williams and cash.
1982-83 Season	Boston wins the three-game first round playoff series from Atlanta ... Dan Roundfield earns his second First Team All Defensive honor ... Dominique Wilkins makes the All-Rookie team ... Kevin Loughery, 43-39 in his second year, departs the Hawks coaching position to take a similar job with Chicago.

June 9, 1983	Michael Fratello named head coach.
July 6, 1983	Hawks acquire rights to Randy Wittman from Bullets in exchange for Tom McMillen.
1983-84 Season	Atlanta makes it to the playoffs for the third straight year after posting a 40-42 record ... Wayne "Tree" Rollins becomes the second Atlanta player to garner First Team All-Defensive honors ... The Hawks are beaten in the first round of the playoffs by Milwaukee, 3-2.
June 18, 1984	Hawks acquire Cliff Levingston, the rights to Antoine Carr and second-round draft picks in 1986 and 1987 from Detroit in exchange for Dan Roundfield.
July 19, 1984	Hawks announce plans to play 12 games in New Orleans during the 1984-85 season.
1984-85 Season	Atlanta finishes the season with a 34-48 record, and misses the playoffs for the first time in four years.
Sept. 27, 1985	Hawks sign free agent guard Anthony "Spud" Webb.
1985-86 Season	Michael Fratello named NBA Coach of the Year after directing the Hawks to a 50-32 mark ... Dominique Wilkins becomes the first Atlanta player to earn First Team All-NBA honors and lead the league in scoring (30.3) ... Wilkins scores a career-high and ies a franchise record with 57 points against New Jersey ... Spud Webb defeats defending champion Wilkins in the 1986 Slam Dunk contest during All-Star Weekend festivities in Dallas ... Atlanta ties franchise marks for most wins in a season (50) and best home record (34-7).
June 4, 1986	Stan Kasten named Executive of the Year and Michael Fratello named Coach of the Year, both by the Sporting News.
1986-87 Season	Hawks win third Division (Central Division) title, conclude season with a franchise-best 57 wins, and the NBA's third-best record (57-25) ... Dominique Wilkins is voted to the Eastern Conference's All-Star Game starting unit for the first time in his career ... Wilkins equals his career high 52 points against Chicago ... Glenn Rivers establishes a new Atlanta team record with 823 assists ... Mike McGee sets an all-time record for three-point FGs (86) and attempts (229).
June 4, 1987	Stan Kasten named NBA Executive of the Year by the Sporting News.
1987-88 Season	Dominique Wilkins and Glenn Rivers earn spots on the Eastern Conference All-Star Game roster, and Michael Fratello and his coaching staff become the first Atlanta staff to represent the Hawks at an All-Star Game ... In an exciting seven-game playoff series, Boston halts Atlanta dreams of reaching the Eastern Conference final as the Celtics defeat the Hawks in the series, 4-3.
June 27, 1988	Hawks acquire guard Reggie Theus from Sacramento for Randy Wittman.
August 16, 1988	Hawks sign unrestricted free agent center Moses Malone.
1988-89 Season	For the fifth straight season, Atlanta establishes a new team attendance record (644,291) at The Omni ... Hawks conclude fourth straight 50-win season - which at the time was the longest streak in the Eastern Conference - but the season ends in disappointing fashion as Milwaukee upsets Atlanta in the first round of the NBA Playoffs.
1989-90 Season	Injuries plague the Hawks throughout the season, and as a result, Atlanta misses the playoffs for the first time in six seasons ... With a 41-41 record, the team drops to sixth place in the Central Division.
April 23, 1990	Michael Fratello resigns as Hawks head coach.
May 22, 1990	Bob Weiss becomes Atlanta's sixth head coach.
January 2, 1991	Bob Weiss named Digital/NBA Coach of the Month for December.
March 3, 1991	Dominique Wilkins named Edge/NBA Player of the Month for February.
1990-91 Season	On the strength of a 22-game home winning streak, Atlanta returns to the playoffs with a 43-39 record ... Detroit edges the Hawks in the first round, 3-2.
June 26, 1991	Hawks trade Glenn Rivers to L.A. Clippers for rights to the ninth pick in the 1991 NBA Draft. Atlanta selects UNLV's Stacey Augmon.
July 1, 1991	Hawks obtain Blair Rasmussen from Denver for the draft rights to Anthony Avent (15th overall pick), and Travis Mays from Sacramento for Anthony "Spud" Webb.
1991-92 Season	It comes down to the final day of the regular season, and Atlanta misses a playoff berth by losing to Cleveland, concluding the year at 38-44 ... Dominique Wilkins and Kevin Willis earn All-Star Game honors, but Wilkins' misses his seventh appearance when he suffers an achilles tendon injury in January against Philadelphia ... Willis is selected to replace Wilkins on the Eastern Conference squad ... Stacey Augmon makes First Team All-Rookie.

HAWKS STARTING LINE-UPS ON OPENING NIGHT

1992-92
Dominique Wilkins	F
Kevin Willis	F
Blair Rasmussen	C
Stacey Augmon	G
Rumeal Robinson	G

1990-91
Dominique Wilkins	F
Kevin Willis	F
Moses Malone	C
Glen Rivers	G
Rumeal Robinson	G

1989-90
Jon Koncak	F
Dominique Wilkins	F
Moses Malone	C
John Battle	G
Glenn Rivers	G

1988-89
Antoine Carr	F
Dominique Wilkins	F
Moses Malone	C
Glenn Rivers	G
Reggie Theus	G

1987-88
Dominique Wilkins	F
Kevin Willis	F
Tree Rollins	C
Glenn Rivers	G
Randy Wittman	G

1986-87
Dominique Wilkins	F
Kevin Willis	F
Tree Rollins	C
Gelnn Rivers	G
Randy Wittman	G

1985-86
Cliff Levingston	F
Kevin Willis	F
Tree Rollins	C
Spud Webb	G
Dominique Wilkins	G

1984-85
Dominique Wilkins	F
Sly Williams	F
Tree Rollins	C
Eddie Johnson	G
Glenn Rivers	G

1983-84
Dan Roundfield	F
Dominique Wilkins	F
Billy Paultz	C
Eddie Johnson	G
Armond Hill	G

1982-83
Dan Roundfield	F
Dominique Wilkins	F
Tree Rollins	C
Eddie Johnson	G
Rory Sparrow	G

1981-82
Rudy Macklin	F
Dan Roundfield	F
Tree Rollins	C
James McElroy	G
Rory Sparrow	G

1980-81
John Drew	F
Dan Roundfield	F
Steve Hawes	C
Armond Hill	G
Eddie Johnson	G

1979-80
John Drew	F
Dan Roundfield	F
Steve Hawes	C
Armond Hill	G
Eddie Johnson	G

1978-79
John Drew	F
Dan Roundfield	F
Steve Hawes	C
Alfred Butch	G
Armond Hill	G

1977-78
John Brown	F
John Drew	F
Steve Hawes	C
Ken Charles	G
Armond Hill	G

1976-77
John Drew	F
Joe C. Meriweather	F
Steve Hawes	C
Tom Henderson	G
Lou Hudson	G

1975-76
Connie Hawkins	F
Lou Hudson	F
Dwight Jones	C
Tom Henderson	G
Tom VanArsdale	G

1974-75
John Brown	F
John Drew	F
Dwight Jones	C
Tom Henderson	G
Dean Meminger	G

1973-74
Lou Hudson	F
Jim Washington	F
Walt Bellamy	C
Herm Gilliam	G
Pete Maravich	G

1972-73
Lou Hudson	F
Jim Washington	F
Walt Bellamy	C
Herm Gilliam	G
Pete Maravich	G

1971-72
Bill Bridges	F
Lou Hudson	F
Walt Bellamy	C
Herm Gilliam	G
Pete Maravich	G

1970-71
Bill Bridges	F
Lou Hudson	F
Walt Bellamy	C
Walt Hazzard	G
Pete Maravich	G

1969-70
Bill Bridges	F
Jimmy Davis	F
Joe Caldwell	C
Walt Hazzard	G
Lou Hudson	G

1968-69
Bill Bridges	F
Joe Caldwell	F
Zelmo Beaty	C
Walt Hazzard	G
Lou Hudson	G

HAWKS THROUGH THE YEARS

Year	Coach	Season W	L	Finish	Playoffs W	L
TRI-CITIES BLACKHAWKS						
1949-50	Roger Potter (1-6)					
	Arnold "Red" Auerbach (28-29)	29	35	3rd	1	2
1950-51	Dave McMillan (9-14)					
	John Logan (2-1)					
	Marke Todorovich (14-28)	25	43	5th	—	—
MILWAUKEE HAWKS						
1951-52	Doxie Moore	17	49	5th	—	—
1952-53	Andrew Lavane	27	44	5th	—	—
1953-54	Andrew Lavane (22-35)					
	William "Red" Holzman (10-16)	21	51	4th	—	—
1954-55	William "Red" Holzman	26	26	4th	—	—
ST. LOUIS HAWKS						
1955-56	William "Red" Holzman	33	39	3rd	4	4
1956-57	William "Red" Holzman (14-19)					
	Slater Martin (5-3)					
	Alex Hannum (15-16)	34	38	1st	8	4
1957-58	Alex Hannum	41	31	1st	8	3
1958-59	Andy Phillip (6-4)					
	Ed Macauley (43-19)	49	23	1st	2	4
1959-60	Ed Macauley	46	29	1st	7	7
1960-61	Paul Seymour	51	28	1st	5	7
1961-62	Paul Seymour (5-9)					
	Andrew Lavane (20-40)					
	Bob Pettit (4-2)	29	51	4th	—	—
1962-63	Harry Gallatin	48	32	2nd	7	5
1963-64	Harry Gallatin	48	34	2nd	7	5
1964-65	Harry Gallatin (17-16)					
	Richie Guerin (28-19)	45	35	2nd	1	3
1965-66	Richie Guerin	36	44	3rd	6	4
1966-67	Richie Guerin	39	42	2nd	5	4
1967-68	Richie Guerin	56	26	1st	2	4
ATLANTA HAWKS						
1968-69	Richie Guerin	48	34	2nd	5	6
1969-70	Richie Guerin	48	34	1st	4	5
1970-71	Richie Guerin	36	46	2nd	1	4
1971-72	Richie Guerin	36	46	2nd	2	4
1972-73	Cotton Fitzsimmons	46	36	2nd	2	4
1973-74	Cotton Fitzsimmons	35	47	2nd	—	—
1974-75	Cotton Fitzsimmons	31	51	4th	—	—
1975-76	Cotton Fitzsimmons					
	Gene Tormohlen (1-7)	29	53	5th	—	—
1976-77	Hubie Brown	31	51	6th	—	—
1977-78	Hubie Brown	41	41	4th	0	2
1978-79	Hubie Brown	46	36	3rd	5	4
1979-80	Hubie Brown	50	31	1st	1	4
1980-81	Hubie Brown (31-48)	31	51	4th	—	—
	Michael Fratello/Brendan Suhr (0-3)					
1981-82	Kevin Loughery	42	40	2nd	0	2
1982-83	Kevin Loughery	43	39	2nd	1	2
1983-84	Michael Fratello	40	42	3rd	2	3
1984-85	Michael Fratello	34	48	5th	—	—
1985-86	Michael Fratello	50	32	2nd	4	5
1986-87	Michael Fratello	57	25	1st	4	5
1987-88	Michael Fratello	50	32	3rd	6	6
1988-89	Michael Fratello	52	30	3rd	2	3
1989-90	Michael Fratello	41	41	6th	—	—
1990-91	Bob Weiss	43	39	4th	2	3
1991-92	Bob Weiss	38	44	5th	—	—

HAWKS COACHING RECORDS

Name	REGULAR SEASON W	L	Pct.	PLAYOFFS W	L	Pct.
Richie Guerin	327	291	.529	26	34	.433
Michael Fratello	324	250	.564	18	22	.450
Hubie Brown	199	208	.489	6	10	.375
Cotton Fitzsimmons	140	180	.438	2	4	.333
Harry Gallatin	111	82	.575	13	10	.565
Ed Macauley	89	48	.650	9	11	.450
Kevin Loughery	85	79	.518	1	4	.200
William "Red" Holzman	83	120	.409	4	4	.500
Andrew Lavane	58	119	.328	—	—	—
Paul Seymour	56	37	.602	5	7	.417
Alex Hannum	56	47	.544	16	7	.696
Bob Weiss	81	83	.495	2	3	.400
Arnold "Red" Auerbach	28	29	.491	1	2	.333
Doxie Moore	17	49	.258			
Marke Todorovich	14	28	.333			
Dave McMillan	9	14	.391			
Andy Phillip	6	4	.600			
Slater Martin	5	3	.625			
Bob Pettit	4	2	.667			
John Logan	2	1	.667			
Roger Potter	1	6	.143			
Gene Tormohlen	1	7	.125			

ATLANTA YEARLY RESULTS

1968-69 GAME-BY-GAME

Date	Opponent	W-L	Score Hawks	Opp.	Record	Date	Opponent	W-L	Score Hawks	Opp.	Record
Oct. 15	CINCINNATI	L	110	125	0-1	Jan. 10	DETROIT	W	104	101	26-17
Oct. 19	MILWAUKEE	W	125	107	1-1	Jan. 11	LOS ANGELES	W	104	100	27-17
Oct. 23	CHICAGO	W	106	91	2-1	Jan. 16	Phoenix at S.C.	W	112	107	28-17
Oct. 25	at Seattle	L	112	123	2-2	Jan. 17	PHOENIX	W	112	107	29-17
Oct. 27	at Phoenix	W	123	100	3-2	Jan. 19	NEW YORK	W	100	96	30-17
Oct. 29	at Los Angeles	L	124	125	3-3	Jan. 21	at San Diego	L	113	124	30-18
Oct. 30	at San Diego	L	116	127	3-4	Jan. 22	at Phoenix	W	125	107	31-18
Nov. 1	SAN FRANCISCO	W	109	105	4-4	Jan. 24	LOS ANGELES	W	110	106	32-18
Nov. 3	BOSTON	L	103	123	4-5	Jan. 25	at Baltimore	W	112	109	33-18
Nov. 6	at Baltimore	L	119	140	4-6	Jan. 26	PHILADELPHIA	L	115	119	33-19
Nov. 8	SAN DIEGO	W	114	101	5-6	Jan. 28	at Boston	L	96	108	33-20
Nov. 9	SAN FRANCISCO	W	113	106	6-6	Jan. 29	at Philadelphia	L	96	119	33-21
Nov. 12	SAN FRANCISCO	L	108	123	6-7	Jan. 31	SEATTLE	L	112	119	33-22
Nov. 13	SEATTLE	W	142	113	7-7	Feb. 1	DETROIT	W	119	99	34-22
Nov. 15	PHILADELPHIA	L	115	116	7-8	Feb. 2	SAN DIEGO	W	115	103	35-22
Nov. 16	at Cincinnati	L	125	130	7-9	Feb. 4	at New York	L	97	122	35-23
Nov. 19	at Milwaukee	L	98	119	7-10	Feb. 7	at Boston	W	109	107	36-23
Nov. 20	NEW YORK	W	111	106	8-10	Feb. 8	CHICAGO	W	106	97	37-23
Nov. 21	at Detroit	W	129	121	9-10	Feb. 9	BALTIMORE	L	101	102	37-24
Nov. 23	at Chicago	W	114	96	10-10	Feb. 11	SAN FRANCISCO	L	87	92	37-25
Nov. 24	BALTIMORE	L	111	118	10-11	Feb. 12	at Milwaukee	W	113	106	38-25
Nov. 26	at Baltimore	L	99	102	10-12	Feb. 14	BOSTON (#)	W	104	101	39-25
Nov. 27	CINCINNATI	W	94	91	11-12	Feb. 16	SAN FRANCISCO	L	106	113	39-26
Nov. 30	at Cincinnati	W	126	109	12-12	Feb. 17	Milwaukee at Baltimore	L	111	123	39-27
Dec. 3	at New York	L	93	126	12-13	Feb. 18	Cincinnati at Cleveland	W	124	123	40-27
Dec. 4	NEW YORK	L	113	121	12-14	Feb. 20	at Detroit	W	97	87	41-27
Dec. 6	LOS ANGELES	L	94	99	12-15	Feb. 23	SAN DIEGO	W	124	92	42-27
Dec. 8	at Phoenix	W	121	99	13-15	Feb. 25	at New York	L	101	122	42-28
Dec. 10	at San Francisco	W	111	100	14-15	Feb. 28	at Boston	L	120	122	42-29
Dec. 12	at Seattle	W	93	91	15-15	Mar. 3	MILWAUKEE	W	112	106	43-29
Dec. 13	at Los Angeles	W	105	103	16-15	Mar. 8	PHILADELPHIA	W	138	99	44-29
Dec. 14	at Chicago	W	87	83	17-15	Mar. 9	CINCINNATI	W	134	107	45-29
Dec. 18	MILWAUKEE	W	122	116	18-15	Mar. 11	at Chicago	L	90	102	45-30
Dec. 21	DETROIT	W	120	110	19-15	Mar. 12	CHICAGO	W	109	90	46-30
Dec. 26	SEATTLE	W	126	96	20-15	Mar. 15	at Philadelphia	L	120	122	46-31
Dec. 28	BOSTON	W	110	97	21-15	Mar. 16	SEATTLE (#)	W	131	127	47-31
Dec. 29	BALTIMORE	W	101	99	22-15	Mar. 18	at San Francisco	W	128	115	48-31
Jan. 2	at Chicago	W	106	88	23-15	Mar. 20	SAN DIEGO	L	97	115	48-32
Jan. 3	DETROIT	W	128	106	24-15	Mar. 21	at Los Angeles	L	103	116	48-33
Jan. 4	LOS ANGELES	L	111	121	24-16	Mar. 23	at San Diego	L	121	128	48-34
Jan. 5	PHOENIX	W	97	96	25-16		(#) overtime; (2#) 2 ot's				
Jan. 8	at Philadelphia	L	111	112	25-17		(3#) 3 ot's; (4#) 4 ot's				

ATLANTA YEARLY RESULTS

1969-70 GAME-BY-GAME

Date	Opponent	W-L	Hawks	Opp.	Record
Oct. 15	SEATTLE	W	124	119	1-0
Oct. 18	PHOENIX	W	121	116	2-0
Oct. 22	SAN FRANCISCO	L	93	94	2-1
Oct. 24	BOSTON	W	122	110	3-1
Oct. 25	at Detroit	L	104	125	3-2
Oct. 28	at New York	L	104	128	3-3
Oct. 29	SAN DIEGO	W	117	114	4-3
Nov. 1	at Baltimore (#)	W	140	137	5-3
Nov. 2	SEATTLE	W	125	113	6-3
Nov. 5	BOSTON	W	128	121	7-3
Nov. 6	at Chicago (#)	W	142	137	8-3
Nov. 8	SAN FRANCISCO	W	106	93	9-3
Nov. 10	Chicago at Auburn	W	133	132	10-3
Nov. 11	PHILADELPHIA	W	124	107	11-3
Nov. 14	at San Francisco	W	120	109	12-3
Nov. 15	at San Diego	L	118	133	12-4
Nov. 16	Phoenix at Albuquerque	L	118	139	12-5
Nov. 19	at Seattle	W	137	116	13-5
Nov. 21	at Detroit	W	118	106	14-5
Nov. 22	PHILADELPHIA	L	116	132	14-6
Nov. 25	Milwaukee at St. Louis	L	115	130	14-7
Nov. 26	NEW YORK	L	103	138	14-8
Nov. 28	at Boston	W	130	105	15-8
Nov. 29	CINCINNATI	W	128	111	16-8
Dec. 4	SEATTLE	W	119	111	17-8
Dec. 5	at Cincinnati	L	127	156	17-9
Dec. 7	at Los Angeles	W	104	103	18-9
Dec. 9	San Francisco at Salt Lake	W	117	115	19-9
Dec. 10	at San Diego	L	107	126	19-10
Dec. 12	LOS ANGELES	W	121	107	20-10
Dec. 13	MILWAUKEE	L	100	121	20-11
Dec. 16	at New York (#)	W	125	124	21-11
Dec. 17	BALTIMORE	L	133	138	21-12
Dec. 18	Chicago at Kansas City	W	112	114	21-13
Dec. 20	BOSTON	W	122	106	22-13
Dec. 21	CHICAGO	W	118	111	23-13
Dec. 26	Cincinnati at Cleveland	L	110	130	23-14
Dec. 27	PHILADELPHIA	W	112	107	24-14
Dec. 29	SAN DIEGO	W	122	118	25-14
Dec. 31	BALTIMORE	W	122	111	26-14
Jan. 2	at Philadelphia	L	117	121	26-15
Jan. 3	CINCINNATI	L	102	104	26-16
Jan. 4	at Milwaukee	W	126	125	27-16
Jan. 6	SEATTLE	W	101	97	28-16
Jan. 7	at Boston	W	112	106	29-16
Jan. 9	LOS ANGELES	L	112	127	29-17
Jan. 10	at Baltimore	L	109	130	29-18
Jan. 12	Detroit at Memphis	L	100	113	29-19
Jan. 13	at Philadelphia	L	105	136	29-20
Jan. 14	SAN FRANCISCO	L	101	103	29-21
Jan. 16	Cincinnati at Columbia, SC	W	117	100	30-21
Jan. 18	CHICAGO	W	125	107	31-21
Jan. 25	MILWAUKEE	L	116	131	31-22
Jan. 26	at San Francisco	W	131	104	32-22
Jan. 28	at Seattle	L	119	120	32-23
Jan. 29	at Phoenix	L	102	111	32-24
Jan. 30	at Los Angeles	L	87	102	32-25
Feb. 1	BALTIMORE	L	124	133	32-26
Feb. 2	DETROIT	W	125	121	33-26
Feb. 4	NEW YORK	W	111	96	34-26
Feb. 6	CHICAGO	W	104	93	35-26
Feb. 8	at Chicago	L	107	117	35-27
Feb. 10	at San Francisco	L	104	113	35-28
Feb. 11	at San Diego	W	155	131	36-28
Feb. 12	at Los Angeles	L	114	136	36-29
Feb. 15	BOSTON	W	146	125	37-29
Feb. 18	at Cincinnati (#)	W	139	125	38-29
Feb. 21	at New York	W	122	106	39-29
Feb. 22	DETROIT	L	114	116	39-30
Feb. 24	at Los Angeles	W	118	105	40-30
Feb. 25	at Seattle	L	112	120	40-31
Feb. 27	at Baltimore	L	107	114	40-32
Mar. 1	PHOENIX	L	98	109	40-33
Mar. 3	LOS ANGELES	W	101	93	41-33
Mar. 5	at Milwaukee	W	126	117	42-33
Mar. 8	at Phoenix	L	119	130	42-34
Mar. 10	MILWAUKEE	W	140	127	43-34
Mar. 11	SAN DIEGO	W	122	121	44-34
Mar. 15	PHOENIX	W	126	111	45-34
Mar. 17	at Philadelphia	W	128	125	46-34
Mar. 20	NEW YORK	W	110	102	47-34
Mar. 22	at Detroit	W	130	126	48-34

1970-71 GAME-BY-GAME

Date	Opponent	W-L	Hawks	Opp.	Record
Oct. 17	MILWAUKEE	L	98	107	0-1
Oct. 21	SAN FRANCISCO	W	102	100	1-1
Oct. 22	at Detroit	L	101	120	1-2
Oct. 24	BOSTON	L	109	113	1-3
Oct. 26	at Cincinnati	L	107	126	1-4
Oct. 31	SAN DIEGO	L	117	121	1-5
Nov. 1	at Cleveland	W	131	107	2-5
Nov. 4	DETROIT	L	105	117	2-6
Nov. 6	at Philadelphia	L	112	118	2-7
Nov. 7	PHOENIX	L	100	107	2-8
Nov. 10	PHILADELPHIA	W	109	104	3-8
Nov. 11	at Buffalo	L	118	134	3-9
Nov. 13	at Boston	W	116	114	4-9
Nov. 14	CHICAGO	L	116	120	4-10
Nov. 17	at Los Angeles	L	105	116	4-11
Nov. 18	at Portland	L	131	146	4-12
Nov. 21	BALTIMORE	W	130	103	5-12
Nov. 22	PHILADELPHIA	W	125	115	6-12
Nov. 24	at New York	L	119	128	6-13
Nov. 25	NEW YORK	L	111	114	6-14
Nov. 27	at San Diego	L	127	128	6-15
Nov. 29	at Seattle	L	107	130	6-16
Dec. 1	at San Francisco	L	106	113	6-17
Dec. 2	at Phoenix	L	112	126	6-18
Dec. 5	SEATTLE	W	106	100	7-18
Dec. 8	at Milwaukee	L	104	125	7-19
Dec. 9	at Cincinnati	L	106	118	7-20
Dec. 11	at Chicago	L	86	87	7-21
Dec. 12	PORTLAND	W	107	101	8-21
Dec. 13	BUFFALO	W	110	91	9-21
Dec. 16	SAN DIEGO	W	128	117	10-21
Dec. 18	at Baltimore	W	116	112	11-21
Dec. 19	LOS ANGELES	L	104	116	11-22
Dec. 22	at Los Angeles	W	119	115	12-22
Dec. 23	at San Diego	L	102	133	12-23
Dec. 25	at Phoenix	L	115	127	12-24
Dec. 26	CINCINNATI	L	118	130	12-25
Dec. 28	SAN FRANCISCO	L	104	115	12-26
Dec. 29	at Detroit	L	97	99	12-27
Dec. 31	CLEVELAND	W	119	85	13-27
Jan. 2	at New York	W	112	108	14-27
Jan. 3	BOSTON	L	128	140	14-28
Jan. 5	DETROIT	L	90	98	14-29
Jan. 7	BALTIMORE	L	102	110	14-30
Jan. 8	at Baltimore	L	104	115	14-31
Jan. 10	PHOENIX	L	105	116	14-32
Jan. 15	at Boston	L	123	134	14-33
Jan. 16	LOS ANGELES	W	127	123	15-33
Jan. 18	at Buffalo	W	123	113	16-33
Jan. 20	SEATTLE	L	108	112	16-34
Jan. 22	at Milwaukee	W	117	110	17-34
Jan. 24	MILWAUKEE	L	120	142	17-35
Jan. 26	at Philadelphia	L	122	129	17-36
Jan. 27	NEW YORK	L	108	116	17-37
Jan. 29	CLEVELAND	W	119	111	18-37
Jan. 31	SAN DIEGO	W	131	120	19-37
Feb. 2	at San Francisco	L	99	101	19-38
Feb. 4	at Portland	L	123	137	19-39
Feb. 5	at Seattle (#)	W	121	120	20-39
Feb. 7	CINCINNATI	W	121	118	21-39
Feb. 9	at New York	W	114	109	22-39
Feb. 10	BOSTON	W	114	102	23-39
Feb. 12	NEW YORK	W	125	116	24-39
Feb. 14	MILWAUKEE	L	88	124	24-40
Feb. 16	at Chicago	L	102	118	24-41
Feb. 20	at Baltimore	W	122	115	25-41
Feb. 21	BALTIMORE	L	119	121	25-42
Feb. 24	PORTLAND	W	118	107	26-42
Feb. 26	at Boston (#)	L	129	137	26-43
Feb. 27	BUFFALO	W	134	117	27-43
Feb. 28	DETROIT	L	105	106	27-44
Mar. 2	at Seattle	W	128	116	28-44
Mar. 3	at San Francisco	W	109	105	29-44
Mar. 5	at Los Angeles	W	105	104	30-44
Mar. 7	CINCINNATI	W	122	112	31-44
Mar. 10	PHOENIX	W	139	98	32-44
Mar. 12	at Cleveland	W	119	107	33-44
Mar. 13	at Cincinnati	L	127	136	33-45
Mar. 14	PHILADELPHIA	W	108	101	34-45
Mar. 16	at Philadelphia	W	130	125	35-45
Mar. 19	CHICAGO (#)	W	112	111	36-45
Mar. 20	at Chicago	L	121	138	36-46

ATLANTA YEARLY RESULTS

1971-72 GAME-BY-GAME

Date	Opponent	W-L	Score Hawks	Opp.	Record
Oct. 2	at Cincinnati	L	113	127	0-1
Oct. 16	PHILADELPHIA	L	102	104	0-2
Oct. 20	LOS ANGELES	L	104	126	0-3
Oct. 22	BOSTON	L	108	115	0-4
Oct. 23	New York	W	95	89	1-4
Oct. 25	at Boston	L	116	136	1-5
Oct. 27	NEW YORK	W	110	96	2-5
Oct. 29	at Cleveland	W	98	97	3-5
Oct. 30	DETROIT	L	99	104	3-6
Nov. 3	CHICAGO	L	100	113	3-7
Nov. 5	BUFFALO (#)	L	117	122	3-8
Nov. 6	at Philadelphia	L	96	101	3-9
Nov. 10	MILWAUKEE	L	100	116	3-10
Nov. 12	GOLDEN STATE	W	106	104	4-10
Nov. 17	SEATTLE	L	104	112	4-11
Nov. 20	PHOENIX	W	115	109	5-11
Nov. 23	at Buffalo	L	97	102	5-12
Nov. 24	at Milwaukee	L	107	141	5-13
Nov. 26	BALTIMORE	L	105	118	5-14
Nov. 27	CLEVELAND	L	95	103	5-15
Nov. 28	at Boston	L	108	130	5-16
Nov. 30	at Chicago	L	85	86	5-17
Dec. 1	at Detroit	W	117	103	6-17
Dec. 4	PHILADELPHIA	W	126	109	7-17
Dec. 7	at Golden State	W	116	113	8-17
Dec. 9	at Phoenix	L	115	135	8-18
Dec. 10	at Houston	L	88	95	8-19
Dec. 12	at Los Angeles		95	104	8-20
Dec. 15	HOUSTON (#)	L	115	117	8-21
Dec. 17	at Baltimore	L	103	114	8-22
Dec. 18	BALTIMORE	W	123	94	9-22
Dec. 19	CINCINNATI	W	101	99	10-22
Dec. 22	at Cincinnati	W	106	103	11-22
Dec. 23	at Cleveland	L	110	115	11-23
Dec. 25	BUFFALO	W	140	117	12-23
Dec. 26	at Milwaukee	L	92	114	12-24
Dec. 27	PORTLAND	W	135	121	13-24
Dec. 30	at Houston	L	115	129	13-25
Jan. 1	at Phoenix	W	116	111	14-25
Jan. 4	at Portland	W	103	91	15-25
Jan. 5	at Seattle	L	116	127	15-26
Jan. 7	LOS ANGELES	L	90	134	15-27
Jan. 8	at Baltimore	L	102	110	15-28
Jan. 12	MILWAUKEE	W	104	102	16-28
Jan. 14	at Cincinnati	L	102	126	16-29
Jan. 15	BOSTON	L	106	122	16-30
Jan. 16	PHILADELPHIA	W	124	116	17-30
Jan. 21	GOLDEN STATE	L	111	113	17-31
Jan. 23	at Milwaukee	W	118	113	18-31
Jan. 25	at Buffalo	W	123	110	19-31
Jan. 26	SEATTLE	L	119	131	19-32
Jan. 28	DETROIT	W	124	108	20-32
Jan. 30	at Phoenix	L	103	105	20-33
Feb. 3	at Golden State	L	115	132	20-34
Feb. 5	CLEVELAND	W	120	117	21-34
Feb. 6	at Houston	L	113	120	21-35
Feb. 9	LOS ANGELES	L	113	117	21-36
Feb. 11	at Chicago	L	91	102	21-37
Feb. 12	CHICAGO	L	106	117	21-38
Feb. 13	BUFFALO	W	133	119	22-38
Feb. 15	at Detroit	W	113	105	23-38
Feb. 16	BALTIMORE	W	105	103	24-38
Feb. 18	at Baltimore	L	81	106	24-39
Feb. 20	CINCINNATI	L	92	101	24-40
Feb. 23	PHOENIX	W	120	118	25-40
Feb. 25	at Philadelphia	L	110	114	25-41
Feb. 27	PORTLAND	W	113	110	26-41
Feb. 29	at Buffalo	W	99	89	27-41
Mar. 3	at Los Angeles	L	104	114	27-42
Mar. 4	at Portland	W	120	101	28-42
Mar. 5	at Seattle	L	110	112	28-43
Mar. 8	CHICAGO	L	96	98	28-44
Mar. 12	CLEVELAND	W	135	114	29-44
Mar. 14	at New York	L	107	115	29-45
Mar. 15	SEATTLE	W	134	96	30-45
Mar. 17	at Detroit	L	112	121	30-46
Mar. 18	CINCINNATI	W	115	106	31-46
Mar. 19	at Cleveland	W	115	105	32-46
Mar. 21	at Philadelphia	W	117	111	33-46
Mar. 22	HOUSTON	W	107	106	34-46
Mar. 24	GOLDEN STATE	W	118	102	35-46
Mar. 26	NEW YORK	W	120	106	36-46

1972-73 GAME-BY-GAME

Date	Opponent	W-L	Score Hawks	Opp.	Record
Oct. 10	at Buffalo	W	120	109	1-0
Oct. 13	at Baltimore	L	98	115	1-1
Oct. 15	NEW YORK	W	109	101	2-1
Oct. 17	BOSTON	L	115	119	2-2
Oct. 20	at Houston	L	108	120	2-3
Oct. 21	at Kansas City	L	101	108	2-4
Oct. 24	at Portland	W	118	110	3-4
Oct. 25	at Seattle	W	118	115	4-4
Oct. 28	at Golden State	L	107	122	4-5
Oct. 31	HOUSTON	L	105	106	4-6
Nov. 3	at Houston	W	114	108	5-6
Nov. 4	PHILADELPHIA	W	128	120	6-6
Nov. 7	BALTIMORE (#)	W	109	107	7-6
Nov. 9	at New York	L	99	101	7-7
Nov. 11	MILWAUKEE	W	111	102	8-7
Nov. 14	GOLDEN STATE	L	105	114	8-8
Nov. 18	PHOENIX	W	126	122	9-8
Nov. 19	at Cleveland	L	98	109	9-9
Nov. 21	at Detroit (#)	L	110	113	9-10
Nov. 23	SEATTLE	W	110	97	10-10
Nov. 25	CHICAGO	L	99	100	10-11
Nov. 26	at Milwaukee	L	96	108	10-12
Nov. 29	at Phoenix	L	98	109	10-13
Dec. 1	at Los Angeles (#)	W	114	109	11-13
Dec. 2	at Portland	W	106	103	12-13
Dec. 5	PORTLAND	W	122	121	13-13
Dec. 7	at Chicago (#)	W	94	89	14-13
Dec. 8	BALTIMORE	W	134	115	15-13
Dec. 9	at Kansas City	L	115	130	15-14
Dec. 12	at New York	L	93	114	15-15
Dec. 13	NEW YORK	W	121	120	16-15
Dec. 16	CLEVELAND	W	100	94	17-15
Dec. 20	KANSAS CITY	W	119	102	18-15
Dec. 22	at Buffalo	W	110	109	19-15
Dec. 23	PHILADELPHIA	W	124	112	20-15
Dec. 26	at Cleveland	L	96	115	20-16
Dec. 27	at Philadelphia	W	121	120	21-16
Dec. 28	BALTIMORE	L	111	112	21-17
Dec. 30	BUFFALO	W	120	110	22-17
Jan. 2	at Chicago	L	90	100	22-18
Jan. 3	at Milwaukee	L	97	105	22-19
Jan. 5	BOSTON	L	108	126	22-20
Jan. 6	at Detroit	W	116	111	23-20
Jan. 9	HOUSTON	W	120	114	24-20
Jan. 11	NEW YORK	L	107	122	24-21
Jan. 12	at Boston	L	109	133	24-22
Jan. 14	LOS ANGELES	L	100	102	24-23
Jan. 16	DETROIT (#)	W	130	129	25-23
Jan. 17	at Philadelphia	W	122	105	26-23
Jan. 18	BUFFALO	L	125	127	26-24
Jan. 20	CLEVELAND	W	96	84	27-24
Jan. 26	at Buffalo	W	118	82	28-24
Jan. 27	KANSAS CITY	W	129	126	29-24
Jan. 28	at Houston	L	108	116	29-25
Jan. 30	DETROIT	L	123	126	29-26
Feb. 2	at Boston	W	100	99	30-26
Feb. 3	BUFFALO	W	105	101	31-26
Feb. 6	BALTIMORE	W	112	106	32-26
Feb. 7	at Baltimore	L	108	137	32-27
Feb. 8	CLEVELAND (#)	L	132	136	32-28
Feb. 10	HOUSTON	W	103	91	33-28
Feb. 11	at Cleveland	W	115	107	34-28
Feb. 16	at Phoenix	W	111	104	35-28
Feb. 18	at Los Angeles	W	99	92	36-28
Feb. 20	at Golden State	L	115	118	36-29
Feb. 23	at Seattle	L	120	124	36-30
Feb. 27	SEATTLE	W	131	130	37-30
Mar. 2	at Philadelphia	W	130	107	38-30
Mar. 3	HOUSTON	W	136	125	39-30
Mar. 4	PHILADELPHIA	W	138	130	40-30
Mar. 8	PORTLAND	W	135	129	41-30
Mar. 10	GOLDEN STATE	W	117	113	42-30
Mar. 11	at Houston	L	118	129	42-31
Mar. 13	at Cleveland	L	107	115	42-32
Mar. 16	PHOENIX	W	135	127	43-32
Mar. 18	MILWAUKEE	L	104	105	43-33
Mar. 20	LOS ANGELES	W	114	112	44-33
Mar. 21	at New York	W	98	93	45-33
Mar. 23	at Boston	L	108	124	45-34
Mar. 24	CHICAGO	W	113	111	46-34
Mar. 25	at Baltimore	L	105	112	46-35
Mar. 27	BOSTON	L	110	117	46-36

ATLANTA YEARLY RESULTS

1973-74 GAME-BY-GAME

Date	Opponent	W-L	Score Hawks	Opp.	Record
Oct. 9	CAPITAL	W	128	114	1-0
Oct. 11	LOS ANGELES	W	129	102	2-0
Oct. 12	at Detroit	L	105	122	2-1
Oct. 13	KC/OMAHA	L	102	117	2-2
Oct. 20	at Phoenix	L	108	118	2-3
Oct. 21	at Los Angeles	W	119	100	3-3
Oct. 24	at Seattle	W	131	106	4-3
Oct. 26	at Portland	L	110	127	4-4
Oct. 27	at Golden State	W	125	116	5-4
Oct. 30	PHOENIX	W	122	101	6-4
Nov. 2	at Houston	W	125	123	7-4
Nov. 3	BOSTON	L	109	122	7-5
Nov. 4	at Cleveland	W	115	110	8-5
Nov. 8	DETROIT	L	115	129	8-6
Nov. 10	PHILADELPHIA	W	120	97	9-6
Nov. 13	at Buffalo	L	114	121	9-7
Nov. 15	PORTLAND	W	123	114	10-7
Nov. 17	CAPITAL	L	109	115	10-8
Nov. 22	GOLDEN STATE	L	99	101	10-9
Nov. 23	at Capital	L	86	101	10-10
Nov. 24	MILWAUKEE	L	92	112	10-11
Nov. 27	at KC/Omaha	W	129	110	11-11
Nov. 28	BUFFALO	W	130	106	12-11
Dec. 1	SEATTLE	W	120	110	13-11
Dec. 5	at KC/Omaha	L	105	117	13-12
Dec. 7	at Boston	L	112	116	13-13
Dec. 8	at New York	L	100	117	13-14
Dec. 11	BUFFALO (#)	W	132	127	14-14
Dec. 15	at Milwaukee	L	82	116	14-15
Dec. 18	at Capital	W	98	91	15-15
Dec. 19	NEW YORK	W	107	105	16-15
Dec. 21	at Houston	W	124	110	17-15
Dec. 22	CLEVELAND	L	98	108	17-16
Dec. 26	PHILADELPHIA	W	145	118	18-16
Dec. 28	at Chicago	L	94	118	18-17
Dec. 29	HOUSTON	W	114	110	19-17
Dec. 30	at Cleveland	W	99	94	20-17
Jan. 1	at New York	L	89	99	20-18
Jan. 2	PHOENIX	L	113	116	20-19
Jan. 5	CLEVELAND	W	99	86	21-19
Jan. 6	at Buffalo	L	109	118	21-20
Jan. 8	at Buffalo	L	96	100	21-21
Jan. 10	CHICAGO	L	104	116	21-22
Jan. 11	at Philadelphia	L	100	121	21-23
Jan. 13	BOSTON	W	128	105	21-24
Jan. 17	PORTLAND	W	126	99	22-24
Jan. 18	at Boston	L	94	98	22-25
Jan. 19	SEATTLE	W	127	109	23-25
Jan. 22	at Chicago	L	89	102	23-26
Jan. 23	HOUSTON	L	104	115	23-27
Jan. 26	BUFFALO	W	132	122	24-27
Jan. 27	NEW YORK	L	89	111	24-28
Jan. 29	at Cleveland	L	111	118	24-29
Jan. 30	GOLDEN STATE	L	122	129	24-30
Feb. 2	HOUSTON	W	117	107	25-30
Feb. 3	at Houston	L	112	123	25-31
Feb. 5	CAPITAL	W	121	103	26-31
Feb. 6	LOS ANGELES	W	107	103	27-31
Feb. 8	at Philadelphia	W	99	90	28-31
Feb. 9	CLEVELAND	L	84	104	28-32
Feb. 11	PHILADELPHIA	L	95	116	28-33
Feb. 14	at Golden State	L	105	121	28-34
Feb. 16	at Phoenix (#)	L	123	124	28-35
Feb. 17	at Los Angeles	W	113	110	29-35
Feb. 20	at Milwaukee	L	94	110	29-36
Feb. 23	at New York	L	90	98	29-37
Feb. 24	at Boston	L	96	111	29-38
Feb. 27	KC/OMAHA	L	76	85	29-39
Mar. 1	MILWAUKEE	W	89	105	29-40
Mar. 2	HOUSTON	W	129	122	30-40
Mar. 5	at Capital	W	89	103	30-41
Mar. 6	NEW YORK	L	94	96	30-42
Mar. 9	CHICAGO	W	106	99	31-42
Mar. 10	DETROIT	L	111	116	31-43
Mar. 12	at Cleveland	L	84	95	31-44
Mar. 15	at Seattle	W	126	107	32-44
Mar. 16	at Portland	L	127	128	32-45
Mar. 20	BOSTON	W	99	89	33-45
Mar. 22	at Philadelphia	W	107	106	34-45
Mar. 23	CAPITAL (#)	W	119	108	35-45
Mar. 24	at Capital	L	92	120	35-46
Mar. 26	at Detroit	L	108	109	35-47

1974-75 GAME-BY-GAME

Date	Opponent	W-L	Score Hawks	Opp.	Record
Oct. 18	at Chicago	L	115	120	0-1
Oct. 19	HOUSTON	W	118	112	1-1
Oct. 22	PHILADELPHIA	W	125	92	2-1
Oct. 24	CLEVELAND	L	97	116	2-2
Oct. 25	at Boston	L	109	116	2-3
Oct. 30	at Detroit	W	104	96	3-3
Oct. 31	at New York	L	90	93	3-4
Nov. 2	BOSTON	L	125	126	3-5
Nov. 7	PHOENIX	W	109	108	4-5
Nov. 9	PORTLAND	L	115	119	4-6
Nov. 10	at Milwaukee	W	99	94	5-6
Nov. 12	at Golden State	L	111	128	5-7
Nov. 14	at Portland	L	92	104	5-8
Nov. 16	NEW ORLEANS	W	130	104	6-8
Nov. 19	SEATTLE	W	122	113	7-8
Nov. 21	NEW YORK	L	95	101	7-9
Nov. 22	at New Orleans	L	86	90	7-10
Nov. 23	KANSAS CITY-OMAHA	L	100	103	7-11
Nov. 26	WASHINGTON	W	119	102	8-11
Nov. 27	at Washington	L	104	114	8-12
Nov. 29	at Houston	W	96	91	9-12
Dec. 3	at Phoenix	W	90	85	10-12
Dec. 6	at Los Angeles	L	84	100	10-13
Dec. 8	at Seattle	W	102	95	11-13
Dec. 10	at Portland	W	107	103	12-13
Dec. 12	GOLDEN STATE	L	109	129	12-13
Dec. 14	BOSTON (#)	L	90	92	12-15
Dec. 17	WASHINGTON	W	96	85	13-15
Dec. 19	CHICAGO	L	80	88	13-16
Dec. 20	at Buffalo	W	113	102	14-16
Dec. 21	HOUSTON	L	96	101	14-17
Dec. 23	at Philadelphia	L	88	100	14-18
Dec. 25	at Washington	L	92	110	14-19
Dec. 26	at Houston	L	86	114	14-20
Dec. 28	LOS ANGELES	W	106	89	15-20
Dec. 29	at Cleveland	L	103	110	15-21
Jan. 1	at KC/Omaha	W	102	97	16-21
Jan. 2	at Milwaukee	L	111	116	16-22
Jan. 4	BUFFALO	L	108	121	16-23
Jan. 7	CLEVELAND (#)	W	113	112	17-23
Jan. 8	at Boston	L	96	104	17-24
Jan. 10	at Chicago	L	113	116	17-25
Jan. 11	DETROIT	L	113	118	17-26
Jan. 16	WASHINGTON	W	108	85	18-26
Jan. 18	BUFFALO	L	115	129	18-27
Jan. 19	SEATTLE	W	117	109	19-27
Jan. 21	NEW ORLEANS	W	135	103	20-27
Jan. 23	HOUSTON	L	95	96	20-28
Jan. 24	at Detroit	L	103	113	20-29
Jan. 25	MILWAUKEE	W	117	101	21-29
Jan. 28	at New York	L	111	115	21-30
Jan. 30	NEW YORK	L	115	117	31-31
Jan. 31	at Buffalo	L	101	111	21-32
Feb. 1	at Cleveland	L	109	112	21-33
Feb. 4	CLEVELAND	W	111	97	22-33
Feb. 6	DETROIT	W	111	98	23-33
Feb. 7	at Houston	L	97	105	23-34
Feb. 8	NEW ORLEANS	L	102	106	23-35
Feb. 10	at New Orleans	L	89	96	23-36
Feb. 14	at Los Angeles	L	100	108	23-37
Feb. 15	at Phoenix	W	111	107	24-37
Feb. 20	at Golden State	L	102	108	24-38
Feb. 21	at Seattle	L	108	110	24-39
Feb. 23	at Cleveland (#)	L	105	111	24-40
Feb. 27	CHICAGO	L	91	111	24-41
Mar. 1	KC/OMAHA	W	108	95	25-41
Mar. 4	LOS ANGELES	W	109	97	26-41
Mar. 5	at Washington	L	112	118	26-42
Mar. 6	GOLDEN STATE	W	110	106	27-42
Mar. 8	NEW ORLEANS	W	113	101	28-42
Mar. 11	WASHINGTON	L	87	99	28-43
Mar. 13	MILWAUKEE	L	104	120	28-44
Mar. 15	at New Orleans	L	123	140	28-45
Mar. 16	PHOENIX	W	117	114	29-45
Mar. 18	at KC/Omaha	L	101	105	29-46
Mar. 21	at Philadelphia	L	103	114	29-47
Mar. 22	PHILADELPHIA	W	104	100	30-47
Mar. 25	PORTLAND	L	89	105	30-48
Mar. 29	CLEVELAND	W	103	97	31-48
Mar. 30	at New Orleans	L	105	108	31-49
Apr. 1	at Houston	L	104	113	31-51
Apr. 5	at Washington	L	115	123	31-51

ATLANTA YEARLY RESULTS

1975-76 GAME-BY-GAME

Date	Opponent	W-L	Hawks	Opp.	Record
Oct. 23	NEW ORLEANS	W	109	91	1-0
Oct. 25	DETROIT	L	102	108	1-1
Nov. 2	at Los Angeles (#)	L	113	116	1-2
Nov. 4	at Portland	W	98	97	2-2
Nov. 6	CLEVELAND	L	108	113	2-3
Nov. 8	SEATTLE	W	107	94	3-3
Nov. 11	BOSTON AT HARTFORD	W	100	91	4-3
Nov. 12	at Detroit	W	109	106	5-3
Nov. 14	WASHINGTON	W	97	88	6-3
Nov. 15	at New York	L	86	92	6-4
Nov. 16	NEW YORK	W	97	96	7-4
Nov. 19	at Golden State (#)	W	104	98	8-4
Nov. 20	at Washington	L	96	105	8-5
Nov. 22	NEW ORLEANS	L	85	89	8-6
Nov. 23	PHILADELPHIA	W	115	111	9-6
Nov. 26	at New Orleans	W	113	108	10-6
Nov. 28	at Boston	L	107	114	10-7
Dec. 4	PORTLAND	W	94	87	11-7
Dec. 6	BOSTON	L	104	111	11-8
Dec. 10	at Kansas City	L	94	100	11-9
Dec. 11	BUFFALO	W	122	99	12-9
Dec. 13	KANSAS CITY	W	115	101	13-9
Dec. 16	at New York	L	96	97	13-10
Dec. 18	LOS ANGELES	W	114	98	14-10
Dec. 19	at Houston	L	107	113	14-11
Dec. 20	HOUSTON	W	123	108	15-11
Dec. 21	CHICAGO (#)	L	90	97	15-12
Dec. 25	at Washington	L	94	99	15-13
Dec. 26	at Cleveland	W	98	97	16-13
Dec. 27	MILWAUKEE	W	87	82	17-13
Jan. 1	at New Orleans	L	95	111	17-14
Jan. 3	PHOENIX	L	89	100	17-15
Jan. 6	at Milwaukee	W	91	87	18-15
Jan. 8	HOUSTON	L	106	115	18-16
Jan. 10	CLEVELAND	L	100	106	18-17
Jan. 11	PORTLAND	L	109	116	18-18
Jan. 14	SEATTLE	L	110	112	18-19
Jan. 15	at Cleveland	W	98	91	19-19
Jan. 17	GOLDEN STATE	W	97	91	20-19
Jan. 20	at Chicago	W	100	86	21-19
Jan. 21	BUFFALO	L	94	102	21-20
Jan. 23	at Buffalo	L	104	119	21-21
Jan. 24	at Philadelphia	L	116	130	21-22
Jan. 25	PHILADELPHIA	L	109	112	21-23
Jan. 27	at New York	W	114	113	22-23
Jan. 28	at Boston	L	99	110	22-24
Jan. 29	NEW YORK	W	112	109	23-24
Jan. 31	NEW ORLEANS	L	95	108	23-25
Feb. 1	CHICAGO	W	84	80	24-25
Feb. 5	DETROIT	L	108	111	24-26
Feb. 7	WASHINGTON	L	90	103	24-27
Feb. 8	LOS ANGELES	L	89	97	24-28
Feb. 10	KANSAS CITY	W	111	89	25-28
Feb. 12	at Golden State	L	104	113	25-29
Feb. 13	at Seattle	L	102	119	25-30
Feb. 15	BUFFALO	W	112	104	26-30
Feb. 17	at Cleveland	L	92	112	26-31
Feb. 21	at Washington	L	95	103	26-32
Feb. 22	at New Orleans	L	94	102	26-33
Feb. 26	at Phoenix	L	97	115	26-34
Feb. 29	at Portland	L	98	102	26-35
Mar. 4	BOSTON	W	103	98	27-35
Mar. 6	at Houston	L	97	101	27-36
Mar. 7	HOUSTON	W	123	106	28-36
Mar. 11	PHOENIX	L	99	104	28-37
Mar. 12	at Philadelphia	L	107	109	28-38
Mar. 14	at Kansas City (#)	L	113	114	28-39
Mar. 17	at Houston	L	112	124	28-40
Mar. 19	at Chicago	L	101	108	28-41
Mar. 20	CLEVELAND	L	99	107	28-42
Mar. 23	at Golden State	L	100	118	28-43
Mar. 25	at Phoenix	L	98	107	28-44
Mar. 26	at Los Angeles	L	85	107	28-45
Mar. 28	at Seattle	L	112	127	28-46
Mar. 30	at Milwaukee (#)	L	126	130	28-47
Apr. 2	at Buffalo	L	93	101	28-48
Apr. 3	MILWAUKEE	L	106	115	28-49
Apr. 4	at Cleveland	L	92	120	28-50
Apr. 5	WASHINGTON	L	105	133	28-51
Apr. 9	at Detroit	L	108	111	28-52
Apr. 10	PHILADELPHIA	W	123	109	29-52
Apr. 11	HOUSTON	L	111	122	29-53

1976-77 GAME-BY-GAME

Date	Opponent	W-L	Hawks	Opp.	Record
Oct. 21	HOUSTON	L	104	120	0-1
Oct. 24	MILWAUKEE	W	115	91	1-1
Oct. 26	SAN ANTONIO	W	122	114	2-1
Oct. 29	at Los Angeles	L	101	118	2-2
Oct. 30	at Golden State	L	106	114	2-3
Oct. 31	at Seattle	L	112	126	2-4
Nov. 2	at Portland	L	116	129	2-5
Nov. 4	CHICAGO	W	97	87	3-5
Nov. 6	DETROIT	L	105	110	3-6
Nov. 7	CLEVELAND	W	107	97	4-6
Nov. 11	PORTLAND	W	107	105	5-6
Nov. 13	NEW ORLEANS	L	87	115	5-7
Nov. 16	at New York Knicks	L	97	100	5-8
Nov. 17	at Boston	L	91	104	5-9
Nov. 20	PHILADELPHIA	L	106	123	5-10
Nov. 21	KANSAS CITY	L	83	106	5-11
Nov. 24	at Indiana	L	93	115	5-12
Nov. 26	at New York Nets	W	109	105	6-12
Nov. 27	BUFFALO	W	101	94	7-12
Nov. 28	GOLDEN STATE	L	98	132	7-13
Dec. 2	WASHINGTON	L	90	102	7-14
Dec. 3	at New Orleans	L	105	121	7-15
Dec. 4	NEW YORK NETS	L	105	107	7-16
Dec. 8	at San Antonio	W	117	108	8-16
Dec. 9	at Kansas City	W	102	100	9-16
Dec. 11	at Cleveland	W	95	94	10-16
Dec. 12	PHOENIX	L	91	106	10-17
Dec. 14	LOS ANGELES	W	106	104	11-17
Dec. 16	at Houston	L	107	118	11-18
Dec. 17	at New Orleans	W	113	109	12-18
Dec. 18	BOSTON	L	110	117	12-19
Dec. 19	at Milwaukee	L	109	126	12-20
Dec. 22	at Detroit	L	94	107	12-21
Dec. 23	at Chicago	L	95	101	12-22
Dec. 26	NEW YORK KNICKS	L	98	103	12-23
Dec. 28	SEATTLE	L	119	120	12-24
Dec. 29	at Washington	L	92	96	12-25
Jan. 2	NEW ORLEANS	L	88	93	12-26
Jan. 4	DENVER	W	113	109	13-26
Jan. 6	INDIANA	L	95	103	13-27
Jan. 10	PHOENIX	L	92	93	13-28
Jan. 12	at Buffalo	W	124	118	14-28
Jan. 14	at New York Nets	W	120	101	15-28
Jan. 15	KANSAS CITY	L	90	115	15-29
Jan. 16	PORTLAND	L	125	120	16-29
Jan. 19	at Philadelphia	L	94	114	16-30
Jan. 21	MILWAUKEE	W	121	101	17-30
Jan. 23	GOLDEN STATE	L	97	104	17-31
Jan. 28	at Houston	L	104	118	17-32
Jan. 29	HOUSTON	W	101	97	18-32
Feb. 1	DETROIT	L	92	95	18-33
Feb. 3	BUFFALO	W	100	98	19-33
Feb. 5	CHICAGO	W	99	96	20-33
Feb. 8	at Phoenix	L	104	117	20-34
Feb. 9	at Seattle	W	99	98	21-34
Feb. 11	at Portland	W	121	108	22-34
Feb. 15	at Golden State	L	111	117	22-35
Feb. 18	at Los Angeles	W	111	101	23-35
Feb. 20	at Denver	L	95	111	23-36
Feb. 24	NEW YORK KNICKS (#)	W	101	98	24-36
Feb. 25	at Chicago	L	87	96	24-37
Feb. 26	SAN ANTONIO	W	119	111	25-37
Mar. 1	LOS ANGELES	L	90	92	25-38
Mar. 4	WASHINGTON	W	100	99	26-38
Mar. 6	at Detroit	L	105	115	26-39
Mar. 8	PHILADELPHIA	W	99	98	27-39
Mar. 11	DENVER	W	100	95	28-39
Mar. 13	CLEVELAND	L	113	115	28-40
Mar. 16	at Philadelphia	L	100	109	28-41
Mar. 18	at Boston	L	96	98	28-42
Mar. 19	at New York Knicks	L	101	107	28-43
Mar. 22	at Buffalo	W	86	84	29-43
Mar. 23	BOSTON	L	96	103	29-44
Mar. 25	at Indiana	L	95	103	29-45
Mar. 26	at Cleveland	L	94	99	29-46
Mar. 30	at Washington	L	103	110	29-47
Mar. 31	NEW YORK NETS	W	95	81	30-47
Apr. 2	INDIANA	L	99	106	30-48
Apr. 3	at San Antonio	W	111	103	31-48
Apr. 5	at Phoenix	L	102	108	31-49
Apr. 6	at Denver	L	95	110	31-50
Apr. 8	at Milwaukee	L	107	118	31-51

ATLANTA YEARLY RESULTS

1977-78 GAME-BY-GAME

Date	Opponent	W-L	Hawks	Opp.	Record
Oct. 22	CLEVELAND	W	107	101	1-0
Oct. 25	at Boston	L	103	110	1-1
Oct. 26	at New Jersey	W	113	110	2-1
Oct. 28	LOS ANGELES	W	102	95	3-1
Nov. 1	SEATTLE	W	102	99	4-1
Nov. 2	at Detroit	W	102	89	5-1
Nov. 4	at Kansas City	W	111	110	6-1
Nov. 5	GOLDEN STATE	W	100	94	7-1
Nov. 10	at Houston	W	132	101	8-1
Nov. 11	PORTLAND	L	92	132	8-2
Nov. 12	at San Antonio	L	99	116	8-3
Nov. 15	PHILADELPHIA	L	93	114	8-4
Nov. 16	at Boston	L	105	131	8-5
Nov. 19	NEW JERSEY	W	129	114	9-5
Nov. 23	DENVER	W	105	104	10-5
Nov. 25	MILWAUKEE	L	115	117	10-6
Nov. 29	BOSTON	W	108	101	11-6
Nov. 30	at Buffalo	L	93	105	11-7
Dec. 3	at Golden State	L	101	118	11-8
Dec. 4	at Phoenix	W	96	89	12-8
Dec. 5	at Seattle	L	88	99	12-9
Dec. 7	at Denver	L	116	123	12-10
Dec. 9	NEW YORK	L	84	103	12-11
Dec. 10	at Cleveland	L	87	102	12-12
Dec. 13	at New York	L	106	107	12-13
Dec. 14	at Philadelphia	W	108	99	13-13
Dec. 16	SAN ANTONIO	W	115	99	14-13
Dec. 18	PHOENIX (#2)	W	134	129	15-13
Dec. 20	at Chicago	L	86	94	15-14
Dec. 21	at Indiana	L	98	109	15-15
Dec. 23	at Milwaukee	W	109	93	16-15
Dec. 25	at Washington	L	93	100	16-16
Dec. 26	WASHINGTON	L	106	113	16-17
Dec. 28	INDIANA	W	99	92	17-17
Dec. 30	DENVER	L	104	106	17-18
Jan. 3	DETROIT	L	103	106	17-19
Jan. 4	at Detroit	L	97	111	17-20
Jan. 6	at New Orleans	L	94	96	17-21
Jan. 7	HOUSTON	W	106	83	18-21
Jan. 11	WASHINGTON	W	100	95	19-21
Jan. 13	SAN ANTONIO	L	92	98	19-22
Jan. 14	at Kansas City	L	101	110	19-23
Jan. 17	KANSAS CITY	W	111	90	20-23
Jan. 18	NEW ORLEANS	L	106	108	20-24
Jan. 19	CHICAGO	L	95	105	20-25
Jan. 21	INDIANA	W	111	100	21-25
Jan. 22	at Cleveland	L	89	93	21-26
Jan. 27	NEW YORK	W	105	96	22-26
Jan. 29	BUFFALO	W	107	102	23-26
Jan. 31	at Chicago (#)	L	103	106	23-27
Feb. 2	at Indiana	W	107	105	24-27
Feb. 8	at Denver	L	109	114	24-28
Feb. 9	at Phoenix	L	98	125	24-29
Feb. 12	at Los Angeles	W	116	103	25-29
Feb. 15	at Portland	L	99	102	25-30
Feb. 17	at New Orleans	W	111	102	26-30
Feb. 18	at Houston	L	112	121	26-31
Feb. 22	PHOENIX	W	107	95	27-31
Feb. 23	at San Antonio	L	105	118	27-32
Feb. 24	GOLDEN STATE	L	96	97	27-33
Feb. 26	BUFFALO	W	119	117	28-33
Feb. 28	BOSTON	W	117	85	29-33
Mar. 1	at New Jersey	L	95	97	29-34
Mar. 3	HOUSTON	W	133	110	30-34
Mar. 5	SEATTLE	W	101	94	31-34
Mar. 7	DETROIT	W	123	109	32-34
Mar. 8	at Philadelphia	L	97	108	32-35
Mar. 10	PORTLAND	W	114	105	33-35
Mar. 12	MILWAUKEE	W	98	93	34-35
Mar. 16	at Golden State	L	98	104	34-36
Mar. 18	at Portland	L	86	105	34-37
Mar. 19	at Los Angeles	L	87	101	34-38
Mar. 21	at Milwaukee	L	86	100	34-39
Mar. 24	NEW ORLEANS	W	96	94	35-39
Mar. 25	at Washington	L	95	98	35-40
Mar. 28	LOS ANGELES	W	105	104	36-40
Mar. 31	PHILADELPHIA (#)	W	111	110	37-40
Apr. 2	NEW JERSEY	W	124	113	38-40
Apr. 4	at New York	W	105	101	39-40
Apr. 5	at Buffalo	W	87	74	40-40
Apr. 7	CLEVELAND	L	109	111	40-41
Apr. 9	CHICAGO	W	99	85	41-41

1978-79 GAME-BY-GAME

Date	Opponent	W-L	Hawks	Opp.	Record
Oct. 13	at Indiana	L	104	117	0-1
Oct. 14	DETROIT	W	122	114	1-1
Oct. 18	BOSTON	L	99	116	1-2
Oct. 21	DENVER	W	130	125	2-2
Oct. 24	at New York	L	109	113	2-3
Oct. 25	at Philadelphia	W	117	118	2-4
Oct. 28	CHICAGO	W	116	92	3-4
Oct. 31	at Washington	W	110	108	4-4
Nov. 2	GOLDEN STATE	L	106	113	4-5
Nov. 4	NEW JERSEY (#)	L	117	118	4-6
Nov. 9	SAN DIEGO	W	125	101	5-6
Nov. 10	at Boston	W	115	103	6-6
Nov. 11	MILWAUKEE	W	105	92	7-6
Nov. 16	at Kansas City	L	100	109	7-7
Nov. 18	PHILADELPHIA	W	124	116	8-7
Nov. 21	at San Diego	W	113	107	9-7
Nov. 22	at Denver	W	113	111	10-7
Nov. 24	at Detroit (#)	L	117	119	10-8
Nov. 25	LOS ANGELES	W	109	103	11-8
Nov. 28	at Cleveland	L	98	112	11-9
Nov. 30	NEW YORK (#)	W	102	96	12-9
Dec. 2	NEW ORLEANS	W	128	94	13-9
Dec. 6	at Phoenix	L	109	136	13-10
Dec. 8	at Seattle	L	106	107	13-11
Dec. 9	at Golden State	L	84	94	13-12
Dec. 10	at Los Angeles	L	86	88	13-13
Dec. 13	INDIANA	W	117	101	14-13
Dec. 15	at New Jersey	W	121	112	15-13
Dec. 17	at New York	L	105	111	15-14
Dec. 19	at Chicago	L	95	101	15-15
Dec. 20	NEW YORK	W	121	112	16-15
Dec. 22	at Boston	L	105	124	16-16
Dec. 23	CLEVELAND	W	109	91	17-16
Dec. 26	at San Antonio	L	111	124	17-17
Dec. 27	SAN ANTONIO	W	115	107	18-17
Dec. 29	at Philadelphia	L	107	113	18-18
Dec. 30	DENVER	W	113	87	19-18
Jan. 3	LOS ANGELES	L	96	99	19-19
Jan. 5	at Houston	W	109	106	20-19
Jan. 6	WASHINGTON	L	102	106	20-20
Jan. 7	at Indiana	L	97	112	20-21
Jan. 10	at Milwaukee (#2)	W	117	113	21-21
Jan. 12	at Chicago	W	100	93	22-21
Jan. 13	SAN DIEGO	W	124	119	23-21
Jan. 14	HOUSTON	W	115	105	24-21
Jan. 17	PORTLAND	W	111	110	25-21
Jan. 20	NEW ORLEANS	W	118	94	26-21
Jan. 21	at New Orleans	L	87	108	26-22
Jan. 23	INDIANA	L	107	110	26-23
Jan. 25	SEATTLE	L	98	100	26-24
Jan. 27	SAN ANTONIO	W	120	113	27-24
Jan. 30	at Washington	L	105	109	27-25
Jan. 31	KANSAS CITY	W	130	118	28-25
Feb. 6	BOSTON	W	104	101	29-25
Feb. 7	at Kansas City	L	108	124	29-26
Feb. 9	at Phoenix	W	105	102	30-26
Feb. 11	at Portland	L	87	91	30-27
Feb. 14	at Seattle	L	104	116	30-28
Feb. 18	at San Diego	L	101	116	30-29
Feb. 20	at Cleveland	W	119	109	31-29
Feb. 21	PORTLAND	W	106	83	32-39
Feb. 24	PHOENIX	W	110	85	33-29
Feb. 27	HOUSTON	W	125	111	34-29
Mar. 1	GOLDEN STATE	W	104	86	35-29
Mar. 3	CHICAGO	W	119	101	36-29
Mar. 6	PHILADELPHIA	W	94	91	37-29
Mar. 7	KANSAS CITY (#)	W	122	120	38-29
Mar. 11	SEATTLE (#)	W	113	111	39-29
Mar. 13	at Portland	L	82	103	39-30
Mar. 14	at Golden State	L	98	113	39-31
Mar. 16	at Los Angeles	L	110	111	39-32
Mar. 17	at Denver	L	111	118	39-33
Mar. 20	CLEVELAND	W	115	109	40-33
Mar. 21	DETROIT	W	111	104	41-33
Mar. 23	at San Antonio	W	115	108	42-33
Mar. 24	at Houston	L	116	120	42-34
Mar. 30	at New Jersey	L	106	117	42-35
Mar. 31	at New Orleans	L	107	109	42-36
Apr. 1	NEW JERSEY	W	109	98	43-36
Apr. 4	MILWAUKEE	W	118	109	44-36
Apr. 6	at Detroit	W	112	96	45-36
Apr. 7	WASHINGTON	W	103	102	46-36

ATLANTA YEARLY RESULTS

1979-80 GAME-BY-GAME

Date	Opponent	W-L	Hawks	Opp.	Record
Oct. 12	NEW YORK	W	121	104	1-0
Oct. 13	at Indiana	L	101	115	1-1
Oct. 16	SAN ANTONIO	L	116	118	1-2
Oct. 17	at Washington	L	97	100	1-3
Oct. 18	INDIANA	W	115	85	2-3
Oct. 20	at Houston	L	102	107	2-4
Oct. 23	at Cleveland	W	121	111	3-4
Oct. 24	CLEVELAND	W	128	118	4-4
Oct. 26	at New Jersey	W	94	90	5-4
Oct. 27	BOSTON	L	95	100	5-5
Oct. 31	PHILADELPHIA	W	102	97	6-5
Nov. 2	at Philadelphia	W	85	81	7-5
Nov. 3	NEW JERSEY	W	110	107	8-5
Nov. 6	at New York	W	98	96	9-5
Nov. 7	at Detroit	W	115	107	10-5
Nov. 10	WASHINGTON	W	109	105	11-5
Nov. 13	at New Jersey	L	82	101	11-6
Nov. 14	UTAH	W	108	97	12-6
Nov. 17	HOUSTON	L	100	102	12-7
Nov. 20	DETROIT	W	109	105	13-7
Nov. 21	at Milwaukee	L	93	96	13-8
Nov. 23	at Chicago	L	98	103	13-9
Nov. 24	BOSTON	L	101	106	13-10
Nov. 27	at San Antonio	W	143	120	14-10
Nov. 28	PORTLAND	W	106	99	15-10
Nov. 30	at Houston	L	95	106	15-11
Dec. 1	SAN DIEGO	W	106	96	16-11
Dec. 2	at Cleveland	L	108	126	16-12
Dec. 5	at Boston	W	120	92	17-12
Dec. 8	at Washington	L	95	96	17-13
Dec. 9	at New Jersey	W	122	85	18-13
Dec. 12	NEW YORK	W	114	102	19-13
Dec. 14	at Philadelphia	W	103	98	20-13
Dec. 15	PHILADELPHIA	W	112	96	21-13
Dec. 18	at New York	L	99	101	21-14
Dec. 19	LOS ANGELES	W	119	112	22-14
Dec. 20	at Detroit	W	122	103	23-14
Dec. 27	HOUSTON	L	112	110	24-15
Dec. 29	DETROIT	W	115	104	25-15
Jan. 3	NEW JERSEY	L	119	126	25-16
Jan. 5	KANSAS CITY	L	107	112	25-17
Jan. 9	CLEVELAND	W	111	107	26-17
Jan. 11	at Boston	L	93	108	26-18
Jan. 12	SAN ANTONIO	W	120	101	27-18
Jan. 13	at San Antonio	W	107	104	28-18
Jan. 16	at San Diego	L	108	111	28-19
Jan. 17	at Phoenix	L	99	101	28-20
Jan. 18	at Los Angeles	L	102	108	28-21
Jan. 22	at Kansas City	L	89	101	28-22
Jan. 23	SEATTLE	L	96	98	28-23
Jan. 26	CHICAGO	W	109	104	29-23
Jan. 27	at San Antonio	W	118	111	30-23
Jan. 29	WASHINGTON	W	98	82	31-23
Jan. 31	GOLDEN STATE (#)	W	111	107	32-23
Feb. 7	at Utah	W	92	90	33-23
Feb. 10	at Golden State (#)	W	98	96	34-23
Feb. 12	at Portland	W	95	89	35-23
Feb. 13	at Seattle	L	86	93	35-24
Feb. 15	at Denver	L	98	111	35-25
Feb. 17	at Detroit	W	108	99	36-35
Feb. 20	MILWAUKEE	W	106	103	37-25
Feb. 22	PHOENIX	W	111	104	38-25
Feb. 26	at Boston	L	97	108	38-26
Feb. 27	INDIANA	W	116	111	39-26
Feb. 29	CLEVELAND (#)	W	111	102	40-26
Mar. 2	DENVER	W	100	93	41-26
Mar. 4	HOUSTON	L	83	93	41-27
Mar. 7	at Indiana	W	99	94	42-27
Mar. 8	at Houston	W	97	79	43-27
Mar. 9	NEW YORK	W	98	92	44-27
Mar. 11	PHILADELPHIA (#)	L	97	102	44-28
Mar. 14	BOSTON	W	88	87	45-28
Mar. 16	INDIANA	W	95	90	46-28
Mar. 18	at New York	L	110	111	46-29
Mar. 19	WASHINGTON	W	109	93	47-29
Mar. 21	DETROIT	W	108	95	48-29
Mar. 23	SAN ANTONIO	W	103	95	49-29
Mar. 26	at Philadelphia	L	81	84	49-30
Mar. 27	NEW JERSEY	W	117	100	50-30
Mar. 28	at Washington	L	80	100	50-31
Mar. 30	at Cleveland	L	102	111	50-32

1980-81 GAME-BY-GAME

Date	Opponent	W-L	Hawks	Opp.	Record
Oct. 11	CHICAGO	W	101	93	1-0
Oct. 14	BOSTON	W	122	116	2-0
Oct. 17	NEW YORK	W	113	101	3-0
Oct. 18	at Detroit (#)	W	125	123	4-0
Oct. 21	INDIANA	L	116	121	4-1
Oct. 24	at Indiana	L	97	104	4-2
Oct. 25	PHILADELPHIA	L	100	113	4-3
Oct. 28	KANSAS CITY	W	119	109	5-3
Oct. 30	at New York (#)	L	115	116	5-4
Oct. 31	at Philadelphia	L	96	107	5-5
Nov. 1	MILWAUKEE	L	93	97	5-6
Nov. 4	at Washington	L	98	122	5-7
Nov. 5	at Boston	L	87	104	5-8
Nov. 7	at Chicago	L	100	103	5-9
Nov. 8	at New Jersey	L	111	115	5-10
Nov. 11	LOS ANGELES	L	97	126	5-11
Nov. 13	at Cleveland	L	111	114	5-12
Nov. 15	WASHINGTON	L	88	100	5-13
Nov. 18	SAN ANTONIO	W	97	93	6-13
Nov. 22	UTAH	W	99	93	7-13
Nov. 25	PORTLAND	W	112	108	8-13
Nov. 26	at Indiana	L	89	110	8-14
Nov. 28	at Milwaukee (#)	L	108	113	8-15
Nov. 29	DETROIT	L	95	98	8-16
Dec. 2	PHILADELPHIA (#)	W	112	108	9-16
Dec. 3	at Boston	L	101	106	9-17
Dec. 5	at Philadelphia	L	100	104	9-18
Dec. 6	DALLAS	W	110	104	10-18
Dec. 9	SAN DIEGO	W	114	87	11-18
Dec. 10	at Detroit	W	100	92	12-18
Dec. 13	MILWAUKEE	W	122	119	13-18
Dec. 16	NEW JERSEY	W	131	114	14-18
Dec. 18	at Utah	W	109	97	15-18
Dec. 19	at Seattle	L	92	95	15-19
Dec. 20	at Portland (#)	L	119	122	15-20
Dec. 23	WASHINGTON	W	100	83	16-20
Dec. 26	at New Jersey	W	108	95	17-20
Dec. 27	BOSTON	L	107	112	17-21
Dec. 30	DETROIT	W	96	89	18-21
Jan. 2	INDIANA	L	106	109	18-22
Jan. 3	at New York	L	95	131	18-23
Jan. 6	PHOENIX	L	106	113	18-24
Jan. 8	at Milwaukee	L	95	98	18-25
Jan. 9	CLEVELAND (#)	L	107	108	18-26
Jan. 13	at Denver	L	132	135	18-27
Jan. 14	at San Diego	L	85	106	18-28
Jan. 16	at Golden State	W	111	110	19-28
Jan. 18	at Phoenix	L	86	120	19-29
Jan. 21	at Los Angeles	L	106	116	19-30
Jan. 23	CLEVELAND	L	98	106	19-31
Jan. 24	CHICAGO	L	102	104	19-32
Jan. 27	WASHINGTON	L	104	105	19-33
Jan. 29	NEW YORK	L	111	114	19-34
Feb. 3	PHILADELPHIA	L	93	97	19-35
Feb. 6	at Dallas	W	100	98	20-35
Feb. 7	at Houston	L	81	87	20-36
Feb. 10	GOLDEN STATE	W	110	100	21-36
Feb. 12	at San Antonio	L	109	110	21-37
Feb. 13	at Kansas City	L	106	118	21-38
Feb. 15	at Philadelphia	L	98	116	21-39
Feb. 18	at Indiana	W	99	96	22-39
Feb. 21	at Cleveland	W	118	105	23-39
Feb. 22	at Chicago	W	121	116	24-39
Feb. 24	NEW YORK (#)	L	117	120	24-40
Feb. 27	BOSTON	L	102	130	24-41
Mar. 1	SEATTLE	W	108	102	25-41
Mar. 3	at New York	W	100	93	26-41
Mar. 5	at Milwaukee	L	91	107	26-42
Mar. 6	NEW JERSEY	W	109	106	27-42
Mar. 7	HOUSTON	W	114	108	28-42
Mar. 10	CHICAGO	L	116	118	28-43
Mar. 11	at Detroit	L	97	100	28-44
Mar. 13	DENVER	W	119	117	29-44
Mar. 14	CLEVELAND	L	110	112	29-45
Mar. 17	at Cleveland	L	107	122	29-46
Mar. 18	at Boston	W	108	97	30-46
Mar. 20	at New Jersey	L	96	108	30-47
Mar. 22	at Washington	L	101	121	30-48
Mar. 24	DETROIT	W	96	91	31-48
Mar. 26	INDIANA	L	115	107	31-49
Mar. 27	at Chicago	L	108	83	31-50
Mar. 29	MILWAUKEE (#)	L	128	132	31-51

ATLANTA YEARLY RESULTS

1981-82 GAME-BY-GAME

Date	Opponent	W-L	Hawks	Opp.	Record
Oct. 31	PHILADELPHIA	L	106	108	0-1
Nov. 3	at Chicago	L	96	104	0-2
Nov. 4	at New Jersey	W	95	86	1-2
Nov. 6	at Philadelphia	W	106	99	2-2
Nov. 10	MILWAUKEE	W	94	83	3-2
Nov. 12	WASHINGTON	L	87	95	3-3
Nov. 14	DETROIT	L	104	117	3-4
Nov. 18	PHOENIX	W	102	97	4-4
Nov. 19	at New York	W	89	84	5-4
Nov. 21	INDIANA	W	107	100	6-4
Nov. 24	CLEVELAND (#)	W	94	92	7-4
Nov. 27	at Detroit (#)	W	114	112	8-4
Nov. 28	BOSTON	L	90	98	8-5
Dec. 1	PHILADELPHIA	L	98	107	8-6
Dec. 4	at Milwaukee	L	80	97	8-7
Dec. 5	SEATTLE	L	85	92	8-8
Dec. 8	NEW JERSEY	L	88	98	8-9
Dec. 9	at Cleveland (#)	L	108	112	8-10
Dec. 11	at Boston	L	86	94	8-11
Dec. 12	BOSTON	W	108	97	9-11
Dec. 15	NEW YORK	W	111	98	10-11
Dec. 17	at Denver	L	103	138	10-12
Dec. 19	at Golden State	L	109	126	10-13
Dec. 20	at Los Angeles	L	94	112	10-14
Dec. 22	at Indiana	L	88	92	10-15
Dec. 26	at San Antonio	W	105	97	11-15
Dec. 29	at Houston	W	102	93	12-15
Dec. 30	SAN DIEGO	L	91	94	12-16
Jan. 2	NEW JERSEY	W	97	95	13-16
Jan. 5	CLEVELAND	W	113	103	14-16
Jan. 8	at Milwaukee	W	90	88	15-16
Jan. 9	NEW YORK	W	102	89	16-16
Jan. 13	at Boston	L	95	116	16-17
Jan. 15	at Philadelphia	W	96	90	17-17
Jan. 17	at Washington	L	78	96	17-18
Jan. 19	PORTLAND	W	112	101	18-18
Jan. 21	at New York	L	101	104	18-19
Jan. 22	SAN ANTONIO	L	107	115	18-20
Jan. 23	at Cleveland	W	109	99	19-20
Jan. 26	DALLAS	L	88	90	19-21
Jan. 27	at Detroit	L	107	108	19-22
Feb. 2	DETROIT	L	105	106	19-23
Feb. 3	at New Jersey	L	103	112	19-24
Feb. 6	CLEVELAND	L	87	88	19-25
Feb. 9	LOS ANGELES	L	117	130	19-26
Feb. 10	at Chicago	L	73	91	19-27
Feb. 12	at Phoenix	L	90	94	19-28
Feb. 16	at San Diego	W	102	91	20-28
Feb. 17	at Utah	W	117	109	21-28
Feb. 19	at Seattle (#4)	W	127	122	22-28
Feb. 21	at Portland	W	109	97	23-28
Feb. 23	KANSAS CITY	W	103	94	24-28
Feb. 26	CHICAGO (#)	L	110	116	24-29
Feb. 28	GOLDEN STATE	L	77	105	24-30
Mar. 3	MILWAUKEE	L	87	96	24-31
Mar. 5	at Philadelphia	L	80	89	24-32
Mar. 6	NEW JERSEY	W	112	92	25-32
Mar. 8	MILWAUKEE	W	98	95	26-32
Mar. 9	DENVER	W	120	106	27-32
Mar. 11	UTAH	W	107	91	28-32
Mar. 13	INDIANA	W	110	90	29-32
Mar. 14	at Washington	L	85	92	29-33
Mar. 17	at Boston	L	109	113	29-34
Mar. 18	HOUSTON	W	95	94	30-34
Mar. 20	at New York	W	104	98	31-34
Mar. 21	DETROIT	W	119	111	32-34
Mar. 23	WASHINGTON	W	107	87	33-34
Mar. 24	at Kansas City	L	106	110	33-35
Mar. 26	at Indiana	W	100	87	34-35
Mar. 27	at Dallas	W	96	85	35-35
Mar. 30	at Chicago	W	107	92	36-35
Apr. 1	at Milwaukee	L	113	117	36-36
Apr. 2	BOSTON	L	107	110	36-37
Apr. 3	WASHINGTON	W	106	101	37-37
Apr. 6	NEW YORK	W	106	104	38-37
Apr. 7	at Detroit	L	115	120	38-38
Apr. 9	PHILADELPHIA	W	103	88	39-38
Apr. 11	CHICAGO	W	108	89	40-38
Apr. 13	at Cleveland	W	119	111	41-38
Apr. 15	at Indiana	L	102	108	41-39
Apr. 16	INDIANA	W	109	91	42-39
Apr. 18	at Washington	L	96	99	42-40

1982-83 GAME-BY-GAME

Date	Opponent	W-L	Hawks	Opp.	Record
Oct. 29	at Detroit	L	86	94	0-1
Oct. 30	BOSTON	L	97	112	0-2
Nov. 2	WASHINGTON	W	105	88	1-2
Nov. 4	MILWAUKEE	L	100	104	1-3
Nov. 6	DETROIT	W	95	93	2-3
Nov. 9	at Denver	W	106	105	3-3
Nov. 12	at Utah	W	106	98	4-3
Nov. 13	at Golden State	L	101	114	4-4
Nov. 16	at Portland	L	87	106	4-5
Nov. 17	at Seattle	L	97	119	4-6
Nov. 20	at Phoenix	L	80	91	4-7
Nov. 23	CHICAGO	W	132	102	5-7
Nov. 27	INDIANA	W	117	98	6-7
Nov. 30	PHILADELPHIA	W	111	97	7-7
Dec. 1	at Boston	L	97	122	7-8
Dec. 3	NEW JERSEY	L	99	107	7-9
Dec. 4	at New York	W	80	79	8-9
Dec. 7	at Cleveland	W	102	90	9-9
Dec. 8	at Philadelphia	L	85	132	9-10
Dec. 10	MILWAUKEE	L	83	104	9-11
Dec. 11	at Chicago	W	117	107	10-11
Dec. 15	at Indiana	W	107	101	11-11
Dec. 16	CLEVELAND	W	106	97	12-11
Dec. 18	BOSTON (#)	L	103	107	12-12
Dec. 21	at Chicago (#2)	L	116	124	12-13
Dec. 23	at Milwaukee	L	90	101	12-14
Dec. 25	at Washington	W	97	91	13-14
Dec. 28	SAN DIEGO	W	123	113	14-14
Dec. 29	at New Jersey	L	99	104	14-15
Jan. 2	KANSAS CITY	L	104	108	14-16
Jan. 4	SAN ANTONIO	L	95	104	14-17
Jan. 6	at New York	W	99	98	15-17
Jan. 7	DALLAS	W	110	102	16-17
Jan. 8	CHICAGO	W	109	89	17-17
Jan. 11	PHILADELPHIA	L	99	109	17-18
Jan. 14	NEW YORK	W	88	80	18-18
Jan. 15	LOS ANGELES	L	101	120	18-19
Jan. 17	at New Jersey	W	102	96	19-19
Jan. 19	SEATTLE	W	116	111	20-19
Jan. 22	at Detroit	L	109	111	20-20
Jan. 24	DETROIT	L	108	112	20-21
Jan. 25	PHOENIX	W	96	94	21-21
Jan. 27	at San Diego	L	100	110	21-22
Jan. 28	at Los Angeles	L	85	109	21-23
Feb. 1	CLEVELAND	W	93	84	22-23
Feb. 3	DENVER	L	112	126	22-24
Feb. 4	at Cleveland	W	92	81	23-24
Feb. 6	at Boston	L	116	111	24-24
Feb. 8	NEW JERSEY	L	109	115	24-25
Feb. 9	at Philadelphia	L	93	106	24-26
Feb. 15	at Houston	W	101	91	25-26
Feb. 19	at Dallas	L	100	122	25-27
Feb. 20	at San Antonio	L	100	103	25-28
Feb. 22	GOLDEN STATE	L	97	109	25-29
Feb. 24	DETROIT	W	116	107	26-29
Feb. 26	NEW JERSEY	W	95	88	27-29
Feb. 27	at Indiana	W	125	107	28-29
Mar. 1	INDIANA	W	109	106	29-29
Mar. 3	WASHINGTON	W	91	89	30-29
Mar. 4	HOUSTON	W	115	87	31-29
Mar. 6	at Washington	L	91	102	31-30
Mar. 8	PORTLAND	W	110	93	32-30
Mar. 9	at Milwaukee	L	100	109	32-31
Mar. 12	at Detroit	W	120	119	33-31
Mar. 15	at New York	L	97	119	33-32
Mar. 16	WASHINGTON (#)	W	94	81	34-32
Mar. 18	at Cleveland	W	97	73	35-32
Mar. 19	UTAH	W	99	94	36-32
Mar. 22	at Indiana	W	111	102	37-32
Mar. 23	at Boston	L	102	114	37-33
Mar. 25	NEW YORK	L	87	104	37-34
Mar. 26	at New Jersey	L	81	102	37-35
Mar. 29	CLEVELAND	W	95	82	38-35
Mar. 30	at Philadelphia	L	113	120	38-36
Apr. 1	at Chicago	W	108	107	39-36
Apr. 2	INDIANA	W	109	99	40-36
Apr. 5	BOSTON	L	95	117	40-37
Apr. 8	CHICAGO	W	138	101	41-37
Apr. 9	at Washington	L	78	100	41-38
Apr. 12	PHILADELPHIA	W	102	97	42-38
Apr. 13	at Kansas City	L	103	114	42-39
Apr. 16	MILWAUKEE	W	96	79	43-39

ATLANTA YEARLY RESULTS

1983-84 GAME-BY-GAME

Date	Opponent	W-L	Hawks	Opp.	Record
Oct. 28	at New Jersey	L	108	126	0-1
Oct. 29	DETROIT	W	117	115	1-1
Nov. 1	WASHINGTON	W	95	92	2-1
Nov. 4	CHICAGO	W	103	90	3-1
Nov. 6	at Milwaukee	L	84	97	3-2
Nov. 8	at Golden State	L	90	97	3-3
Nov. 11	at Seattle	L	93	104	3-4
Nov. 13	at Portland	L	105	135	3-5
Nov. 15	SAN DIEGO	W	107	102	4-5
Nov. 17	PHILADELPHIA	W	99	94	5-5
Nov. 19	SEATTLE	W	104	92	6-5
Nov. 22	INDIANA	W	104	93	7-5
Nov. 25	at Boston	L	102	109	7-6
Nov. 26	HOUSTON	W	115	109	8-6
Nov. 29	DENVER	L	96	105	8-7
Nov. 30	at Philadelphia	L	110	122	8-8
Dec. 2	at Detroit	L	92	128	8-9
Dec. 3	CLEVELAND	W	102	91	9-9
Dec. 6	PHOENIX	W	95	88	10-9
Dec. 7	at Cleveland	L	92	106	10-10
Dec. 9	at Indiana	L	104	110	10-11
Dec. 10	BOSTON	L	87	104	10-12
Dec. 13	at Washington	W	94	89	11-12
Dec. 14	WASHINGTON	L	96	99	11-13
Dec. 17	SAN ANTONIO	W	113	108	12-13
Dec. 20	NEW JERSEY	W	98	87	13-13
Dec. 21	at Boston	L	96	107	13-14
Dec. 23	NEW YORK (#)	W	114	113	14-14
Dec. 27	DALLAS	W	112	109	15-14
Dec. 29	at Cleveland	L	77	88	15-15
Dec. 30	CLEVELAND	W	109	98	16-15
Jan. 2	at Indiana	L	86	96	16-16
Jan. 4	NEW JERSEY	L	88	91	16-17
Jan. 6	MILWAUKEE	W	91	87	17-17
Jan. 7	at New Jersey	L	104	108	17-18
Jan. 10	GOLDEN STATE	W	103	101	18-18
Jan. 12	at Washington	W	106	91	19-18
Jan. 13	INDIANA	W	117	108	20-18
Jan. 17	UTAH	W	112	106	21-18
Jan. 18	at Milwaukee	L	90	99	21-19
Jan. 20	at Detroit	L	94	116	21-20
Jan. 21	at New York	W	97	95	22-20
Jan. 23	at Chicago	W	100	93	23-20
Jan. 25	MILWAUKEE	W	109	105	24-20
Jan. 31	at Washington	L	94	118	24-21
Feb. 1	CHICAGO	W	116	103	25-21
Feb. 3	at Philadelphia	W	99	88	26-21
Feb. 4	PHILADELPHIA	W	102	97	27-21
Feb. 7	NEW JERSEY	W	109	102	28-21
Feb. 9	at Phoenix	L	105	118	28-22
Feb. 10	at San Diego	L	101	113	28-23
Feb. 12	at Los Angeles	L	87	108	28-24
Feb. 14	at Utah	L	98	100	28-25
Feb. 16	at Denver	L	102	117	28-26
Feb. 18	at Kansas City	L	106	111	28-27
Feb. 21	CLEVELAND	W	102	84	29-27
Feb. 24	NEW YORK (#)	W	105	104	30-27
Feb. 25	CHICAGO	W	122	87	31-27
Feb. 27	at New York	L	92	96	31-28
Feb. 28	DETROIT	L	96	101	31-29
Mar. 2	LOS ANGELES	L	94	98	31-30
Mar. 3	at Chicago	L	98	102	31-31
Mar. 6	MILWAUKEE (#)	L	104	109	31-32
Mar. 7	at Detroit	L	93	107	31-33
Mar. 9	PORTLAND	L	101	104	31-34
Mar. 11	at Milwaukee	W	108	94	32-34
Mar. 13	at Cleveland	L	83	92	32-35
Mar. 14	KANSAS CITY	L	93	101	32-36
Mar. 16	at Philadelphia	W	105	102	33-36
Mar. 17	BOSTON	L	88	103	33-37
Mar. 20	at San Antonio (#3)	L	132	135	33-38
Mar. 21	at Dallas	L	101	102	33-39
Mar. 24	at Houston	L	102	103	33-40
Mar. 27	PHILADELPHIA	W	97	78	34-40
Mar. 30	at Boston	L	96	105	34-41
Mar. 31	NEW YORK	W	109	106	35-41
Apr. 4	WASHINGTON	W	99	92	36-41
Apr. 6	at Chicago	L	103	111	36-42
Apr. 7	INDIANA	W	122	103	37-42
Apr. 11	at Indiana	W	114	111	38-42
Apr. 13	at New Jersey	W	118	112	39-42
Apr. 14	DETROIT	W	115	107	40-42

1984-85 GAME-BY-GAME

(*) played in New Orleans

Date	Opponent	W-L	Hawks	Opp.	Record
Oct. 26	at New Jersey	W	119	104	1-0
Oct. 27	PHILADELPHIA	L	108	111	1-1
Oct. 30	at Washington	L	104	119	1-2
Nov. 1	DETROIT	L	114	118	1-3
Nov. 3	WASHINGTON	W	127	107	2-3
Nov. 7	at Milwaukee	L	99	103	2-4
Nov. 8	at Dallas (#)	L	105	112	2-5
Nov. 10	at Phoenix	W	114	107	3-5
Nov. 13	MILWAUKEE	L	99	110	3-6
Nov. 15	CLEVELAND	L	99	102	3-7
Nov. 17	INDIANA	W	118	108	4-7
Nov. 21	UTAH (*)	W	122	90	5-7
Nov. 24	NEW JERSEY	W	101	99	6-7
Nov. 25	at Cleveland	L	111	118	6-8
Nov. 27	at New York	L	96	97	6-9
Nov. 28	MILWAUKEE (*)	W	95	83	7-9
Nov. 30	HOUSTON	L	102	116	7-10
Dec. 4	at San Antonio	L	106	114	7-11
Dec. 5	at Kansas City	L	100	121	7-12
Dec. 7	L.A. CLIPPERS	W	101	89	8-12
Dec. 9	at Boston	L	127	128	8-13
Dec. 10	at Indiana	W	104	98	9-13
Dec. 12	CLEVELAND (*)	W	116	99	10-13
Dec. 13	at Houston	L	93	96	10-14
Dec. 15	BOSTON	L	94	101	10-15
Dec. 18	L.A. LAKERS	L	116	117	10-16
Dec. 20	CHICAGO (#2) (*)	L	129	132	10-17
Dec. 22	WASHINGTON	W	119	101	11-17
Dec. 25	at Cleveland	L	106	109	11-18
Dec. 26	NEW YORK (#)	W	117	105	12-18
Dec. 28	at Washington	L	111	125	12-19
Dec. 29	at Chicago	W	104	101	13-19
Jan. 2	CHICAGO	W	121	107	14-19
Jan. 4	at Detroit	L	111	134	14-20
Jan. 5	NEW JERSEY	W	124	114	15-20
Jan. 11	at New Jersey	L	103	122	15-21
Jan. 12	BOSTON	L	111	119	15-22
Jan. 15	at Indiana	W	120	113	16-22
Jan. 16	at Philadelphia	L	99	122	16-23
Jan. 18	SEATTLE	W	104	90	17-23
Jan. 19	at New York	L	86	88	17-24
Jan. 22	DETROIT (*)	L	113	130	17-25
Jan. 23	PHOENIX	W	101	100	18-25
Jan. 26	at Chicago	L	104	117	18-26
Jan. 29	INDIANA (*)	W	115	106	19-26
Feb. 1	CLEVELAND	W	126	108	20-26
Feb. 2	at Detroit (#)	L	102	110	20-27
Feb. 4	at Philadelphia	L	92	106	20-28
Feb. 5	DALLAS (*)	L	103	112	20-29
Feb. 7	at Milwaukee (#)	W	94	91	21-29
Feb. 12	at Denver	L	107	131	21-30
Feb. 13	at Utah	W	94	88	22-30
Feb. 15	at L.A. Lakers	L	111	120	22-31
Feb. 17	at L.A. Clippers	W	91	90	23-31
Feb. 19	GOLDEN STATE	W	107	104	24-31
Feb. 22	New York	L	105	113	24-32
Feb. 26	DENVER	L	94	106	24-33
Feb. 27	at New Jersey	L	91	114	24-34
Mar. 1	at Boston	W	114	105	25-34
Mar. 2	SAN ANTONIO	L	92	105	25-35
Mar. 5	PORTLAND (*)	L	91	100	25-36
Mar. 6	at Philadelphia	L	86	96	25-37
Mar. 9	DETROIT	L	113	115	25-38
Mar. 11	MILWAUKEE	L	115	121	25-39
Mar. 12	BOSTON (*)	L	115	126	25-40
Mar. 14	at Golden State	W	120	112	26-40
Mar. 16	at Seattle	L	99	108	26-41
Mar. 17	at Portland	L	101	114	26-42
Mar. 19	WASHINGTON (*)	W	103	97	27-42
Mar. 22	KANSAS CITY	L	102	121	27-43
Mar. 23	at Cleveland (#)	W	91	86	28-43
Mar. 26	NEW JERSEY (*) (#)	L	108	109	28-44
Mar. 27	at Indiana	W	125	99	29-44
Mar. 30	at Milwaukee	L	95	106	29-45
Apr. 1	at Detroit	W	114	100	30-45
Apr. 2	PHILADELPHIA	L	91	102	30-46
Apr. 4	at New York	W	100	79	31-46
Apr. 6	CHICAGO	L	114	117	31-47
Apr. 9	at Washington	L	110	130	31-48
Apr. 10	NEW YORK	W	98	94	32-48
Apr. 12	at Chicago	W	119	108	33-48
Apr. 13	INDIANA	W	122	117	34-48

ATLANTA YEARLY RESULTS

1985-86 GAME-BY-GAME

Date	Opponent	W-L	Score Hawks	Opp.	Record
Oct. 25	WASHINGTON	L	91	100	0-1
Oct. 26	at Milwaukee	L	91	117	0-2
Oct. 29	NEW YORK	W	102	87	1-2
Nov. 1	at Boston	L	105	109	1-3
Nov. 2	PHILADELPHIA (#)	W	114	113	2-3
Nov. 5	at Denver	L	113	128	2-4
Nov. 6	at Phoenix	W	114	106	3-4
Nov. 8	at Golden State	L	119	130	3-5
Nov. 9	at L.A. Clippers	W	97	94	4-5
Nov. 13	PHOENIX	W	108	101	5-5
Nov. 15	DETROIT	W	122	118	6-5
Nov. 16	at New York	L	96	103	6-6
Nov. 20	CHICAGO	W	116	101	7-6
Nov. 23	UTAH	L	106	116	7-7
Nov. 24	at Cleveland	L	90	98	7-8
Nov. 26	NEW YORK	W	104	94	8-8
Nov. 27	at Milwaukee	L	96	114	8-9
Nov. 29	at New Jersey	L	97	107	8-10
Nov. 30	BOSTON	L	97	102	8-11
Dec. 4	PORTLAND	W	109	98	9-11
Dec. 6	MILWAUKEE	W	94	93	10-11
Dec. 10	at Boston	L	110	114	10-12
Dec. 11	SEATTLE	W	105	97	11-12
Dec. 13	at Indiana	L	89	109	11-13
Dec. 14	PHILADELPHIA	W	107	103	12-13
Dec. 17	NEW JERSEY	W	104	103	13-13
Dec. 19	DALLAS	L	108	120	13-14
Dec. 21	HOUSTON	W	123	122	14-14
Dec. 27	at Washington	L	109	111	14-15
Dec. 28	at New York	W	100	80	15-15
Jan. 3	DETROIT	W	111	101	16-15
Jan. 4	at Chicago	W	111	100	17-15
Jan. 7	L.A. CLIPPERS	W	117	103	18-15
Jan. 9	at Detroit	W	110	99	19-15
Jan. 10	at Boston	L	108	115	19-16
Jan. 14	SACRAMENTO	W	115	104	20-16
Jan. 16	CLEVELAND	W	116	99	21-16
Jan. 18	BOSTON (#)	L	122	125	21-17
Jan. 20	MILWAUKEE	W	101	98	22-17
Jan. 22	GOLDEN STATE	W	131	100	23-17
Jan. 24	NEW YORK	W	117	100	24-17
Jan. 25	at Washington	L	103	111	24-18
Jan. 28	INDIANA	W	123	92	25-18
Jan. 29	at Detroit	L	94	107	25-19
Jan. 31	DETROIT	W	116	103	26-19
Feb. 1	at New Jersey	L	100	108	26-20
Feb. 4	at Cleveland	W	105	104	27-20
Feb. 6	at Indiana	W	100	85	28-20
Feb. 11	at Houston	L	100	113	28-21
Feb. 13	at Sacramento	W	123	114	29-21
Feb. 14	at L.A. Lakers	L	117	141	29-22
Feb. 16	at Portland	W	110	101	30-22
Feb. 17	at Seattle	L	87	100	30-23
Feb. 19	at Utah (#)	L	105	109	30-24
Feb. 21	INDIANA	W	106	98	31-24
Feb. 22	NEW JERSEY	W	112	83	32-24
Feb. 24	L.A. LAKERS	W	102	93	33-24
Feb. 26	CLEVELAND	W	129	109	34-24
Feb. 28	at Detroit	L	103	115	34-25
Mar. 1	SAN ANTONIO	W	116	108	35-25
Mar. 4	PHILADELPHIA	W	128	121	36-25
Mar. 5	at Philadelphia (#)	W	122	114	37-25
Mar. 7	at Chicago	W	112	108	38-25
Mar. 8	MILWAUKEE	W	111	109	39-25
Mar. 11	DENVER	W	128	116	40-25
Mar. 12	at New Jersey	W	113	97	41-25
Mar. 14	BOSTON	L	114	121	41-26
Mar. 15	at New York	W	106	101	42-26
Mar. 17	CHICAGO	W	106	96	43-26
Mar. 19	at San Antonio	L	112	115	43-27
Mar. 21	at Dallas	W	107	103	44-27
Mar. 22	at Milwaukee	L	98	113	44-28
Mar. 25	at Cleveland	W	97	91	45-28
Mar. 26	at Philadelphia	L	103	112	45-29
Mar. 28	at Indiana	W	100	92	46-29
Mar. 29	CLEVELAND	L	105	123	46-30
Apr. 1	WASHINGTON	W	107	91	47-30
Apr. 4	at Washington (#)	L	129	135	47-31
Apr. 5	at Chicago	L	97	102	47-32
Apr. 8	CHICAGO	W	131	118	48-32
Apr. 10	NEW JERSEY	W	126	117	49-32
Apr. 12	INDIANA	W	108	91	50-32

1986-87 GAME-BY-GAME

Date	Opponent	W-L	Score Hawks	Opp.	Record
Nov. 1	NEW JERSEY	W	131	111	1-0
Nov. 2	at Philadelphia	W	122	113	2-0
Nov. 4	MILWAUKEE	W	107	98	3-0
Nov. 7	PHOENIX	W	106	86	4-0
Nov. 8	WASHINGTON	W	110	91	5-0
Nov. 11	at Chicago	L	110	112	5-1
Nov. 14	at Detroit	W	105	100	6-1
Nov. 15	at New Jersey	W	109	90	7-1
Nov. 19	at Boston	L	107	111	7-2
Nov. 20	CLEVELAND	W	108	89	8-2
Nov. 22	BOSTON	W	97	96	9-2
Nov. 25	at L.A. Lakers	W	113	107	10-2
Nov. 26	at Phoenix	L	106	120	10-3
Nov. 28	at Utah	W	97	88	11-3
Nov. 30	at Sacramento	W	113	109	12-3
Dec. 2	DENVER	W	116	100	13-3
Dec. 4	at Houston	W	109	93	14-3
Dec. 5	at Indiana	L	113	119	14-4
Dec. 9	at Cleveland	W	122	96	15-4
Dec. 10	CHICAGO	W	123	95	16-4
Dec. 12	SACRAMENTO	W	130	120	17-4
Dec. 13	at New York	W	122	110	18-4
Dec. 16	DETROIT	L	100	111	18-5
Dec. 18	at Milwaukee	L	95	104	18-6
Dec. 20	SAN ANTONIO	W	111	96	19-6
Dec. 27	GOLDEN STATE	W	119	108	20-6
Dec. 29	at Cleveland	L	106	107	20-7
Jan. 2	at Washington	W	118	101	21-7
Jan. 3	NEW YORK	W	114	92	22-7
Jan. 6	at New York	L	86	118	22-8
Jan. 7	PHILADELPHIA	L	102	109	22-9
Jan. 10	CLEVELAND	W	129	104	23-9
Jan. 12	L.A. CLIPPERS	W	125	115	24-9
Jan. 14	at Philadelphia	L	93	96	24-10
Jan. 15	MILWAUKEE	W	130	91	25-10
Jan. 18	at Milwaukee	L	91	100	25-11
Jan. 19	at Detroit	L	98	108	25-12
Jan. 21	L.A. LAKERS	L	109	112	25-13
Jan. 23	at Boston	L	106	126	25-14
Jan. 24	SEATTLE	W	97	87	26-14
Jan. 27	INDIANA	W	114	98	27-14
Jan. 29	at Cleveland	L	91	102	27-15
Jan. 30	NEW YORK	W	106	98	28-15
Feb. 1	HOUSTON	L	104	106	28-16
Feb. 3	BOSTON (#)	W	126	123	29-16
Feb. 10	at Seattle	W	125	113	30-16
Feb. 11	at L.A. Clippers	W	109	82	31-16
Feb. 14	at Golden State	L	96	103	31-17
Feb. 15	at Portland	L	93	98	31-18
Feb. 17	DETROIT	W	107	103	32-18
Feb. 20	INDIANA	L	105	107	32-19
Feb. 21	at Detroit	L	97	102	32-20
Feb. 23	PHILADELPHIA	W	112	103	33-20
Feb. 24	at Chicago	L	103	113	33-21
Feb. 27	BOSTON	W	115	105	34-21
Feb. 28	PORTLAND	W	123	102	35-21
Mar. 2	WASHINGTON	W	121	99	36-21
Mar. 3	at Indiana	W	109	108	37-21
Mar. 6	at New Jersey	W	111	83	38-21
Mar. 7	UTAH	W	122	97	39-21
Mar. 9	CHICAGO	W	108	103	40-21
Mar. 10	at San Antonio (#)	W	113	106	41-21
Mar. 13	at Dallas	W	113	105	42-21
Mar. 15	at Denver	W	104	100	43-21
Mar. 17	WASHINGTON	W	118	98	44-21
Mar. 18	at Philadelphia	L	107	109	44-22
Mar. 20	MILWAUKEE	W	114	97	45-22
Mar. 21	at New York	W	97	85	46-22
Mar. 24	at Washington	W	96	87	47-22
Mar. 26	DALLAS	W	120	112	48-22
Mar. 28	INDIANA	L	114	120	48-23
Apr. 1	at Milwaukee	L	92	104	48-24
Apr. 3	NEW YORK	W	126	89	49-24
Apr. 4	CHICAGO	W	110	97	50-24
Apr. 6	CLEVELAND	W	110	105	51-24
Apr. 8	PHILADELPHIA	W	110	92	52-24
Apr. 10	DETROIT	W	101	99	53-24
Apr. 12	at New Jersey	W	115	88	54-24
Apr. 13	at Indiana	W	102	101	55-24
Apr. 15	NEW JERSEY	W	136	116	56-24
Apr. 16	at Chicago	W	117	114	57-24
Apr. 19	at Boston	L	107	118	57-25

ATLANTA YEARLY RESULTS

1987-88 GAME-BY-GAME

Date	Opponent	W-L	Hawks	Opp.	Record
Nov. 6	WASHINGTON	W	114	97	1-0
Nov. 7	CLEVELAND	W	113	105	2-0
Nov. 10	CHICAGO	L	95	105	2-1
Nov. 11	at New York	W	94	93	3-1
Nov. 14	PHILADELPHIA	W	104	83	4-1
Nov. 15	at Milwaukee	L	103	112	4-2
Nov. 18	GOLDEN STATE	W	95	92	5-2
Nov. 20	at Chicago	L	92	94	5-3
Nov. 21	HOUSTON	W	104	94	6-3
Nov. 25	at Boston	L	102	117	6-4
Nov. 27	at Indiana	L	86	88	6-5
Nov. 28	SAN ANTONIO	W	124	100	7-5
Dec. 1	BOSTON	W	120	106	8-5
Dec. 3	at Washington	W	102	94	9-5
Dec. 4	NEW JERSEY	W	139	102	10-5
Dec. 8	at L.A. Clippers	W	90	79	11-5
Dec. 9	at Phoenix	L	105	117	11-6
Dec. 11	at Golden State	W	109	93	12-6
Dec. 13	at Sacramento	W	106	100	13-6
Dec. 15	INDIANA	W	93	91	14-6
Dec. 18	at Milwaukee	W	94	87	15-6
Dec. 19	UTAH (#)	W	130	124	16-6
Dec. 22	at Houston	L	103	122	16-7
Dec. 25	at Philadelphia	W	106	100	17-7
Dec. 26	NEW YORK	W	125	98	18-7
Dec. 29	at Chicago	W	108	98	19-7
Dec. 30	at Cleveland	W	117	110	20-7
Jan. 3	L.A. CLIPPERS	W	121	84	21-7
Jan. 5	DETROIT	W	81	71	22-7
Jan. 6	at Detroit	L	87	90	22-8
Jan. 8	CLEVELAND	W	101	97	23-8
Jan. 9	DENVER	W	113	105	24-8
Jan. 13	at San Antonio	W	120	110	25-8
Jan. 14	at Denver	L	112	115	25-9
Jan. 16	at Dallas	W	101	98	26-9
Jan. 18	at New York	L	102	110	26-10
Jan. 19	CHICAGO	W	106	94	27-10
Jan. 21	at Cleveland	W	101	93	28-10
Jan. 22	at Boston	L	106	124	28-11
Jan. 24	NEW JERSEY	W	118	111	29-11
Jan. 26	BOSTON	L	97	102	29-12
Jan. 29	at L.A. Lakers	L	107	117	29-13
Jan. 30	at Utah	L	109	115	29-14
Feb. 2	at Portland	L	118	121	29-15
Feb. 4	at Seattle	W	119	109	30-15
Feb. 9	PHILADELPHIA	W	112	110	31-15
Feb. 12	at Detroit	L	92	108	31-16
Feb. 13	WASHINGTON	W	105	103	32-16
Feb. 15	at Chicago	L	107	126	32-17
Feb. 16	SACRAMENTO	L	115	118	32-18
Feb. 19	L.A. LAKERS (#)	L	119	126	32-19
Feb. 21	SEATTLE	W	129	113	33-19
Feb. 23	INDIANA	W	131	111	34-19
Feb. 26	at Indiana	W	116	101	35-19
Feb. 27	PORTLAND	L	120	123	35-20
Mar. 1	DETROIT	L	104	117	35-21
Mar. 5	MILWAUKEE	L	101	104	35-22
Mar. 8	PHOENIX	W	143	113	36-22
Mar. 11	NEW YORK	W	122	115	37-22
Mar. 13	at Boston	L	100	117	37-23
Mar. 15	PHILADELPHIA	W	104	90	38-23
Mar. 18	at New Jersey	W	106	104	39-23
Mar. 19	at New York	L	110	116	39-24
Mar. 21	MILWAUKEE	W	115	105	40-24
Mar. 22	at Milwaukee	L	98	111	40-25
Mar. 24	at Washington	L	91	94	40-26
Mar. 26	CLEVELAND	W	109	102	41-26
Mar. 29	DALLAS	W	120	106	42-26
Mar. 30	at Detroit	W	103	102	43-26
Apr. 1	at Philadelphia	W	105	93	44-26
Apr. 4	at Indiana	W	102	100	45-26
Apr. 5	MILWAUKEE	W	121	110	46-26
Apr. 7	NEW JERSEY	W	120	94	47-26
Apr. 9	DETROIT	L	102	115	47-27
Apr. 11	WASHINGTON	L	85	86	47-28
Apr. 12	at Cleveland	L	103	116	47-29
Apr. 15	at Philadelphia (#)	W	103	101	48-29
Apr. 16	NEW YORK	L	93	95	48-30
Apr. 19	at New Jersey (#)	W	119	109	49-30
Apr. 20	INDIANA	L	98	116	49-31
Apr. 22	BOSTON	W	133	106	50-31
Apr. 23	at Washington	L	96	106	50-32

1988-89 GAME-BY-GAME

Date	Opponent	W-L	Hawks	Opp.	Record
Nov. 4	at New Jersey	W	113	105	1-0
Nov. 5	at Milwaukee	W	107	94	2-0
Nov. 8	INDIANA	W	112	107	3-0
Nov. 9	at Detroit (#)	L	95	101	3-1
Nov. 11	at Philadelphia	L	105	107	3-2
Nov. 12	CHARLOTTE	W	132	111	4-2
Nov. 15	at Cleveland	W	97	95	5-2
Nov. 18	at Chicago (#)	L	112	115	5-3
Nov. 19	GOLDEN STATE	W	111	92	6-3
Nov. 21	at Houston	L	113	117	6-4
Nov. 23	at San Antonio	L	109	119	6-5
Nov. 25	at Dallas	L	95	100	6-6
Nov. 26	BOSTON	W	104	91	7-6
Nov. 29	SAN ANTONIO	W	120	104	8-6
Dec. 1	WASHINGTON	W	127	115	9-6
Dec. 3	PORTLAND	W	115	97	10-6
Dec. 6	SACRAMENTO	W	123	113	11-6
Dec. 7	at Boston	W	106	103	12-6
Dec. 9	DETROIT	L	82	92	12-7
Dec. 10	DENVER	L	130	133	12-8
Dec. 13	at Chicago	W	106	88	13-8
Dec. 14	PHILADELPHIA	W	103	96	14-8
Dec. 16	MILWAUKEE	W	115	112	15-8
Dec. 17	at Cleveland	L	94	120	15-9
Dec. 20	SEATTLE	W	121	118	16-9
Dec. 23	INDIANA	W	131	114	17-9
Dec. 27	NEW YORK	W	128	126	18-9
Dec. 30	at Milwaukee	W	117	113	19-9
Jan. 3	DETROIT	W	123	104	20-9
Jan. 4	at Indiana	L	113	116	20-10
Jan. 6	at Detroit	L	88	111	20-11
Jan. 7	NEW JERSEY	W	103	93	21-11
Jan. 10	CHICAGO	L	101	104	21-12
Jan. 13	at Philadelphia	L	101	114	21-13
Jan. 14	at New York	L	122	132	21-14
Jan. 16	at Washington	W	117	106	22-14
Jan. 17	MILWAUKEE	W	111	98	23-14
Jan. 21	CHARLOTTE	W	137	113	24-14
Jan. 24	CLEVELAND	W	121	105	25-14
Jan. 27	at Seattle	L	112	119	25-15
Jan. 28	at Portland	L	94	110	25-16
Jan. 30	at L.A. Clippers	W	130	101	26-16
Feb. 1	at Utah	W	94	93	27-16
Feb. 2	at Denver	L	103	112	27-17
Feb. 4	at Phoenix (#)	W	118	116	28-17
Feb. 8	NEW YORK	L	101	113	28-18
Feb. 9	at Charlotte	L	108	110	28-19
Feb. 14	at Chicago	W	106	98	29-19
Feb. 15	at New Jersey	W	119	112	30-19
Feb. 17	CLEVELAND	W	108	100	31-19
Feb. 19	at Miami	L	115	124	31-20
Feb. 20	L.A. CLIPPERS	W	114	100	32-20
Feb. 23	INDIANA	W	100	97	33-20
Feb. 25	CHICAGO	W	125	95	34-20
Feb. 27	DALLAS	W	105	83	35-20
Mar. 2	at Boston	L	90	104	35-21
Mar. 3	CHARLOTTE	W	133	109	36-21
Mar. 5	UTAH	L	83	85	36-22
Mar. 7	L.A. LAKERS	L	97	106	36-23
Mar. 8	at Washington	L	111	119	36-24
Mar. 11	MIAMI	W	111	78	37-24
Mar. 14	PHOENIX	L	112	114	37-25
Mar. 16	at Sacramento	W	119	103	38-25
Mar. 17	at Golden State (#)	L	118	127	38-26
Mar. 19	at L.A. Lakers	W	113	111	39-26
Mar. 21	DETROIT	L	95	110	39-27
Mar. 25	at New York	W	115	108	40-27
Mar. 28	at New Jersey	L	108	111	40-28
Mar. 29	WASHINGTON	W	120	102	41-28
Mar. 31	NEW JERSEY	W	116	99	42-28
Apr. 2	at Indiana	W	132	109	43-28
Apr. 4	at Cleveland	L	91	105	43-29
Apr. 5	PHILADELPHIA	W	135	93	44-29
Apr. 7	HOUSTON (#)	W	120	112	45-29
Apr. 9	CHICAGO	W	108	100	46-29
Apr. 10	at Charlotte	W	112	105	47-29
Apr. 13	BOSTON	W	132	118	48-29
Apr. 15	MILWAUKEE	W	125	100	49-29
Apr. 18	at Indiana	W	121	114	50-29
Apr. 19	at Milwaukee	W	100	92	51-29
Apr. 21	CLEVELAND	W	92	89	52-29
Apr. 23	at Detroit	L	81	99	52-30

ATLANTA YEARLY RESULTS

1989-90 GAME-BY-GAME

Date	Opponent	W-L	Score Hawks	Opp.	Record
Nov. 3	INDIANA	L	103	126	0-1
Nov. 7	WASHINGTON	L	114	118	0-2
Nov. 10	at Boston	L	106	117	0-3
Nov. 11	ORLANDO	W	148	109	1-3
Nov. 13	at Orlando	W	112	104	2-3
Nov. 17	at Cleveland (#)	L	125	131	2-4
Nov. 18	GOLDEN STATE	W	112	96	3-4
Nov. 21	at Detroit	W	103	96	4-4
Nov. 22	at Milwaukee	L	100	118	4-5
Nov. 24	at Miami	W	103	87	5-5
Nov. 25	BOSTON	W	108	100	6-5
Nov. 28	at Chicago	L	98	113	6-6
Nov. 29	at Washington	W	111	104	7-6
Dec. 1	UTAH	W	114	103	8-6
Dec. 2	PHILADELPHIA	W	102	92	9-6
Dec. 6	at Orlando	W	118	100	10-6
Dec. 8	PORTLAND	W	127	120	11-6
Dec. 9	MINNESOTA	W	104	91	12-6
Dec. 12	SAN ANTONIO	W	102	94	13-6
Dec. 13	at Philadelphia	L	103	112	13-7
Dec. 15	NEW YORK	L	109	113	13-8
Dec. 19	SACRAMENTO	W	115	112	14-8
Dec. 21	at Miami	W	117	115	15-8
Dec. 22	CHICAGO	L	113	125	15-9
Dec. 25	CLEVELAND	W	115	104	16-9
Dec. 27	at Dallas	L	101	114	16-10
Dec. 30	at Indiana	L	98	105	16-11
Jan. 2	MILWAUKEE	W	113	107	17-11
Jan. 4	at New York	L	95	100	17-12
Jan. 6	NEW JERSEY	W	105	96	18-12
Jan. 7	at New Jersey	L	93	98	18-13
Jan. 10	L.A. CLIPPERS	L	109	115	18-14
Jan. 13	at Seattle	L	106	113	18-15
Jan. 16	at Sacramento	L	91	108	18-16
Jan. 17	at Utah	L	88	95	18-17
Jan. 19	CHICAGO	L	84	92	18-18
Jan. 23	at Charlotte	W	106	101	19-18
Jan. 24	CLEVELAND	W	103	86	20-18
Jan. 27	at Orlando	W	114	96	21-18
Jan. 29	at Chicago	L	111	121	21-19
Jan. 30	DETROIT	L	95	112	21-20
Feb. 1	at Phoenix	L	90	102	21-21
Feb. 2	at L.A. Lakers	L	106	112	21-22
Feb. 4	at Denver	L	113	125	21-23
Feb. 6	at San Antonio	L	94	105	21-24
Feb. 8	at Houston	W	110	108	22-24
Feb. 13	NEW YORK	L	109	114	22-25
Feb. 15	ORLANDO	W	130	123	23-25
Feb. 16	at Cleveland	L	101	109	23-26
Feb. 18	at Minnesota	L	98	108	23-27
Feb. 20	WASHINGTON	L	107	110	23-28
Feb. 21	at Indiana	L	96	123	23-29
Feb. 23	DETROIT	W	112	103	24-29
Feb. 24	HOUSTON	W	104	96	25-29
Feb. 26	MIAMI	W	123	114	26-29
Feb. 28	INDIANA	W	102	99	27-29
Mar. 2	MILWAUKEE	W	132	110	28-29
Mar. 3	at New Jersey	L	109	114	28-30
Mar. 6	PHOENIX	L	111	113	28-31
Mar. 9	SEATTLE	W	107	97	29-31
Mar. 11	L.A. LAKERS	L	115	123	29-32
Mar. 13	BOSTON	L	100	112	29-33
Mar. 16	at Indiana (#)	W	106	104	30-33
Mar. 17	at Washington	W	119	92	31-33
Mar. 19	DALLAS	L	110	117	31-34
Mar. 21	CHICAGO	L	89	99	31-35
Mar. 23	at Boston	L	98	101	31-36
Mar. 24	CHARLOTTE	W	122	109	32-36
Mar. 26	DENVER	W	113	102	33-36
Mar. 29	at Portland	L	106	112	33-37
Mar. 30	at L.A. Clippers	W	122	118	34-37
Apr. 1	at Golden State	W	142	116	35-37
Apr. 4	at Cleveland	L	95	101	35-38
Apr. 5	DETROIT	L	99	104	35-39
Apr. 7	PHILADELPHIA	W	108	112	35-40
Apr. 10	at Philadelphia	W	123	111	36-40
Apr. 11	MILWAUKEE	W	106	94	37-40
Apr. 13	at Detroit	W	115	111	38-40
Apr. 14	at Milwaukee	L	93	109	38-41
Apr. 17	NEW JERSEY	W	118	95	39-41
Apr. 20	at New York	W	126	112	40-41
Apr. 21	MIAMI	W	130	109	41-41

1990-91 GAME-BY-GAME

Date	Opponent	W-L	Score Hawks	Opp.	Record
Nov. 2	ORLANDO	W	115	111	1-0
Nov. 3	INDIANA	W	121	120	2-0
Nov. 6	@Sacramento	W	102	85	3-0
Nov. 9	@Golden State	L	128	143	3-1
Nov. 10	@Clippers	W	112	94	4-1
Nov. 13	CLEVELAND	L	104	121	4-2
Nov. 14	@Philadelphia	L	104	112	4-3
Nov. 16	CHARLOTTE	L	109	119	4-4
Nov. 17	@Detroit	L	83	91	4-5
Nov. 20	@Charlotte	L	121	128	4-6
Nov. 21	@Milwaukee	L	93	105	4-7
Nov. 24	PHILADELPHIA	L	121	124	4-8
Nov. 27	DETROIT	L	97	120	4-9
Nov. 30	CLEVELAND	L	93	101	4-10
Dec. 4	@Houston	W	113	110	5-10
Dec. 5	@San Antonio	W	110	108	6-10
Dec. 7	MILWAUKEE	L	103	104	6-11
Dec. 8	NEW YORK	W	99	86	7-11
Dec. 12	@Miami	W	118	93	8-11
Dec. 13	NEW JERSEY	W	106	97	9-11
Dec. 15	WASHINGTON	W	125	113	10-11
Dec. 17	@Cleveland	W	109	98	11-11
Dec. 20	UTAH	W	105	87	12-11
Dec. 21	@Detroit	L	87	113	12-12
Dec. 23	@Boston	L	104	132	12-13
Dec. 26	@New Jersey	W	113	111	13-13
Dec. 28	BOSTON	W	131	114	14-13
Dec. 29	GOLDEN STATE	W	134	130	15-13
Jan. 02	CLIPPERS	W	120	107	16-13
Jan. 04	INDIANA	W	111	96	17-13
Jan. 05	MINNESOTA (#)	W	117	112	18-13
Jan. 08	SAN ANTONIO	W	109	98	19-13
Jan. 11	@Chicago	L	96	99	19-14
Jan. 12	@New York	L	92	99	19-15
Jan. 14	NEW YORK	W	96	82	20-15
Jan. 15	@Indiana	W	117	106	21-15
Jan. 18	CHICAGO	W	114	105	22-15
Jan. 19	NEW JERSEY	W	114	84	23-15
Jan. 22	MIAMI	W	118	107	24-15
Jan. 23	@Washington	L	99	104	24-16
Jan. 26	@Seattle	L	102	103	24-17
Jan. 28	@Portland	L	111	116	24-18
Jan. 29	@Utah	L	105	116	24-19
Jan. 31	@L.A. Lakers	L	103	116	24-20
Feb. 02	@Denver	L	125	126	24-21
Feb. 05	CLEVELAND	W	118	114	25-21
Feb. 07	CHARLOTTE	W	127	114	26-21
Feb. 12	@Chicago	L	113	122	26-22
Feb. 13	@New Jersey	L	106	140	26-23
Feb. 16	SEATTLE	W	122	113	27-23
Feb. 19	@New York	W	110	102	28-23
Feb. 20	@Detroit	L	89	97	28-24
Feb. 22	L.A. LAKERS	W	111	102	29-24
Feb. 23	DALLAS	W	122	107	30-24
Feb. 25	SACRAMENTO	W	96	88	31-24
Feb. 27	@Philadelphia	L	103	107	31-25
Feb. 28	PORTLAND	W	117	109	32-25
Mar. 03	@Milwaukee	W	115	106	33-25
Mar. 05	DENVER	W	139	127	34-25
Mar. 07	PHOENIX	L	104	106	34-26
Mar. 08	@Miami	W	102	96	35-26
Mar. 10	CHICAGO	L	87	122	35-27
Mar. 12	PHILADEL (#).	L	129	133	35-28
Mar. 15	@Dallas	W	127	117	36-28
Mar. 16	@Phoenix	L	116	128	36-29
Mar. 19	BOSTON	W	104	92	37-29
Mar. 20	@Chicago	L	107	129	37-30
Mar. 22	@Washington	L	116	121	37-31
Mar. 23	MIAMI	W	108	93	38-21
Mar. 26	@Indiana	L	113	123	38-32
Mar. 28	HOUSTON	L	111	112	38-33
Mar. 30	@Milwaukee	L	96	104	38-34
Apr. 04	@Charlotte	L	91	98	38-35
Apr. 06	INDIANA	W	137	110	39-35
Apr. 08	WASHINGTON	W	105	94	40-35
Apr. 09	@Cleveland	W	104	98	41-35
Apr. 11	@Minnesota	L	98	112	41-36
Apr. 13	MILWAUKEE	W	97	91	42-36
Apr. 16	@Orlando	L	106	113	42-37
Apr. 17	CHARLOTTE	L	111	123	42-38
Apr. 19	DETROIT	L	120	126	42-39
Apr. 21	@Boston	W	117	105	43-39

1991-92 Atlanta Hawks Game-By-Game Results

Date	Opponent	W -	L/Score	Home	Date	Opponent	W -	L/Score	Home
11-2	DETROIT		L/ 87- 89	0-1	1-28	PHILADELPHIA	W	/110-109	22-20
11-5	UTAH	W	/ 98- 94	1-1	1-29	At Milwaukee	W	/110-100	23-20
11-6	At Charlotte		L/104-114	1-2	1-31	At Indiana		L/106-115ot	23-21
11-8	AT Boston	W	/ 97- 93	2-2	2/01	DETROIT		L/ 80- 89	23-22
11-9	MIAMI	W	/ 97- 93	3-2	2/03	SEATTLE		L/110-112	23-23
11-12	CHARLOTTE	W	/118-100	4-2	2-06	ORLANDO	W	/123-112	24-23
11-14	At Sacramento		L/ 96- 98	4-3	2-11	CHARLOTTE		L/108-113	24-24
11-15	At Phoenix	W	/119-115	5-3	2-13	At Miami		L/119-121	24-25
11-17	At LA Lakers		L/ 89-111	5-4	2-14	At Orlando	W	/112-107	25-25
11-20	SACRAMENTO	W	/116-104	6-4	2-17	At Washington	W	/117-110	26-25
11-22	At Philadelphia	W	/ 99- 92	7-4	2-19	WASHINGTON		L/102-103ot	26-26
11-23	At Washington		L/115-126	7-5	2-21	CHICAGO		L/ 88-103	26-27
11-26	DETROIT		L/ 93-103	7-6	2-22	NEW JERSEY	W	119-107	27-27
11-27	At Detroit		L/ 91-100	7-7	2-24	DENVER	W	/117- 95	17-11
11-29	SAN ANTONIO		L/ 85- 88	7-8	2-28	BOSTON	W	/102- 90	29-27
11-30	BOSTON	W	/129-102	8-8	3-01	At Milwaukee		L/106-109ot	29-28
12-3	At Dallas	W	/103- 99	4-5	3-04	At Philadelphia		L/102-107	29-29
					3-06	INDIANA		L113-115ot	29-30
12-5	At Houston	W	/109- 97	10-8	3-07	CLEVELAND		L/ 94-110	29-31
12-7	NEW YORK		L/128-137ot2	10-9	3-10	At SanAntonio		L/ 92-103	29-32
12-10	MILWAUKEE	W	/118-104	11-9	3-11	L.A. LAKERS		L/ 98-109	29-33
12-12	At Cleveland		L/107-134	11-10	3-13	PORTLAND		L/ 95-106	29-34
12-14	At Miami		L/101-121	11-11	3-14	MIAMI	W	/115-102	30-34
12-17	INDIANA	W	/117-113	12-11	3-16	At Detroit	W	/ 89-77	31-34
12-20	CLEVELAND		L/ 99-122	12-12	3-18	ORLANDO		L/ 96- 99	31-35
12-21	At Chicago		L/103-117	12-13	3-20	At Charlotte	W	/112-110	32-35
12-23	At New Jersey		L/ 93-105	12-14	3-22	At Cleveland		L/ 80-123	32-36
12-26	CHICAGO		L/111-122	12-15	3-23	GOLDEN STATE	W	/107- 95	34-36
12-28	MINESOTA	W	/125-122ot	13-15	3-26	WASHINGTON	W	/107- 95	34-36
1-02	PHOENIX	W	/123-105	14-15	3-27	At Boston		L/ 93-117	35-36
1-04	L.A. CLIPPERS	W	/ 97- 95	5-15	3-29	At Boston		L/ 93-117	35-37
1-06	HOUSTON	W	/109- 97	16-15	4-01	At Indiana		L/117-137	35-38
1-07	At New York	W	/109- 94	17-15	4-03	At New York		L/ 94-115	35-39
1-09	DALLAS	W	/124-108	18-15	4-04	PHILADELPHIA		L/121-126	35-40
1-11	At Indiana		L/115-138	18-16	4-07	At New Jersey	W	/104- 97	36-40
1-14	MILWAUKEE	W	/ 93- 88	19-16	4-09	At Orlando		L/ 94- 96	36-41
1-16	At Utah		L/111-116	19-17	4-11	NEW JERSEY	W	/118- 98	37-41
1-17	At L.A. Clippers		L/107-111ot	19-18	4-13	At Chicago		L/ 93-100	37-42
1-19	At Denver	W	/119- 93	20-18	4-15	NEW YORK	W	/ 95- 94	38-42
1-21	At Seattle	W	/128/119	21-18	4-17	CHICAGO		L/ 95-121	38-43
1-22	At Golden StAte		L/124-136	21-19	4-19	At Cleveland		L/108-112	38-44
1-24	At Portland		L/117-125	21-20					

CONTRIBUTORS

Editor

Arthur Triche, 31, is entering his fourth year as the Hawks' Public Relations Director. A native of New Orleans and a Tulane graduate, Triche worked extensively in the sports information departments at Tulane and LSU until he joined the NFL's Detroit Lions in 1988 as assistant director of public relations.

Writers

Jeffrey Denberg, 50, is embarking upon his tenth season covering the Hawks for the *Atlanta Journal-Constitution*. A New York native, he is a senior NBA writer. Denberg covered the 1969-70 world champion New York Knicks for *Newsday*. He has also worked at the *Miami News*. Denberg. His favorite Hawk over the years has been Glenn "Doc" Rivers.

Roland Lazenby, 40, is a free-lance writer and book producer living in Roanoke, Virginia, with his wife and three children. He has written more than two dozen books, including *The NBA Finals, The Official Illustrated History*. He has also written four titles with CBS college basketball analyst Billy Packer.

Tom Stinson has worked at the Atlanta Journal-Constitution for 12 years. He covered the Hawks in 1980-82 and now works as a columnist and general assignment reporter. Stinson, 40, has also worked at the Washington Star, the Naples Daily News and the Beaver Falls News Tribune. His favorite Atlanta player during his stint on the beat was Wayne "Tree" Rollins.

Furman Bisher, author of the foreword, has been writing about sports since 1948 and his column has graced the pages of the *Atlanta Journal-Constitution* almost as long. Honored 18 times as the winner of the Associated Press Sports Award and 14 times as the Georgia Sportswriter of the Year, he is also the author of numerous books, including *Aaron* and *Miracle in Atlanta*.

CREDITS

Cover photo credits: Front—Nathaniel Butler/ NBA Photos, Dominique Wilkins. Scott Cunningham: Ted Turner and Mike Fratello. Dick Raphael: Lou Hudson. Back cover—Raphael: Richie Guerin and bench, and Pete Maravich. Scott Cunningham, all others.

Interior photo credits: Scott Cunningham—1, 8, 9, 12, 13, 51, 54, 55, 58, 59, 60, 61, 62, 63, 66, 68, 59, 70, 71, 72, 73, 77, 80.
C.W. "Bud" Skinner, 2, 4. Wendell Webb, 70. Jimmy Cribb, 82. Dick Raphael, 8, 17. Calvin Cruce, 85. Buzz Taylor, 32. Jerry Buckley, 16. Jack Reismer, 50. Mack Giblin, 18.
Atlanta Hawks, 6, 19, 24, 25, 26, 27, 28, 31, 32, 34, 35, 41, 45, 48, 50, 69, 78, 79.
The Naismith Memorial Basketball Hall of Fame, 21, 22, 23, 29.
The Atlanta Journal-Constitution, 28, 37, 39, 43, 44, 46, 50, 52, 53, 56, 57, 64, 102.
NBA Photos, 29, 30, 36, 38, 40, 42, 48, 64, 76.